Anti-Blackness and Christian Ethics

ANTI-BLACKNESS AND CHRISTIAN ETHICS

Edited by
VINCENT W. LLOYD *and* ANDREW PREVOT

ORBIS BOOKS
Maryknoll, New York

ORBIS BOOKS
Maryknoll, New York 10545

Fathers and Brothers
MARYKNOLL™

Founded in 1970, Orbis Books endeavors to publish works that enlighten the mind, nourish the spirit, and challenge the conscience. The publishing arm of the Maryknoll Fathers and Brothers, Orbis seeks to explore the global dimensions of the Christian faith and mission, to invite dialogue with diverse cultures and religious traditions, and to serve the cause of reconciliation and peace. The books published reflect the views of their authors and do not represent the official position of the Maryknoll Society. To learn more about Maryknoll and Orbis Books, please visit our website at www.maryknollsociety.org.

Manufactured in the United States of America.

Library of Congress Cataloging-in-Publication Data

Names: Lloyd, Vincent W., 1982- editor. | Prevot, Andrew L., editor.
Title: Anti-Blackness and Christian ethics / Vincent W. Lloyd and Andrew Prevot, editors.
Description: Maryknoll, NY : Orbis Books, [2017] | Includes bibliographical references and index.
Identifiers: LCCN 2017017344 (print) | LCCN 2017039827 (ebook) | ISBN 9781608337163 (e-book) | ISBN 9781626982512 (paperback)
Subjects: LCSH: Racism—United States. | United States—Race relations. | Race relations—Religious aspects—Christianity. | Church and social problems—United States. | White supremacy movements—United States. | Black lives matter movement.
Classification: LCC E185.615 (ebook) | LCC E185.615 .A725 2017 (print) | DDC 241/.675—dc23
LC record available at https://lccn.loc.gov/2017017344

Contents

Part II: Black Bodies and Selves

Part III: Black Loves

Acknowledgments

The papers collected here were first presented at a symposium on anti-blackness and Christian ethics held at Boston College from September 14 through 16, 2016. This event and the resulting volume were made possible by a major grant from Boston College's Institute for the Liberal Arts, as well as generous support from the Dean's Office of the Morrissey College of Arts and Sciences, the Theology Department, and the Program of African and African Diaspora Studies. Villanova University's Department of Theology and Religious Studies also contributed funding for which we are very grateful. Special thanks to Gregory Kalscheur, S.J., Robert Ellsberg, Catherine Cornille, Richard Gaillardetz, Nancy Pineda-Madrid, Andre Willis, Martin Summers, Maria Clara Bingemer, Pamela Lightsey, James Keenan, S.J., Lisa Cahill, Kim Humphrey, Craig Ford, Eduardo Gonzalez, Jaisy Joseph, Amaryah Armstrong, Elizabeth Antus, and Steven Battin.

Contributors

M. SHAWN COPELAND is Professor of Theology and Core Faculty in the Program of African and African Diaspora Studies at Boston College. Recent publications include *Enfleshing Freedom: Body, Race, and Being* (Fortress Press, 2010); *The Subversive Power of Love: The Vision of Henriette Delille* (Paulist Press, 2009); and a coedited volume, with LaReine Marie Mosely and Albert J. Raboteau, *Uncommon Faithfulness: The Black Catholic Experience* (Orbis Books, 2009).

ASHON CRAWLEY is Assistant Professor jointly appointed in Religious Studies and in the Carter G. Woodson Institute for African-American and African Studies at the University of Virginia. He is the author of *Blackpentecostal Breath: The Aesthetics of Possibility* (Fordham University Press, 2017); "Circum-Religious Performance: Queer(ed) Black Bodies and the Black Church," *Theology & Sexuality* 14, no. 2 (2008): 201–22; and "'Let's Get It On!' Performance Theory and Black Pentecostalism," *Black Theology* 6, no. 3 (2008): 308–29.

KELLY BROWN DOUGLAS is Dean of Episcopal Divinity School at Union Theological Seminary. She is the author of *Stand Your Ground: Black Bodies and the Justice of God* (Orbis Books, 2015); *What's Faith Got to Do with It? Black Bodies/Christian Souls* (Orbis Books, 2005); *Sexuality and the Black Church: A Womanist Perspective* (Orbis Books, 1999); and *The Black Christ* (Orbis Books, 1994). She is the coeditor, with Marvin M. Ellison, of *Sexuality and the Sacred: Sources for Theological Reflection*, 2nd ed. (Westminster John Knox, 2010).

KATIE WALKER GRIMES is Assistant Professor of Theology and Religious Studies at Villanova University. Her works include *Fugitive Saints: Catholicism and the Politics of Slavery* (Fortress Press, 2017); *"Christ Divided": Antiblackness as Corporate Vice* (Fortress Press, 2017); "Breaking the Body of Christ: The Sacraments of Initiation in a Habitat of White Supremacy," *Political Theology* 18, no. 1 (2017): 22–43.

VINCENT W. LLOYD is Associate Professor of Theology and Religious Studies at Villanova University. He is the author of *Religion of the Field Negro: Black Secularism and Black Theology* (Fordham University Press, 2017) and *Black Natural Law* (Oxford University Press, 2016). He edited *Race and Political Theology* (Stanford University Press, 2012) and coedited, with Jonathan Kahn, *Race and Secularism in America* (Columbia University Press, 2016) and, with Molly Bassett, *Sainthood and Race: Marked Flesh, Holy Flesh* (Routledge, 2014).

EBONI MARSHALL TURMAN is Assistant Professor of Theology and African American Religion at Yale Divinity School. Recent publications include *Toward a Womanist Ethic of Incarnation: Black Bodies, the Black Church, and the Council of Chalcedon* (Palgrave Macmillan, 2013); "'The Greatest Tool of the Devil': Mamie, Malcolm X, and the PolitiX of the Black Madonna in Black Churches and the Nation of Islam in the United States," *Journal of Africana Religions* 3, no. 1 (2015): 130–50; and "Black & Blue: Uncovering the Ecclesial Cover-Up of Black Women's Bodies through a Womanist Reimagining of the Doctrine of the Incarnation," in *Reimagining with Christian Doctrines: Responding to Global Gender Injustices*, ed. Grace Ji-Sun Kim and Jenny Daggers (Palgrave Macmillan, 2014).

BRYAN N. MASSINGALE is Professor of Theology at Fordham University. He is the author of *Racial Justice and the Catholic Church* (Orbis Books, 2010); "Has the Silence Been Broken? Catholic Theological Ethics and Racial Justice," *Theological Studies* 75, no. 1

(2014): 133–55; and "James Cone and Recent Catholic Episcopal Teaching on Racism," *Theological Studies* 61, no. 4 (2000): 700–730.

ELIAS ORTEGA-APONTE is Associate Professor of Afro-Latino/a Religions and Cultural Studies at Drew University. He is the coeditor, with Melanie Johnson-DeBaufre and Catherine Keller, of *Common Goods: Economy, Ecology, and Political Theology* (Fordham University Press, 2015), in which he has a chapter entitled "Democratic Futures in the Shadow of Mass Incarceration: Toward a Political Theology of Prison Abolition." Other works include "Epistemology," in *Hispanic American Religious Cultures*, ed. Miguel De La Torre (ABC-CLIO, 2009), and "An Africana Reading of Complexity" (forthcoming).

ANDREW PREVOT is Assistant Professor of Theology and Affiliate Faculty in the Program of African and African Diaspora Studies at Boston College. He is the author of *Thinking Prayer: Theology and Spirituality amid the Crises of Modernity* (University of Notre Dame Press, 2015); "Divine Opacity: Mystical Theology, Black Theology, and the Problem of Light-Dark Aesthetics," *Spiritus: A Journal of Christian Spirituality* 16, no. 2 (2016): 166–88; and "The Aporia of Race and Identity: J. Kameron Carter and the Future of Black Liberation Theology," in *Religion, Economics, and Culture in Conflict and Conversation*, ed. Laurie Cassidy and Maureen O'Connell (Orbis Books, 2010).

SANTIAGO SLABODSKY is Associate Professor of Religion and the Florence and Robert Kaufman Chair in Jewish Studies at Hofstra University. Recent publications include *Decolonial Judaism: Triumphal Failures of Barbaric Thinking* (Palgrave Macmillan, 2014) and "Emmanuel Levinas's Geopolitics: Overlooked Conversations between Rabbinical and Third World Decolonialisms," *Journal of Jewish Thought and Philosophy* 18, no. 2 (2010): 147–65. He is also the coeditor, with Roland Faber, of *Living Traditions and Universal Conviviality: Prospects and Challenges for Peace in Multireligious Communities* (Lexington, 2016).

Preface

We are angry. We see gross racial injustice in the United States today. We see the anti-black violence committed by the police, by the prison system, by poverty, by environmental racism, by racial bias, and by hateful words and deeds. We know that this violence is pervasive and connected, and we know that it results from this nation's deep, longstanding commitment to denying black humanity. Many of us, as people of color, have not only observed this violence at a distance; we have felt it on our own bodies and souls.

We are heartened by grassroots organizing demanding racial justice, and we join in the affirmation that *Black Lives Matter*. We seek to learn from activists and to struggle together with them, both to challenge the white supremacy that infects this nation and to envision what racial justice may look like. We are grateful to movement organizers for crafting an inspiring platform that calls for an end to the war on black people, reparations, investment in black communities, economic justice, community control of police, and black political power. We are inspired by the movement's deep analysis of anti-black racism and by the connections that the movement makes with other struggles for justice.

We acknowledge the complicity of religious communities in perpetuating anti-black racism, and we acknowledge the deafening silence of many religious communities in the face of racial injustice. But we also remember the long, inspiring tradition of religious organizing and analysis aimed at challenging anti-black racism. We remember the invitation to believe in a God who is black. We remember the ideals of love and nonviolence, and we remember how these ideals have been perverted by those who privilege hollow peace over justice. We learn from the movement that advancing justice requires disrupting ordinary life.

Affirming that black lives matter is necessary, but it is not enough. We call on our fellow theologians and scholars of religion to articulate how religious traditions speak to anti-black racism in their research and teaching. We also call on our colleagues to personally join the movement, in the streets. We call on religious leaders to interrogate the ways their institutions have been complicit in anti-black racism and to mobilize institutional resources in support of the struggle for racial justice—and to personally join the movement, in the streets. Finally, we call on religious practitioners to discern the resources in their faith traditions to struggle against anti-black racism—and, as well, to personally join the movement, in the streets.

We are an ecumenical group, Catholic and Protestant, Jewish and agnostic. We are predominantly black, but we are also Latino and white. We are gay and straight, immigrants and U.S.-born, clergy and laity. We are theologians and secular scholars of religion. Collectively, we lament that the grip of anti-black racism remains so tight. We denounce the false god of whiteness that is worshiped throughout this nation. We know that changes to a few laws will not suffice. We demand a revolutionary transformation in souls and in society, in universities and in political institutions. We believe that struggle and worship can be one and the same. Let us follow the lead of the black youths blocking highways and disrupting brunches, organizing together to recognize the inherent worth and dignity of black life.

Introduction

VINCENT W. LLOYD AND
ANDREW PREVOT

It was just shy of two months after white police officer Darren Wilson shot to death black teenager Michael Brown—whom Wilson would later describe as appearing "like a demon." Protests continued night after night in Ferguson, Missouri, capturing national attention just as the shooting of Trayvon Martin and subsequent protests had two years earlier. On this night, September 29, 2014, just after 11 pm, a dozen clergy members kneeled to pray in front of the Ferguson Police Department. It was a diverse group, including a Reform rabbi, Susan Talve; an African American United Church of Christ minister, Traci Blackmon; several white Episcopal priests; and Osagyefo Uhuru Sekou, a Pentecostal minister. As Reverend Sekou led a prayer, the police interrupted, demanding that the clergy and other protesters disperse. Reverend Sekou kneeled, continued his prayer—and was arrested by the police. He spent two hours in a blood-stained police van, one of scores of arrests in the Ferguson uprising.[1]

Reverend Sekou, who was born in St. Louis but was at the time pastoring a Massachusetts congregation, spent three months in

---

1. Kenya Vaughn, "Praying While Black: Rev. Osagyefo Sekou Detained by Police," *St. Louis American* (October 2, 2014), http://www.stlamerican.com. On February 9, 2016, a jury took just twenty minutes to acquit Rev. Sekou. See Steve Giegerich, "Cleric Acquitted in Ferguson Protest Case," *St. Louis Post-Dispatch* (February 9, 2016), http://www.stltoday.com.

Ferguson participating in protests and conducting trainings in non-violent civil disobedience for fellow protestors. He has a dim view of the potential for churches to take the lead in struggles for racial justice. During the iconic Montgomery and Birmingham protests, he notes, only a tiny fraction of churches participated. "I'm not terribly hopeful for the church. I think queer, black, poor women are the church's salvation. They don't need to get saved. The church needs to get saved." Reverend Sekou is not contrasting a religiously (or specifically Christian) inspired civil rights movement with a secular, twenty-first-century racial justice movement. Rather, he is pointing to the shared religious spirit that animates both, a spirit found in "the least of these"—a spirit of love. He points to a protest in San Francisco's financial district where black women bared their breasts while stopping traffic to call attention to the police shootings of Yuvette Henderson, Rekia Boyd, and Kayla Moore. Those women were "presenting their bodies as living sacrifices," according to Rev. Sekou. "This generation has made a commitment to love its way out."[2] Loving black flesh that is deemed by the world unloveable—doing so publicly, disturbingly, ritually—this dramatizes systemic injustice and forces us to ask difficult questions that are political, personal, and inescapably theological.

It is not only ministers who see love ethics at the core of the #BlackLivesMatter movement. The hashtag originated with a queer black woman, Alicia Garza, a California-based organizer with the National Domestic Workers Alliance. The night neighborhood-watch volunteer George Zimmerman was acquitted of Trayvon Martin's murder, Garza was angry and grieving. The next morning, she composed her thoughts and shared them on Facebook, concluding, "Black people. I love you. I love us. Our lives matter." Her friend Patrice Cullors, another queer black activist, shared the Facebook status and added #BlackLivesMatter. With the participa-

---

2. Sarah van Gelder, "Rev. Sekou on Today's Civil Rights Leaders," *Yes! Magazine* (July 22, 2015), http://www.yesmagazine.org; Tanvi Misra, "San Francisco's Topless Protest Against Police Brutality," *Citylab* (May 22, 2015), http://www.citylab.com.

tion of Opal Tometi of the Black Alliance for Just Immigration, the three created a digital platform to facilitate organizing based on the simple principle encapsulated in the hashtag. "The project that we are building is a love note to our folks," Garza reflects. When a Ferguson grand jury acquitted Officer Wilson, Garza was involved in planning nonviolent civil disobedience in California as a response. She explains that protests and marches did not seem like the appropriate response: "What our spirits need right now is really to stop the wheels"—to block highways, paralyze public transportation systems, and interrupt brunches.[3]

A swirl of religious ideas, symbols, rituals, and feelings surround today's racial justice movement. While a half century ago the role of religion in struggles for racial justice might be symbolized by the image of a respectable black preacher standing in front of the masses—though certainly the story was much more complicated even then—today, in our spiritual-but-not-religious age, in our age of social-media-savvy millennial activists, in our age that is so new but also, in the pains inflicted by systemic injustice, so old, religion and struggles for justice are closely, complexly entangled.

There is religion on the surface, in the presence of clergy and ideas of love and spirit, but there is also religion below, present but unspoken. There is religion that inheres to the long history of struggles for racial justice, from the memories of African traditional religions and Islam that motivated resistance to enslavement to the ambivalent responses to Christianity that sometimes fueled rebellion to the Black Panthers' effort to build a secular temple to black humanity in Oakland.[4] Today, this religious tradition is often forgotten, or

3. Alicia Garza, "A Love Note to Our Folks," *n + 1* (January 20, 2015), https://nplusonemag.com.

4. See Albert J. Raboteau, *Slave Religion: The "Invisible Institution" in the Antebellum South* (New York: Oxford University Press, 1978); Gary Dorrien, *The New Abolition: W. E. B. Du Bois and the Black Social Gospel* (New Haven, CT: Yale University Press, 2015); Barbara Savage, *Your Spirits Walk Beside Us: The Politics of Black Religion* (Cambridge, MA: Belknap Press of Harvard University Press, 2008); "Son of Man Temple," in *The Black Panther Party:*

repressed, with freedom struggles described as a part of the (ostensibly secular) black radical tradition. The last half century has seen a rapid transformation of the religious landscape in the United States, together with a dramatic shift in the religious ideas and languages that are legible to a broad public audience. Religion has become more individualized, many staid religious institutions have declined in their membership and moral influence, and intellectual elites have often become invested in a deep secularism. Certainly these shifts play out in black communities differently than in white, but they are essential to understanding how religion relates to struggles for social justice today. They explain, in part, why grander visions of social justice that transcend the religious-secular divide have been neglected. Today, it is necessary to ask: How might we understand the black radical tradition as a black *religious* radical tradition—or a black *Christian* radical tradition?

It is our contention that those struggling for racial justice would do well to reflect on religion, and specifically on Christianity. There are obvious, practical reasons for racial justice organizers to deepen their understanding of Christianity: there are lessons to be learned from history; there are institutional resources to be tapped; there is rhetoric that moves the masses to action; and there are spiritual disciplines that enable the emotional balance necessary to persist in struggle. There are also less obvious reasons. Some scholars have contended that the very idea of race may have a provenance that is not only economic and political, but also religious—so grappling with religious ideas can offer critical leverage for challenging racist practices and for dismantling white supremacy. Further, religion offers more than a set of resources to be mobilized: at their best, religious traditions offer a way of seeing the world at odds with the status quo—that is, at odds with the way the wealthy and the powerful would like us to see the world. Because of the importance of Christianity in shaping American culture and in shaping Americans (whether they admit it or not), retrieving that world-defying

Service to the People Programs, ed. David Hilliard (Albuquerque: University of New Mexico Press, 2008).

potential of Christianity holds the possibility of critical leverage for seeing the world otherwise—and seeing another world absent injustice.

We further contend that Christians discerning how to live ethically (lay and clerical and academic) would do well to reflect on the insights found in struggles for racial justice. Again, there are obvious, practical reasons: race is one among the list of ethical issues that every congregation's social justice committee contemplates along with the other usual suspects: environment, women's rights, workers' rights, immigration, poverty, and so on. The race-specific injustices of the prison system, drug laws, the education system, and everyday interactions (microaggresions) have captured media attention and demand a response from religious communities. But there are subtler reasons, too. Something like race has long played a central, if ambiguous, role in Christian self-understanding—*neither Jew nor Greek*. Racial injustice is not only a problem out there, in the secular world; it also infects religious congregations that remain deeply segregated and at times incubate rather than combat prejudice. But most importantly, *God is black*. This was the provocation of Albert Cleage and James Cone, the first formalizers of black theology, in the 1960s, and, for Christians, it should be straightforwardly true. God identifies with the most marginalized, those who suffer from systemic injustice. In twenty-first-century America, those are blacks, so that is where God is to be found, with all this claim implies. To understand Christian ethics, studying the practices of black communities, particularly black communities struggling against injustice, is more likely to yield insights than studying the works of European theologians alone. An even higher yield will come when that study of black struggle is accompanied by participation in struggle. In the formulation of black theologians, this is the imperative to become black.[5]

---

5. See Albert Cleage, *The Black Messiah* (Kansas City: Sheed & Ward, 1969); James Cone, *A Black Theology of Liberation* (Maryknoll, NY: Orbis Books, 1970); and Kelly Brown Douglas, *The Black Christ* (Maryknoll, NY: Orbis Books, 1994).

At the heart of racial justice organizing today, expressed in the unifying principle *Black Lives Matter*, is a commitment irreducible to secular terms. This commitment is misunderstood if it is taken quantitatively: that white lives count as, say, 10, perhaps Latino lives as 6, Native American lives as 4, Muslim lives as 2, and black lives as 0, with the goal being to raise all lives to a 10. The absurdity of such a formulation points to the inadequacy of scalar frameworks. Indeed, what is at stake is the belief that no lives are disposable, that there is something about human life that deserves reverence, not calculation. Human life has inherent worth and dignity, or, in a more theological idiom, sacredness—it images and shelters the divine. In a sense, the claim of racial justice organizers today is that white lives are treated with reverence, accorded dignity; black lives are treated as disposable, subject to crude calculation that could result in their end. The police officer is charged with protecting sacred (white) life by means of calculating and neutralizing threats from disposable (black) life. As disposable, as object of calculation, black life is stripped of spirit. At the extreme, what remains is only the black body, object of repulsion and attraction, of fantasy, transformed into a demon in the mind of Officer Wilson, warehoused in prisons, executed by lethal injection or by environmental racism or by inadequate health care. What remains is flesh without feeling, incapable of being loved by others, let alone loving itself, let alone loving the world that so humiliates it.

But *Black Lives Matter*. This is not only shorthand for a political program, it is also an affirmation of a truth that the world denies. Black women and men, girls and boys, young and old, straight and queer, northern and southern, and immigrant and biracial—black humanity in all its variety—is beautiful. Is dignified. Is sacred. Loves. Is loved. Doing all this, *being human*, when the world treats black life as disposable—that takes something special, something powerful, something supernatural. In black life, denied but irrepressible, we see the divine imaged in the human clearly. For those who do not face racial oppression, the dignity or sacredness of life may become but an abstract principle to be affirmed, and one that is sometimes affirmed at the same time black humanity is denied. This is the tragic gift that black folks bring to the world, a reminder that to be human is to struggle against the powers that be, against the wisdom of the world, at once personally and collectively. This is what we see in black communities: in the songs, the art, the wit, the ingenuity, and most especially the collective action, all of which evidences both grave oppression and an ability to transcend the limits on personality and community prescribed by the world.

This story seems too stark, too black and white. Why not speak more generally about racial justice? Why slip into a seemingly old-fashioned, simplistic opposition? There is something very specific to anti-black racism—and very enduring. Anti-blackness is a key term animating both theoretical discussions of race today and grassroots organizing for racial justice. In both, this term indicates that the racial oppression faced by blacks in America (and, on some accounts, globally) is more than can be expressed by a collection of empirical evidence. Housing and employment discrimination, enormous wealth inequities, police harassment, disproportionate incarceration—these are all realities of black American life, but they are symptoms of a chronic ailment. The same ailment expressed itself in de jure segregation until a half century ago, and the same ailment expressed itself in slavery before that. Unless this disease is named and addressed, whatever remedies are offered for the specific forms of oppression faced by black Americans today will prove to be no more than short-term solutions. If mass incarceration is ended, some other, equally if not more grotesque social institution will take its place.

Anti-blackness is the key term employed in struggles for racial justice today. The key term for an earlier generation was *racism*. As a category of critical analysis, racism has two major limitations. First, it is very general. It can refer to any set of beliefs or practices that disadvantages one race more than another. Conversations about racism can tend, therefore, to remain at an unhelpful level of abstraction. They can also be easily sidetracked by appeals to so-called reverse racism. Second, despite many efforts to define racism as a structural evil, many people still associate it with prejudice on the part of individuals, of *racists*.[6] In contrast, the term anti-blackness draws particular attention to harms done to black people, and it points to both the interpersonal and structural dimensions of these harms.

What is this disease of anti-blackness, where does it reside, and how did it come about? Accounts vary. Some locate it in the institution of slavery: it is so unnatural to treat another human being as nonhuman that a mythology, diffused through not only stories and images but also habits and feelings, had to develop for slavery to seem plausible and remain sustainable. On such accounts, black Americans today are still, effectively, enslaved, because the racial ontology developed during slavery persists.[7] Others—of particular interest in the present context—tell an even longer history of anti-blackness, one in which anti-blackness is a transformation of the anti-Indian cultural metaphysics developed during colonialism, itself a transformation of the anti-Jewish logics developed in the early days of Christianity.[8] In other words, the structure of anti-

---

6. See Eduardo Bonilla-Silva, *Racism without Racists: Color-Blind Racism and the Persistence of Racial Inequality in the United States* (Lanham, MD: Rowman & Littlefield, 2003); and Bryan Massingale, *Racial Justice and the Catholic Church* (Maryknoll, NY: Orbis Books, 2010).

7. The most prominent account along these lines is Frank B. Wilderson, *Red, White, and Black: Cinema and the Structure of U.S. Antagonisms* (Durham, NC: Duke University Press, 2010). See also Achille Mbembe, *Critique of Black Reason* (Durham, NC: Duke University Press, 2017); Linda Martín Alcoff, "Afterword: The Black/White Binary and Antiblack Racism," *Critical Philosophy of Race* 1, no. 1 (2013): 121–24; Jared Sexton, *Amalgamation Schemes: Antiblackness and the Critique of Multiracialism* (Minneapolis: University of Minnesota Press, 2008); João H. Costa Vargas, *Never Meant to Survive: Genocide and Utopias in Black Diaspora Communities* (Lanham, MD: Rowman & Littlefield, 2008); Lewis Gordon, *Bad Faith and Antiblack Racism* (Amherst, NY: Humanity Books, 1995); Hortense Spillers, "Mama's Baby, Papa's Maybe: An American Grammar Book," *Diacritics* 17, no. 2 (1987): 65–81.

8. Sylvia Wynter "Unsettling the Coloniality of Being/Power/Truth/ Freedom: Towards the Human, After Man, Its Overrepresentation—An Argument," *CR: The New Centennial Review* 3, no. 3 (2003): 257–333;

blackness is really a new form of the theological problem of anti-Judaism, or supersessionism.[9]

Regardless of which theoretical picture of anti-blackness seems most persuasive, it is clear that anti-blackness is deeply entrenched. So combatting racism requires more than policy fixes, and more than changing individuals' hearts and minds. Transforming something so broadly and firmly held is daunting, and secular theorists often appear stumped (hence the label for such theoretical frameworks: Afro-pessimism). The critical leverage offered by religious traditions promises a response. If the problem is fundamentally about theology infected by supersessionist heresy, then fixing theology should fix anti-blackness, but of course that is too simple. Theorists probing the depths of theology or cultural metaphysics for the hidden roots of our current racial dilemmas can be compelling storytellers, but their stories are not particularly useful as specific guides for ethical and political action. The essays in this volume are mindful and appreciative of the insights of such theorists, but they equally attend to the practical challenges of living together today, in a nation debilitated by anti-blackness.

Why focus on anti-blackness instead of *white privilege* or *white supremacy*? The category of white privilege names the unearned, disproportionate benefits that white people regularly receive just because of their whiteness. Scholars who want to stress the oppressive power dynamics involved in this arrangement tend to prefer the

J. Kameron Carter, *Race: A Theological Account* (Oxford: Oxford University Press, 2008).

9. Jared Hickman offers an alternative theological account where the figure of Prometheus, a human stealing power from the gods, is central. Whites aspire to be Prometheus, themselves stealing fire, while blacks attempt to dethrone the gods without occupying the newly emptied throne. "That empty throne ... grounds an alternative tradition of radicalism, a political theology arrayed against Euro-Christian apotheosis via non-Euro-Christian debasement, perhaps captured in W. E. B. Du Bois's resonant phrase, 'Divine Anarchy.'" Jared Hickman, *Black Prometheus: Race and Radicalism in the Age of Atlantic Slavery* (New York: Oxford University Press, 2017), 147.

category of white supremacy.[10] Both of these are valuable analytical tools, and valuable tools for self-reflection. However, they also place whites at the center of struggles for racial justice. Although conversations surrounding these terms have helped some whites take responsibility for the functioning of whiteness in contemporary societies, these conversations also risk taking attention away from the harms that are being done to black bodies, selves, and communities. The term anti-blackness concentrates precisely on these harms and primes black communities to fight back. (Katie Walker Grimes's chapter in this volume makes the intriguing argument that we ought to shift the discussion further toward the category of "anti-blackness supremacy.")

This book does not consider anti-blackness in isolation from other social problems. On the contrary, it examines concrete connections between anti-blackness and colonialism, capitalism, patriarchy, and homophobia, to mention but a few, and it relates anti-blackness to similar harms done to other nonwhite groups, such as immigrant communities from Latin America and Asia and indigenous peoples of the Americas. Clarity about the role of anti-blackness in this interconnected web of social crises and oppressions is possible only if we can appreciate anti-blackness as a distinct category of critical analysis that is not reducible to the others. All of the contributions to this volume exhibit the intersectionality of the term in one way or another. To mention just two examples: Santiago Slabodsky draws connections between anti-blackness and other forms of colonial oppression, and Eboni

---

10. See Paula S. Rothenberg, ed., *White Privilege: Essential Readings on the Other Side of Racism*, 3rd ed. (New York: Worth, 2008); Laurie M. Cassidy and Alex Mikulich, eds., *Interrupting White Privilege: Catholic Theologians Break the Silence* (Maryknoll, NY: Orbis Books, 2007); Moon-Kie Jung, João H. Costa Vargas, and Eduardo Bonilla-Silva, eds., *State of White Supremacy: Racism, Government, and the United States* (Stanford, CA: Stanford University Press, 2011); and George Lipsitz, *The Possessive Investment in Whiteness: How White People Profit from Identity Politics*, rev. ed. (Philadelphia: Temple University Press, 2009).

Marshall Turman analyzes the gendering of anti-blackness as a particular assault against black girls and women.

The focus on anti-blackness does not require any allegiance to a racial essentialism that would reduce the meaning of black existence to some fixed essence or set of narrow stereotypes. Nevertheless, resistance to anti-blackness has the potential to mobilize people for social action in much the same way that appeals to black identity have done in the past. The double negative—resisting anti-blackness—allows the meaning of black life to remain open-ended. Yet the political stakes of resisting anti-blackness are clear and urgent, in contrast to the risks of political inactivity and discursive confusion that come with some postmodern performances of indeterminacy. Without telling black people what they must do or be to achieve black authenticity, it is clear that we are engaged in a determinate struggle for black lives and black futures. (On the question of black authenticity, see Andrew Prevot's chapter.)

The movement-mobilizing power of *anti-blackness* is arguably much stronger than that of *diversity, inclusion,* or *multiculturalism.* Although these terms represent positive social values that we do not want to dismiss, they lack the precision and critical edge that come with an explicit struggle against anti-blackness. There can be no justice in the celebration of multiple ways of being human unless and until there is also firm commitment to overcome the negations of black life that are rampant today. Nonetheless, the struggle against anti-blackness is, and must be, inclusive. Diverse persons, groups, and institutions must come together to build up a more black-loving and black-friendly world that can be genuinely hospitable to all.

Without providing a comprehensive list of types of anti-blackness, we can point to a few examples that reveal some of the harmful realities that this category is meant to name and address: colonial domination of African nations by European imperial powers, which expropriated their resources, destabilized their politics and economies, and fueled apartheids and genocides; the trans-Atlantic slave trade, with its uniquely devastating forms of dehumanization, violence, and rape (see the chapters by Walker Grimes, M. Shawn

Copeland, and Kelly Brown Douglas); Jim Crow era discrimination and lynching, continued in new forms today; unjust policing practices, including killings of unarmed black adults and children and "stop-and-frisk" policing strategies targeting black communities; the mass incarceration of black persons, including many persons convicted of only nonviolent crimes; sexualized violence against black bodies in policing and in the pornography industry (see especially Bryan Massingale's chapter); structural inequalities that disadvantage black persons in areas of housing, education, health care, and employment; negative cultural tropes about the meaning of blackness, perpetuated through popular culture and the viral distribution of lynching videos (see especially Elias Ortega-Aponte's chapter); physiological, psychological, sociological, and spiritual effects of being perpetually excluded, marginalized, and feared; and microaggressions permeating the quotidian experiences of black life.

The category of anti-blackness enables us to reflect critically on the concrete ways that Christian persons and institutions, including the very discipline of Christian ethics, have failed to resist the multifaceted harm that is being heaped upon black people. Ashon Crawley's chapter makes the thought-provoking suggestion that resistance against anti-blackness must begin from an "anethical" attention to performance, beyond the bounds of what we normally understand by "Christian ethics." Slabodsky argues that "religion," particularly the Christianity that allied itself with colonial powers, functioned as a tool to dehumanize black peoples. Copeland shows that the Catholic Church has been an active participant in the forging of anti-blackness. Brown Douglas makes a similar point about Anglo-Saxon civil religion of the United States, which has been historically blended with and misconstrued as Christianity. Marshall Turman argues that even the Black Church, in its various denominational forms, remains complicit in certain anti-black and other oppressive dynamics.

A large-scale struggle against anti-blackness is already underway. This book seeks to affirm, participate in, and contribute to this struggle. It does not put forward a completely new agenda but instead builds on the already-existing momentum and emerging consensus within critical race theories and activist communities. Working in solidarity with the Movement for Black Lives and other similar initiatives, the contributors to this volume not only reflect on various aspects of the social evil of anti-blackness (including aspects linked to religion and Christianity) but also seek positive ways forward, drawing on religious and specifically Christian ideas and practices. This volume presupposes no single definition of "Christian ethics" but instead engages it as a category that can be questioned, concretized, and developed in different ways.

The range of interpretations of Christian ethics that follows reveals a variety of ways that Christian ideas and practices can contribute positively to the struggle against anti-blackness. First, as Copeland, Massingale, Brown Douglas, and others show, Christian ethics can give voice to God's righteous anger against societies that abuse the poor and oppress the stranger. Christian ethics can condemn as idolatrous any cultural tropes or religious institutions that explicitly or implicitly identify divinity, purity, and holiness with whiteness and associate evil with blackness. Christian ethics can urge individuals and communities to cry out in lamentation at the horrors of anti-blackness, mourning those who have been wounded and destroyed by it. In these ways, Christian ethics can function as a powerful, prophetic critique. Precisely as a theological discourse, Christian ethics has the ability and the obligation to invoke God's name against this blasphemous violence.

Christian ethics can engage particular Christian doctrines in areas such as theological anthropology, Christology, pneumatology, trinitarian theology, ecclesiology, soteriology, and eschatology in its fight against anti-blackness. For instance, Copeland argues that anti-blackness contradicts the basic tenet of theological anthropology that all persons are created in the image of God and have rights and dignity on that basis, regardless of their race. She also raises ecclesiological issues when she discusses Catholic bishops who were supporting anti-black policies, not only in defiance of Rome, but also in direct opposition to the efforts of certain local pastors and the resilience of black Catholic laypersons. Marshall Turman offers a christological and soteriological reading of black girl suffering and resistance. Massingale turns to social forms of trinitarian theology for a model of just, loving relationships that can assist us in the struggle against sexualized anti-black violence. Vincent Lloyd discovers a quasi-theological eschatology in the writings of the imprisoned Black Power leaders George Jackson and Eldridge Cleaver, which helps them order their loves and locates them in an Augustinian ethical tradition.

Within Christian ethics, and within other ethical and anethical traditions, resistance against anti-blackness may involve reconnecting with oneself, with one's communities, with the land, with aesthetic experiences of body and soul, and with a spiritual life of prayer and contemplation. Crawley finds hope in the sounds, vibrations, and affects that the character Helga Crane experiences in Nella Larson's *Quicksand*. For Crane, these experiences were a "path toward some other sociality." Prevot seeks to recover Sojourner Truth's life of mystical prayer, which begins on "a small island in a small stream, covered with large willow shrubbery," as the hidden source of her prophetic witness.

Confronted by the complexity, malleability, and persistence of anti-blackness in modern societies, it can be difficult to know how to proceed ethically. Even when the problems are clear, the solutions are often less so. Ortega-Aponte wrestles with perplexing questions about the shape of a liberationist ethics in a digital culture, where anti-blackness happens at the intersections of virtuality and reality. Lloyd retrieves powerful insights from Jackson and Cleaver, while recognizing that there is significant moral ambiguity, and even moral failure, in their treatment of women. Slabodsky shows that the entanglement between anti-blackness and Western religious culture has deep roots that cannot be easily undone. Walker Grimes considers challenging questions about how anti-blackness and other social problems, such as economic inequality and mistreatment of immigrants, can be combated at the same time and with equal vigor.

Many such questions remain open. This book does not purport to offer the final word about how Christian ethics can best respond to the social evil of anti-blackness. Our hope is only that it may be a spur for further reflection and action.

A recent collection of essays about racism today by leading American writers took as its patron saint James Baldwin, and borrowed its title from him, *The Fire This Time*.[11] Baldwin used similar words to conclude his classic jeremiad against American racism, published in 1963 as *The Fire Next Time* to wide acclaim, and the poets, journalists, and novelists of *The Fire This Time* riff off Baldwin's meditations on the depths of American anti-black racism in elegant, varied ways. Totally absent from this, the state of the art in the literary world's engagement with race, is religion—despite the ubiquity of religion in Baldwin's own thought, and the religious source of Baldwin's title. Indeed, the alteration to the title in the twenty-first-century volume marks its secularization. The climax of Baldwin's book is a citation of a slave spiritual: "God gave Noah the rainbow sign / No more water, the fire next time"—itself a paraphrase of 2 Peter 3:6-7. Following the classic form of the American jeremiad, refined over the centuries from John Winthrop on the *Arbella* to Abraham Lincoln's summoning of a New Israel to Martin Luther King Jr.'s vision from the mountaintop, Baldwin warns of potential doom if the ways of the world are not radically altered.[12] Implicit in Baldwin's words is a vision of world-transcending justice, a vision that would guide the dramatic transformation of our nation that Baldwin believed is so urgent. Baldwin forced his readers to choose: accept the ways of the world or have faith that another world is possible.

In contrast, *The Fire This Time* offers no time or space to turn away from the world. Anti-black racism is permanent and suffocating. The fire is upon us now: We can't breath. What Baldwin does

---

11. Jesmyn Ward, ed., *The Fire This Time: A New Generation Speaks about Race* (New York: Scribner, 2016).

12. Sacvan Bercovitch, *The American Jeremiad* (Madison, WI: University of Wisconsin Press, 1978).

so magnificently, and what the essays in our volume attempt, is at once to recognize the horror and intransigence of anti-black racism and, at the same time, to recognize that we have the opportunity to imagine otherwise—and we have the ability to build another world. The Christian tradition offers resources to vision and build. Crucially, the Christian tradition offers a peculiar hope—not that our struggles will inevitably result in victories, not that white supremacy will soon be relegated to the history books, but that the world does not have the final word on what is possible. The world is not in flames, but it could soon be. Whether it burns will not be determined by the decisions of the wealthy and powerful and white. It will be determined by God. Our task is to respond—not with melancholy to the possibility of destruction, but with faith in a world-transcending, world-transforming God, a God who is to be found among the weakest as they organize and struggle, a God who calls for our participation in the divine, through struggle.

PART I

Theorizing Anti-Blackness

CHAPTER 1

More Than Skin Deep
The Violence of Anti-Blackness

KELLY BROWN DOUGLAS

Some 170 years ago Frederick Douglass wrote, "Killing a slave, or any colored person, ... is not treated as a crime, either by the courts or the community."[1] From the age of slavery through the era of a black president, deadly violence continues to be visited upon black bodies, with relative impunity. What is it about America that has made the black body a prime target for unrelenting violence? In a 1967 speech defending black protestors' rights to use violence "to rid ourselves of oppression," Jamil Abdullah Al-Amin, then known as H. Rap Brown, said, "Violence is a part of America's culture. It is as American as cherry pie." While Al-Amin's words received much criticism at the time, he actually spoke a truth about America—especially when it came to the black body—that perhaps even he did not fully grasp. For the violence to which black bodies fall prey in America reflects an often-ignored narrative that is integral to America's very violent identity—an identity that indeed fosters the violent culture that Al-Amin named. It is the narrative of anti-blackness.

---

1. *Narrative of the Life of Frederick Douglass, An American Slave. Written by Himself.* Boston: Published at the Anti-Slavery Office, no.25 Cornhill 1845, docsouth.unc.edu, 24.

In order to understand the complex unremitting violence that is perpetrated upon black bodies, this chapter explores the narrative of anti-blackness and its relationship to America's very identity. It is impossible to examine thoroughly all aspects of this theme in the space of a chapter. The purpose of this chapter is simply to clarify the inherent violence of anti-blackness so as to discern how the cycle of anti-black violence might be broken.

Anti-Blackness: A Narrative of Violence

The narrative of anti-blackness became most palpable with Europeans' earliest incursions into the African continent. While ancient Greek and Roman scholars were certainly chauvinistic when it came to appraising the body aesthetic of their own people, there is little evidence that color prejudice was integral to their thought or culture. Even as the Greeks described the Africans as "burnt people," this did not imply any stigma of color. Rather it pointed to their belief concerning the impact that living close to the sun had on a people's pigmentation. In the main, the reality of color prejudice is of Western origination, coming into full relief with the earliest European encounters with Africa.

While the belief that Africans were meant to be slaves was prevalent prior to European encroachments on the African continent, an anti-black narrative was not as apparent until their arrival. As the historian Winthrop Jordan says, "One of the fairest-skinned nations [the English] suddenly came face to face with one of the darkest peoples on the earth."[2] The color difference was so "arresting" that these early European "explorers" of Africa made little of the diverse skin tones among African people. Instead, they typically described them all as "blacke." In the travel collections of Englishman Richard Hakluyt he illustrates the point in his description of Africans: "This is also to be seen as a secrete work of Nature that throughout all

---

2. Winthrop D. Jordan, *White over Black: American Attitudes toward the Negro, 1550–1812* (Chapel Hill: University of North Carolina Press, 1968), 6.

Africke, the regions are extreme hote, and the people very blacke."[3] English explorer John Hawkins was much more succinct but no less direct in his description of the people on Cape Verdes. "They are all black," he exclaimed.[4]

Whether describing Africans as black was initially done with malicious intent is debatable; what is clear is that skin color mattered to the Europeans in their encounters with a people seemingly starkly different from themselves. Furthermore, black was not a benign signifier. No less an authority than the *Oxford English Dictionary* had already established whiteness as a sign of innocence, purity, and goodness while blackness signified vileness, danger, and evil. As far apart as the English complexion was from the African, the meaning of whiteness was from blackness. Consequently, to describe the Africans as black ensured that the Eurocentric color-defined gaze would not remain innocent, if it ever was. It was only the beginning of an anti-blackness that provided the aesthetic justification for the enslavement and other violent acts against the bodies of "black" men and women.

As crucial as skin color was, it was not the only physical feature that astonished these early white intruders and soon-to-be pillagers of Africa, nor was it the only aspect of the anti-black narrative. Europeans also noted, with ominous condescension, the fullness of the Africans' lips, the broadness of their noses, and the texture of their hair. It soon became very clear that there was more at play than just a shocked realization of the diversity among human creation. In the European imagination, the Africans' physiognomy signaled a genetic difference. When coupled with the dissimilarity of dress and customs, not to speak of religions, the European interlopers became convinced that the "blackness" of the Africans was more

---

3. *The Principal Navigations, Voyages, Traffiques and Discoveries of the English Nation* ed. Richard Hakluyt and Edmund Goldsmid, onlinebooks.library. upenn.edu (volume xi, 102).

4. Quoted by Charles Johnson, Patricia Smith, and the WGBH Series Research Team, in *Africans in America: America's Journey through Slavery* (San Diego: Harvest Books, 1999), 11.

than skin deep. They believed it penetrated through to the very character and soul (which some Europeans claimed Africans did not possess) of the people, thereby signaling a people who were so thoroughly uncivilized that they were more beastly than human. Hakluyt gives evidence of this belief when he reports, "Moores, Morrens, or Negroes a people of beastly living, without a God, lawe, religion, a common wealth, and so scorched and vexed with the heat of the sunne, that in many places they curse it when it riseth."[5]

That Africans were likened to beasts was consequential. This beastly descriptor implied not simply that they were wild and uncivilized but also hypersexualized. As Jordan points out, the terms "beastial" and "beastly" carried with them sexual connotations. Thus, when an Englishman described the Africans as beastly "he was frequently as much registering a sense of sexual shock as describing swinish manners. . . ."[6] The similarities that the Europeans registered between Africans and "apes" gave way to further insinuations concerning the Africans' sexual habits. The unfortunate circumstance was that the Europeans' first encounter with apes and orangutans coincided with their first encounter with the people of Africa. Hence, they were just as startled by these animals' similarities to humans as they were by what they considered the Africans' "sub-human" qualities. It required, therefore, only a small leap in the European imagination to conceive of an inherent connection between the African "apes" and the African people. As Jordan argues, it was practically inevitable that Europeans would see a genetic tie between the "beast-like humans," and the "human-like beasts." Once such a tie was forged, it was an even easier leap of logic for the Europeans to assume, as Jordan remarks, "a beastly copulation or conjuncture" between the two species.[7] By crafting such an indecent link, again as pointed out by Jordan, Europeans were able to "give vent to their feelings that Negroes [Africans] were a lewd,

---

5. Hakluyt and Goldsmid, eds., *Principal Navigations*, 94.
6. Jordan, *White over Black*, 33.
7. Ibid., 31.

lascivious and wanton people."[8] It was in this way that "blackness" came to signal a people who were grossly uncivilized and dangerously hypersexualized. René Girard's observations concerning the connection between sexuality and violence are instructive in this regard.

Girard describes sex and violence as different sides of the same coin. He explains that sexual excitement and violent impulses elicit identical "bodily reactions." He goes on to say, "Thwarted sexuality leads naturally to violence."[9] That the early European encroachers onto the African continent posited a *sexual* connection between wild animals and "uncivilized" Africans only fortified the notion that African men and women were dangerous. If nothing else, it was clear to the white interlopers that these were a people who needed to be patrolled and controlled given their dissolute character and "beastly" disposition.

The violent nature of the anti-black narrative itself now becomes clear. It is about more than a chauvinistic repulsion to skin color. It is a narrative that negates the very humanity of a people; therefore, it is inherently violent. Any ideology or system of thought that objectifies another human being must be understood as violent. Borrowing from the words of Paulo Freire, that which "fails to recognize others as persons," hence dehumanizes them, is by definition violent. Furthermore, such a system of thought initiates a cycle of violence in which the oppressed, in this instance black bodies, become entrapped. As Freire explains, "There would be no oppressed had there been no prior situation of violence to establish their subjugation."[10] The "prior system" that renders black bodies oppressed bodies is the narrative of anti-blackness (later we shall see how that colludes with the ideology of white supremacy/culture of whiteness). It is in this way that Freire is also right to say that the

---

8. Ibid. 32.

9. René Girard, *Violence and the Sacred*, trans. Patrick Gregory (Baltimore: Johns Hopkins University Press, 1979), 35–36.

10. Paulo Freire, *Pedagogy of the Oppressed*, 30th anniversary ed. (New York: Continuum, 2005), 55.

oppressed are not the initiators of violence.[11] In short, the narrative of anti-blackness spawns a multidimensional cycle of violence against black bodies. This brings us to the centrality of this narrative to the American identity.

The anti-black narrative arrived in America with the Puritans and Pilgrims. When America's Pilgrim and Puritan forebears fled England in search of freedom, they believed themselves descendants of an ancient Anglo-Saxon people, "free from the taint of intermarriages," who uniquely possessed high moral values and an "instinctive love for freedom."[12] Their beliefs reflected an Anglo-Saxon myth that originated with the first-century Roman philosopher Tacitus, who, in his book *Germania,* touted the unique superiority of these Anglo-Saxon people from the ancient woods of Germany. Fueled by this myth, Americans crossed the Atlantic with a vision to build a nation that was politically and culturally—if not demographically—true to their "exceptional" Anglo-Saxon heritage. As such, America was envisioned as a testament to the sacredness of Anglo-Saxon character and values, if not people. American exceptionalism was Anglo-Saxon exceptionalism. In this regard, to be an Anglo-Saxon was the measure of what it meant to be an American. American identity was equated with Anglo-Saxon identity. In order to safeguard America's mythic Anglo-Saxon vision and sense of self a pervasive culture of whiteness was born. Thus, whiteness became the perfect way to mask the fact that America was an immigrant nation with migrants—even from Europe—who were not actually Anglo-Saxon.

The elevation of whiteness was inevitable since—as noted earlier—whiteness had come to signify purity and moral innocence, a skin tone therefore befitting exceptional Anglo-Saxons. Invariably, therefore, whiteness forged an impregnable wall between America's myth of Anglo-Saxon exceptionalism and that which might compromise it—such as those persons on the other side of whiteness. Hence the birth of white culture, with an anti-black narrative as its defining feature. After all, there was nothing more opposed to white-

---

11. Ibid.

12. Tacitus, *Germania*, Medieval Sourcebook, http://www.fordham.edu.

ness than blackness—not only in color but also in what it signified about a people. To reiterate, blackness signified a lewd, dangerous, and immoral people, while whiteness signaled a chaste, innocent, and virtuous people. In the words of legal scholar Cheryl Harris, "The amalgamation of various European strains into an American identity [that is, Anglo-Saxon identity] was facilitated by an oppositional definition of Black as other."[13] It is this opposition between whiteness and blackness that forms the basis of white supremacist ideology.

With the emergence of a white supremacist ideology two things become clear. First, to state the obvious, the ideology of white supremacy depends on the narrative of anti-blackness, since the notion of white superiority rests on the idea of black inferiority. Second, whiteness itself must be regarded as a violent identity construct inasmuch as it is defined by denigrating that which is non-white, notably blackness. This brings us back to the fact of white culture. To reiterate, if America's mythic Anglo-Saxon/white identity was to be protected, then blackness had to be repelled at all cost. This is the work of white culture.

White culture in its various manifestations is that which perpetuates the idea of white superiority and—especially through its legal and extralegal expressions—helps whiteness to stand its ground against any corrupting or threatening intrusions into the white Anglo-Saxon space (such as black bodies). And so once again the reality of America's inherent violence becomes evident. For like white identity, white culture in all of its expressions is intrinsically violent, given its necessary anti-black nature. The fact of the matter is that as long as American identity is grounded in the myth of Anglo-Saxon exceptionalism (and it is), then it is grounded in violence. In this regard, there is no getting around it: anti-black violence is a part of America's original DNA.

---

13. Cheryl I. Harris, "Whiteness as Property," *Harvard Law Review* 106, no. 8 (June 1993): 1742. In this article Harris provides a comprehensive and insightful analysis of the meaning of whiteness as property through scrupulous examination of case law.

No one better reflects the violent anti-black narrative inherent in American identity than America's preeminent founding father, Thomas Jefferson. In pondering the possibility of emancipation and whether or not blacks and whites could live together in the same land, Jefferson points to the differences between the two races. As he argues, "The first difference which strikes us is that of colour. . . . And is this difference of no importance? Is it not the foundation of a greater or less share of beauty in the two races. . . . Besides those of color, figure and hair, there are other physical distinctions proving a difference of race." Jefferson goes on in great detail to explain how such physical differences are part and parcel of the differences in work ethic, intelligence, judgment, and sexual propriety between black and white people. Jefferson ultimately concludes, "This unfortunate difference of color, and perhaps of faculty, is a powerful obstacle to the emancipation of these people," and if emancipated they are to "be removed beyond the reach" of mixing with white people.[14] Jefferson was speaking of an involuntary emigration of black people from America, commensurate to their forced migration to the land. Given the fact that such plans never came to fruition, measures to insure the purity of whiteness were extended to a program of unrelenting violence perpetrated against black bodies. Before exploring this further, it is important to look specifically at the impact of the anti-black narrative on black women's bodies to appreciate the particular forms of anti-black violence that affect their bodies.

Anti-Blackness and the Black Female Body

As grave as the impact that the European anti-black gaze had on black people in general, it had a unique bearing upon black women. This gaze was shaped not only by color but also by gender. Thus, it involved a racialized standard of beauty that indicated whether or not one was a "proper woman." The visage of a beautiful woman

----

14. "Thomas Jefferson on the African Race 1781," excerpted from *Notes on the State of Virginia*, http://www.historytools. org.

in the English mind was well established during the Elizabethan period, with the queen serving as the perfect exemplar:

> Her cheeke, her chinne, her neck, her nose,
> This was a lillye, that was a rose;
> Her hande so white as whales bone,
> Her finger tipt with Cassidone;
> Her bosome, sleeke as Paris plaster,
> Held upp twoo bowles of Alabaster.[15]

Shakespeare would give further evidence of this racially determined gendered aesthetic in his sonnet to the "Dark Lady." In this sonnet the poet defends his attraction to the "dark lady," well aware that "In the old age black was not counted fair/Or if it were, it bore not beauty's name." In describing the dark lady he writes:

> My mistress' eyes are nothing like the sun;
> Coral is far more red than her lips' red:
> If snow be white, why then her breasts are dun;
> If hairs be wires, black wires grow on her head.
> I have seen roses damask'd, red and white,
> But no such roses see I in her cheeks.[16]

Once again, this aesthetic assessment was not benign when it came to black women in America—especially given the enslaved realities of their lives. As far as black women were from the standard of "white" beauty, they were also far removed from the standard of femininity and what it meant to be a "lady." If "fair skin" and "rosy cheeks" suggested what would come to be known as a "Victorian lady"—pure, chaste, in need of being protected from the hardships and evils of life—the dark skin, wiry hair, "dun" breasts suggested just the opposite. As is well documented, black women

---

15. Richard Puttenham and George Puttenham, *Partheniades (1579),* quoted in Winthrop D. Jordan, *White over Black,* 8.

16. William Shakespeare, Sonnet 130, quoted in ibid., 9.

became the perfect foil to white women. While white women were considered virginal, pure angels in need of protection, black women were considered wanton, lascivious Jezebels in need of controlling.[17] To reiterate an earlier point, according to early European logic, black African women were so lewd that even the African apes were sexually drawn to them. Once again, such logic did not escape the white imagination of Thomas Jefferson as he argued that the orang-utan has more of a preference for black women than for "his own species."[18]

Black women were essentially entrapped within the Catch-22 of a violent "intersection." Inasmuch as they did not meet the white female standard of beauty, they were not regarded as "ladies" to be respected; the more that their black skin marked them for a way of living that defied ideal "womanhood," the more validity was given to the meaning of their black body aesthetic. Their blackness signified that they were in fact not proper women; they were not Victorian ladies, even as it ensured that they would never enjoy the privilege of being treated as a Victorian lady. Worse yet, it ensured brutal assaults against their bodies. Most particularly, it enabled white men literally to rape black women with moral and legal impunity. In the logic of the anti-black narrative, a black woman could never be raped since she was an unabashed temptress and thus responsible for any such assault against her body.

To understand this anti-black Catch-22 is to appreciate the layered meaning in Sojourner Truth's now famous 1851 "Ain't I a Woman" speech, delivered at a Women's Convention in Akron, Ohio. In this speech Sojourner is at once affirming her black-bodied self and defending her womanhood. She is contesting the very notion that her skin color, hair texture, and physical features mark her as anything less than a woman even if they relegate her to a way of life that betrayed Victorian notions of womanhood. She is virtually contesting the anti-black narrative that has consigned her to a

---

17. See, for instance, Kelly Brown Douglas, *Sexuality and the Black Church* (Maryknoll, NY: Orbis Books, 1999).

18. Jefferson, *Notes*.

life of denigration and brutality. She is essentially trying to escape the violent cycle of anti-blackness by offering a nonviolent narrative of resistance—to which we will return. For now it is important to understand the profoundly violent reality of the narrative of anti-blackness and its centrality to American identity.

In short, the narrative of anti-blackness itself is violent. It therefore spawns a cycle of violence with fatal results for black bodies. Worse yet, this violent narrative is integral to America's very identity. And so it seems that not only is violence in general "as American as cherry pie" but so too is violence against black bodies.

The Deadly Impact of America's Anti-Blackness

That black bodies bare the brunt of America's war on drugs, biased policing, and "tough-on-crime" measures is well documented. However, what is not recognized is the fact that these assaults on black bodies reflect the unspoken violence of the anti-black narrative that is woven into the fabric of America's mythic Anglo-Saxon identity. It is no wonder, therefore, that African Americans are 5.1 times more likely than whites to be incarcerated. In fact, in twelve states blacks make up over 50 percent of the prison population, with Maryland heading the list at 72 percent. Black people make up 13.2 percent of the U.S. population, but almost 40 percent of the prison population. An even more disconcerting manifestation of the anti-black narrative is its impact on young black bodies, thus assuring what has become known as a school-to-prison pipeline. This pipeline is evident in the racially disproportionate rates of school suspensions and juvenile sentencing. According to recent Department of Education data, black males are three times more likely than their white counterparts to be suspended from school, while black girls are six times more likely than their white counterparts, perhaps reflecting the intersecting realities of race and gender. In fact, black girls are the fastest growing population in the juvenile justice system. The anti-black narrative is also realized through socioeconomic policies that trap over 27 percent of black bodies in a cycle of poverty, thus rendering black children four times more likely than white or Asian children and significantly more likely than Hispanic children to be likewise trapped. In short, because of the violent anti-black narrative that helps to define America's identity, black bodies are trapped in a cycle of violence from poverty to incarceration to death. This brings us to the reality of fatal policing.

Again, inasmuch as the anti-black narrative is central to America's collective identity, it has insinuated itself into the collective American consciousness. Consequently, it has successfully implanted deep within the American psyche the image of the black body as a dangerously criminal body and an ever-present threat to whiteness. Numerous studies show this to be the case. They reveal that when white people, in particular, see a black body, they see a criminal. In one study conducted to investigate the impact that the perception of a black person as criminal might have on police officers, a video game was used to present a series of young men. Some of the men were armed, while others were unarmed. Half of each category of men were white, the other half black. The object of the game was to shoot the armed targets. The study found that the participants were more likely to shoot an unarmed black target, and rarely missed shooting the armed black target. At the same time, they were least likely to shoot the white target, whether or not armed. There are numerous other studies that reveal almost "automatic, unconscious" responses to black bodies, as if those bodies are threatening or criminal in and of themselves.[19]

While the above study focused on black male bodies, it should be noted that the black female body is seen as a dangerous and immoral body as well, perhaps in a more gender-specific way. While not regularly portrayed as particularly predatory, she is often portrayed as criminally immoral and most times mean and angry. The Jezebel has

---

19. Joshua Correll et al., "The Police Officer's Dilemma: Using Ethnicity to Disambiguate Potentially Threatening Individuals," *Journal of Personality and Social Psychology* 83 (2002): 1314–29, discussed in "Across the Thin Blue Line: Police Officers and Racial Bias in the Decision to Shoot," http://www.fairandimpartialpolicing.com.

morphed into the "welfare queen." Various studies have shown that the image of the black female welfare offender is just as implanted within the public consciousness as the criminal black male.[20]

Given the pervasive impact of the anti-black narrative on the white imagination it is no wonder that the officer who shot and killed eighteen-year-old Michael Brown thought it reasonable to describe Brown as a "demon," just as it seemed reasonable that the officer who killed twelve-year-old Tamir Rice might mistake him for a twenty-one-year-old man, or that an officer would perceive Sandra Bland as threatening during a traffic stop that led to her arrest and death. The point of the matter is, as long as the violent narrative of anti-blackness is a decisive aspect of America's Anglo-Saxon identity, then black bodies will be disproportionately impacted by denigrating and deadly violence.

To reiterate, the narrative of anti-blackness is inherently violent, as its sole purpose is the denigration and dehumanization of black people. This narrative alone would have a devastating impact on black lives. However, as it has interacted with America's narrative of Anglo–Saxon exceptionalism and thus become an integral part of America's identity, it is even more deadly. Consequently, as it is a part of America's very sense of self it has practically eliminated the possibility for black bodies to be truly safe in America. Therefore, if black bodies are ever to be safe to survive and thrive with dignity in America then the violent cycle of anti-blackness must be broken.

Breaking the Cycle of Anti-Blackness

How are we to break the cycle of violence perpetuated by the violent narrative of anti-blackness? It is here where Jesus's crucifying death and resurrection speak to our situation.

---

20. See, for instance, Mark Peffley, Jon Hurwirtz, and Paul M. Sniderman, "Racial Stereotypes and Whites' Political Views of Blacks in the Context of Welfare and Crime," *American Journal of Political Science* 41, no. 1 (January 1997): 30–60.

The cross represents the power that denigrates human bodies, destroys life, and preys on the most vulnerable in society. As the cross is defeated, so too is that power. The impressive factor is how it is defeated. It is defeated by a nonviolent, life-affirming force that is none other than God's resurrection of Jesus. It cannot be stressed enough that God's resurrecting power is one that by definition respects the sacred integrity of all human bodies and the sanctity of all life. This is significant in two ways as we reflect on the narrative of anti-blackness.

Black feminist literary artist and social critic Audre Lorde once said, "The master's tools will never dismantle the master's house. They may allow us to temporarily beat him at his own game, but they will never enable us to bring about genuine change."[21] What the crucifixion–resurrection event reveals is that God does not use the master's tools. God does not utilize the violence exhibited in the cross to defeat deadly violence itself. As Lorde suggests, while this may bring a temporary solution, it does not bring an end to the culture of deadly violence itself. Rather, one stays entrapped in that very culture. As such, "only the most narrow parameters of change are possible and allowable." This implies therefore that the only way to defeat violent power is by nonviolent means.

There is no doubt that the cross reflects the depth and scope of human violence. The cross in this respect represents the consuming violence of the world. It points to a world that is saturated with violence. This violence includes not simply the physical brutality meant to harm bodies, but also the systems, structures, narratives, and constructs that do harm, including the narrative of anti-blackness and the systems and structures it fosters in conjunction with the narrative of Anglo-Saxon exceptionalism. To reiterate, anything that would devalue the life of another is violent. Through Jesus, God enters into this world of violence, yet does not take it into God's

---

21. Audre Lorde, "The Master's Tools Will Never Dismantle the Master's House," in *Sister Outsider: Essays and Speeches* (Berkeley, CA: Crossing Press, 2007), 110–13.

very self. Thus, God responds to the violence of the world not in an eye-for-an-eye manner. Instead, God responds in a way that negates and denounces the violence that perverts and demeans the integrity of human lives. God accomplishes this by affirming life, as seen in the very resurrection of Jesus. Essentially, God responds to the violence of the cross—the violence of the world—in a nonviolent but forceful manner.

It is important to understand that nonviolence is not the same as passivity or accommodation to violence. Rather, it is a forceful response that protects the integrity of life. This is even clearer as one recognizes that Jesus was crucified in the first place because of his active resistance to the violent political and religious powers of his time, which trapped various people in violent, hence crucifying, realities of living. The point is that while violence seeks to denigrate and do harm to the bodies of people, nonviolence seeks to free bodies from denigrating and deadly violence. By not resorting to violence, it seeks to break the very cycle of violence itself. It is in this way that the crucifixion–resurrection event reflects nothing less than a counternarrative to the crucifying narrative of violence. This has implications for breaking the cycle of violence perpetuated by the narrative of anti-blackness.

Anti-Blackness and the Matter of Black Lives

Even as people must consistently resist and dismantle the systems and structures of anti-black violence that serve to protect the myth of Anglo-Saxon (white) exceptionalism, something just as essential must be done to counter the narrative of anti-blackness. That is an actual counternarrative that affirms the value of black bodies. This narrative must disturb the collective consciousness of America—especially white America—if black bodies are ever truly to be safe. As noted above, Sojourner Truth attempted to put forth such a counternarrative in her "Ain't I a Woman" speech. In that speech she contested the notion that black women were anything less than women. With the repeated refrain of "ain't I a woman?," she was attempting to sever the link in the white male imagination, especially between black female bodies and lewd, bestial bodies. The refrain *black lives matter* represents a counternarrative similar to that of Sojourner Truth's. It attempts to sever the link within the collective white imagination between black bodies and criminal bodies. In this regard, the refrain *black lives matter* is just as significant as the movement's active protest against the systemic and structural violence perpetrated against black bodies. For again, the refrain itself offers a direct counternarrative to the narrative of anti-blackness as it loudly affirms the sacred value of black lives. With this being the case, it was inevitable that as the #BlackLivesMatter hashtag went viral and as it moved into the public square, whiteness would stand its ground with the refrain "all lives matter." Essentially, this latter refrain was nothing less than an utter refusal to acknowledge the value of black lives, and thus a refusal to reject the narrative of anti-blackness. So, in the end, it is essential that the *black lives matter* refrain be consistently repeated in the public square. It must constantly counteract the hold of the narrative of anti-blackness on the white American psyche. Until such time as that is achieved, the words of Jamil Abdullah Al-Amin will continue to speak a truth: violence against black bodies will remain as American as cherry pie.

CHAPTER 2

It's the Theology, Stupid!
Coloniality, Anti-Blackness, and the Bounds of "Humanity"

SANTIAGO SLABODSKY

Interrogating Theology

Readers of this chapter may bring to it a logical expectation of reading an erudite essay in Christian ethics, U.S. history, and anti-blackness in North America. This is, after all, the central topic of this book.[1] If this is the case, I regret to inform them that they will be roundly disappointed. But there is no reason to despair. This volume contains wonderful essays that accomplish this goal much better than I could. My work intends to complement these studies. The author of this essay is not a Christian but a Jew; I am not an ethicist but a sociologist of knowledge; and, finally, my work does not frame the problem of anti-blackness in the context of the United

---

1. This essay was first presented in the conference on "Anti-Blackness and Christian Ethics" organized by Andrew Prevot and Vincent Lloyd at Boston College. I would like to thank the organizers and other authors for their feedback during the conference. A very brief discussion of some of my key points was presented in a symposium format as Santiago Slabodsky, "You Don't Need a Rabbi: Interrogating the Privilege of Theological Discourses after Ferguson," *Journal of Asian/North American Theological Educators* 2, no. 1 (2016): 124–28.

States. It explores how this problem affects a network of racialized peoples beyond the borders of the nation-state. More precisely, in this essay I explore how the patterns of domination that were developed during colonialism have transcended this temporal political context and have been reproduced until today under the rubric of "coloniality."[2]

My intention in this essay is to study how the relation between theology and coloniality has played on a global scale. Coloniality here refers to the patterns of domination developed during colonial times that persist beyond this political format. We will explore the role of religious discourses in the reproduction of a system of racial hierarchies that were in play since the sixteenth century. I will explain how, from very early on in modernity, theology had been granted the privilege of pontificating about the extension of humanity, and how this extension very often excluded non-Europeans. One of the most pernicious examples of this privilege can be found in the fact that a large number of collectives and individuals externally identified as "black" were denied their humanity because they presumably "lacked" the minimal conditions to be considered human (those conditions included religion, history, civilization, development, and ultimately democracy, depending on the period). This logic placed "blacks" in a network of racial hierarchization that put them on the underside of history. I will argue, furthermore, that this exclusion is one side of a more pernicious coin. Even those discourses that did include "black" people within the realms of the human hardly questioned theology's role in defining humanity. This strategy became a totalizing tactic to maintain in the hands of those authorized to produce knowledge the right to limit entire populations' access to humanity. In other words, it functioned as a form of blackmail to correct alternative behaviors, consciously or unconsciously rebellious, and to ensure that black-

---

2. For this essay, I employ the approach to coloniality developed by the decolonial school of modernity/coloniality in general and by Walter Mignolo in particular. See Walter Mignolo, *Local Histories/Global Designs* (Princeton, NJ: Princeton University Press, 2000), 17–51.

ness would functionally serve first as free and later underpaid labor in the capitalist system.[3]

I argue that this privilege has been reproduced until today. I contend that the problem is not whether or not the theologies are socially exclusive or inclusive, but, rather, the role both versions play in the reproduction of the same system of hierarchization. But this essay does not partake in the well-known (and truly constructive) pessimism that this topic has inspired in colleagues around issues of blackness. I will show that current activism is questioning from outside what theology did not dare to do from the inside. My primary example of this hopeful break is the interpretation that the Black Lives Matter movement offers of theology. The movement does not confront the answer that theology gives to the extension of humanity but chooses instead to target the privilege of religious discourses to talk about this question.[4] In no way do I argue that theologians, ethicists, religious studies scholars or clerics should not uphold a committed solidarity with the movement(s). On the contrary, I propose to practice a commitment of humility that pays close attention to the challenges the umbrella of movements is presenting, independently of whatever we consider ourselves to be part of or external to. I propose to offer our solidarity not from the privilege that theology has been granted but from an attitude of humility (or weakness) that is able to question our proposal.

Constructing Others

Let me start this exploration by surveying one of the most revealing paradoxes we find today in the public sphere: the uneven hierarchy between religious and racial discourses. Every time we witness a

---

3. On the construction of a world system of economics that required a division of labor and racial hierarchies to justify it, see the early Africanist Immanuel Wallerstein, *World-System Analysis* (Durham, NC: Duke University Press, 2004).

4. "11 Major Misconceptions about the Black Lives Matter Movement," http://blacklivesmatter.com.

racially motivated attack, progressive and well-intentioned religious leaders are quickly summoned to the site. They show their solidarity with the victims by proclaiming the existence of a unified humanity. In the event of a racial attack, religious diversity becomes a necessary response. Religiously motivated attacks, however, elicit a different reaction. On most of these occasions, unless there is a clear intersectionality, it is very rare to see organizers summoning a group of racially diverse leaders to support the same call for humanity. On these occasions, racial or ethnic diversity just become superfluous, unnecessary. Some may even argue that is a competitive claim that blurs the protest against the religious attack.

This distinction leaves us with a very clear lesson: while religious diversity comes to represent the solidarity of a unified humanity, racial diversity has become unnecessary and is viewed as incapable of encompassing the same universal collectivity. This is not necessarily surprising. From very early modernity, religious discourses have arrogated to themselves the right to define the extension and bounds of humanity. Racial discourses have stemmed from their definitions. Today some of the best-intentioned religious leaders (and often scholars of religion) who intend to support anti-racist movements such as Black Lives Matter end up reifying the right of theological language to pontificate about the extension of humanity. Naturally, we cannot overlook the distinct responses to the question of who is or is not human. We should differentiate between discourses that limit humanity to the perpetrators of "just wars" and arguments that also extend this humanity to their victims. Yet what the entire spectrum has in common is that none of these positions questions the discursive privilege of religion to define the extension and bounds of humanity.

While this may not be a problem for most secular readers interested in the role of religion in modern societies, contemporary activists post-Ferguson have understood and denounced, probably before scholars, the trap that this discourse entails. They have even gone further by explaining the connection between this religious privilege and the trap posed by discourses on civility that limit the possibility of rebellion against the inhumanity that religious discourses have created. This essay, then, intends to look into the *longue durée* of coloniality to evaluate the tension between the goodwill of religious discourses and their actual social role.

Racial constructions have frequently been a central criterion for organizing societies in the modern world. On some occasions one perverse pattern becomes so evident that mediations crack and the struggle against the structure crystalizes. During the last years we have seen a particularly crude manifestation of some of these social constructions. Between 2014 and 2016, this pattern was reproduced in Ferguson and its multiple aftermaths in various cities across the nation, and in the rampant Islamophobia that manifested itself following the Charlie Hebdo attacks in Paris.

In this context a wonderful drawing began to appear across various social media forums. This drawing was reproducing common-sense perceptions of an act of violence according to the race of the person who was perpetrating it. The first two drawings on the right reproduce the common-sense perception of a white person as a perpetrator of a shooting. If "he" is representative of the state's "legitimate" monopoly of violence (police, army, etc.) "he" becomes a hero; if not, "he" is characterized as a lone wolf with emotional issues (or parking problems). But crossing to the left side, the author draws two people of color, and the perception is completely different. If a Muslim is a shooter in the "barbaric" act, all 1.3 billion Muslims are held responsible. Furthermore, the entire *Ummah* is asked to show its solidarity with victims, who could well be some of the perpetrators of the harshest Islamophobia. If the shooter is a black person, "he" is quickly linked with "gang" violence, and the occurrence is portrayed as a nonsensical attack perpetrated by those who are inherently incapable of engaging with the progress of civilization. The racial minorities, in other times called barbarians or primitives, take out their frustration on the fittest, those who allegedly achieved their success by merit alone.

These two ideal types are not new. Today's Muslims are attacked for allegedly trying to conquer the world and impose an alternative way of life against the will of a free West. Not too long ago, it was the figure of the Jewish Bolshevik, and not that of the Islamic jihadist, that fulfilled the same role. It comes as no surprise, then, that the discourses that today challenge the absorption of Syrian refugees reproduce almost the same stereotypes that were applied to Jews who failed to find asylum and perished in the Holocaust. Today African Americans are attacked for allegedly perpetrating nonsensical violence that disrupts the "natural" progressive development of civilized life. Yesterday, the figure of the Native American fulfilled the same role. One need only to open a browser in Netflix to see how Hollywood defines to our day the figure of the "Indian" as inherently incapable of understanding the "advance" of civilization and as randomly using crude "savagery" to try to stop the inevitable European settlement.

These two collaborative types of otherness are not novel. They respond to over five centuries of Euro-Christian discursive privilege in defining the extension of humanity. The narrative that interprets black/Native behavior describes them as monolithic collectives who *lack* the precondition of humanity. In different periods this precondition was redefined in response to epistemological changes in the system. In the sixteenth to seventeenth centuries the precondition was that of having a soul or religion; in the eighteenth to nineteenth centuries, it was history; in the nineteenth to twentieth, it was civilization; in the twentieth, development; and in the twenty-first, democracy. Throughout this period, discourses questioned whether or not enslaved Africans, Natives, and then African and Latin Americans (among others) met the precondition. While modern society may have "advanced" for the privileged, this discourse continued to be entrenched in modern structures and has actualized itself in ways that continue victimizing the same populations.[5]

The second narrative, which was traditionally applied to Jews and Muslims, presents collectives accused of opposing Euro-Chris-

---

5. Ramon Grosfougel, "The Structure of Knowledge in Westernized Universities: Epistemic Racism/Sexism and the Four Genocides of the Long 16th Century," *Human Architecture* 11, no. 1 (2013): 78–89.

tianity and, therefore, of having the *wrong* precondition. So, again, between the sixteenth and nineteenth centuries they were defined as having the wrong (or being stuck on) religion, history, and civilization. In the nineteenth century two interrelated factors, imperialism in Muslim majority regions and the complex exteriority of European Jews on the continent, forcibly incorporated Muslims and Jews into the system as Africans and Natives had been. It is no surprise, then, that they started to be defined by their *lack* of civilized behavior, development, and currently (especially for Muslims) democracy. So, in Euro-Christian discourses, these two parallel narratives of racialization, which had overlapped for centuries in other areas, started to converge in the Euro-Christian right to define the extension and bounds of humanity. Even those who fought to affirm the humanity of these victims rarely challenged the Euro-Christian right to delimit these victims' humanity.[6]

Coloniality and People Who "Lack" Religion

Indians/Natives, blacks/Africans, Jews/Muslims have walked different trajectories that should not be confused. Not only among the different groups but also within each externally created collective. Merging them in a single line of oppression confounds the specificity of each experience. Yet there is a reason why some of the leading decolonial Afro-Caribbean intellectuals insisted on making a connection with the other groups. To take just one example, Aimé Césaire invited those who were horrified at the Holocaust to explore the natural connection with the experiences of Africans in the Caribbean and Africa, adding that the Jewish genocide cannot be explained exclusively by European history.[7] His pupil, Frantz

---

6. See further interrelation among different types in Ella Shohat and Robert Stam, *Race in Translation* (Durham, NC: Duke University Press, 2012), 1–25.

7. Aimé Césaire, *Discours sur le colonialisme* (Paris: Présence Africaine, 1955), 31. John Pinkham, trans., *Discourse on Colonialism* (New York: Monthly Review Press, 2001), 36.

Fanon, first mentioned that "his teacher" had told him that he should notice that an anti-Semite was very often also anti-black, and took this thought further by defining "the Jew" as his "brother in suffering," using 1960s terminology.[8] Following this longstanding tradition, the Black Lives Matter movement risked its political capital by developing, pursuing, and welcoming a fraternal relationship with the Palestinian struggle in the so-called Middle East.[9]

In parallel to local studies on anti-black racism, I would like to follow Césaire, Fanon, and the Black Lives Matter movement by exploring the global networks of racialization that started in the sixteenth century, and that came to be denounced in the twentieth and twenty-first centuries. It was starting in the period that symbolically begins in 1492 that the first modern empires, Spain and Portugal, conquered the last bastion of Muslim rule in the Iberian peninsula, expelled Jews, colonized "indigenous" populations in the Americas, and, perhaps more importantly for this essay, started to kidnap individuals on the coasts of Africa, destroying communities, and enslaving these individuals for free labor. The development of "modern race thinking," as has been characterized by leading anthropologist Irene Silverblatt, put these different experiences in a common network that has continued until our day.[10] This network of racialization at times confounded the different populations, lumping together the distinct experiences, while, at other times, it split them to divide and conquer, creating hierarchies that often relegated "black" people to the bottom of the social structure. While others will eloquently explore the distinction between historical

---

8. Frantz Fanon, *Peau noire, masques blancs* (Paris: Éditions du Seuil, 1952), 98. Charles Markmann trans., *Black Skin/White Masks* (New York: Grove Press, 1991), 122.

9. See the platform of Black Lives Matter regarding the mutual solidarity with Palestine here: https://policy.m4bl.org/platform/. For an excellent exploration of the implications of this move read Hamid Dabashi's, "Black Lives Matter and Palestine: A Historical Alliance," *Al Jazeera* (September 6, 2016), http://www.aljazeera.com.

10. Irene Silverblatt, *Modern Inquisitions* (Durham, NC: Duke University Press, 2004), 16–21.

experiences of suffering, I opt here to follow Césaire, Fanon, and Black Lives Matter by exploring the common core among the different experiences.

This center, I will argue here, is coloniality. I would like to distinguish coloniality from other common terms used by colleagues including colonialism, settler colonialism, or neocolonialism. Colonialism is the imposition of political power of one civilization over another. Settler colonialism is the construction of an alternative society in that location in a way that makes the colonizer invert the understanding of him-/herself as an invader and think of him-/herself as a native, deeming the native as a foreigner. Neocolonialism is the reinvention of economic, cultural, or political ties that are structured after the formal process of political decolonization. Coloniality is a different analytical tool, which, I argue, can clarify the extension of our problem for over five hundred years. Without disregarding the usefulness of the other terms to explain parallel phenomena, coloniality describes a subtle and pernicious reality. It refers, and here I use Walter Mignolo's term, to the patterns of domination that were developed during colonial times and that continue to reproduce themselves beyond formal colonialism. In other words, it is the construction of racial hierarchies set in the sixteenth century that helped to define, for example, blackness by its "lack" (of soul, religion, history, civilization, development, etc.). This lack would then be used to question the humanity of those identified as blacks and put them in the service of a global division of work as first "free" (i.e., slave) labor and then underpaid labor.[11]

The denial of humanity on the basis of this argued "lack" was not accidental, nor was it a collateral effect of the system. It would be a mistake to think it can be solved with further inclusion in a system that was built on the backs of those who were caught in the tentacles of coloniality. For epistemological, anthropological, and economic reasons, it has been a constitutive part of a framework that enabled a geopolitical system since the sixteenth century. And this is where

---

11. See Mignolo, *Local Histories/Global Designs*, 17–51.

religious discourses played a key role in justifying the system from the very beginning. Again, we see how the problem is not necessarily the answer that theologians could offer to the question of the extension of humanity to those enslaved. The problem here is the refusal to abdicate the privilege of defining the bounds of humanity. This double game can be seen particularly clearly when we explore racist anti-blackness not as an independent problem but as part of a global program.

In order to describe this trajectory, I opt to start with one of the first debates on the humanity of non-Europeans that took place in the courts of Valladolid in the sixteenth century. Between 1550 and 1551 the head of the first modern empire, Charles I of Spain, summoned two iconic theologians, Juan Ginés de Sepúlveda and Bartolomé de Las Casas, to discuss a pressing issue: the humanity of the recently "discovered" Natives. The role of the court of Valladolid, where the debate between the two theologians was to take place, was not to pass judgment but to offer theopolitical justification for the crown's decision.

Sepúlveda described the Natives as "barbarians" who virtually lacked any "trace of humanness." This description, buttressed by both Christian theology and gradually monopolized Greek philosophy, inaugurated one of the longest-standing justifications for modern imperialism: the right of the presumably civilized power to subjugate an entire population based on their lack of what this civilization defined as the basic requirements to become human. After defining the collective for their lack (of religion, economy, laws, civility, sexual morals, etc.), Sepúlveda argued that there was only one way of achieving salvation: complete submission to the Christian faith and the nascent European civilization. Sepúlveda reasoned that, given the limited faculties of the Natives, this submission needed to be accomplished by force, in an exercise of what would be defined as a "just war," made "just" by the Natives' ignorance. The coercion, then, would be both epistemological (eradicating any pre-European "superstition") and economical (free labor in the extractive mercantilist economy that laid the ground for the primitive accumulation for capitalism). Sepúlveda, in this way, inaugurates a longstanding colonial tradition of framing the denial of humanity in an altruistic project: it is the responsibility of Christianity to help those who lack humanity to achieve it. The forced labor and consequent material gain and the cost in human lives (lost either to the harshness of labor or in resistance to European designs) were understood as collateral damage in a larger divine altruistic enterprise.[12]

In the court of Valladolid, Sepúlveda was opposed by Bartolomé de Las Casas. The latter had been bishop in the Americas and, contrary to Sepúlveda, had firsthand experience with Spanish actions on the continent. His work confronting arguments like Sepúlveda's gained him the motto of "defender of Indian tears." Eventually he would become an icon for the progressive church in Latin America in general and for liberation theologians during the 1970s and 1980s in particular. A priori this recognition seems to be deserved. He described the Natives as indeed human and denounced the brutal practices that the Spaniards were conducting on the continent. But critics who have taken a closer look at his work point out the collaborationism of his proposal. In the first place he insisted on the evangelization of the Natives, discarding any other possibility than Christianity as a way of achieving full humanity and salvation. He did argue that this should be done with love and not coercion, but this path still situated European Christianity as the deciding power that should dictate the extension of humanity. In effect this created a hierarchy in which the Europeans, having already achieved full humanity, had the privilege of dividing the population into good/ bad Natives and used this divide to correct behavior, limit access, and ultimately reproduce their hierarchical privilege.[13]

---

12. Juan Ginés de Sepúlveda, *Demócrates Segundo; o De las justas causas de la guerra contra los indios* (Madrid: CSIC, 1951), 35–88 and 120–35. See critical engagement in Luis Rivera-Pagan, *A Violent Evangelism* (Louisville, KY: Westminster/John Knox Press, 1992), 135; and Hebert Frey, "La Mirada de Europa y el 'otro' indoamericano," *Revista Mexicana de Sociología* 58, no. 2 (1996): 61–62.

13. Bartolomé de Las Casas, *Brevísima relación de la destrucción de las*

The bishop's affinity with the reproduction of hierarchies becomes particularly clear when we discuss his proposal to replace with African "slaves" the labor of Natives who were dying by the hundreds of thousands because of the impossible work conditions. In doing this, his proposal was partaking in an elaborate theological justification for the enslavement of Africans that was already a century old and justifying it with a well-known metaphor from the animal world: speaking about the racial animal characteristics of Africans, who were naturally fit for hard work. This strategy shows two sides of the same coin in terms of the relation between populations under the effects of coloniality. On the one hand, Natives and Africans were going to be linked through labor in the primitive accumulation of capitalism in the Americas that eventually helped Europe become Europe and launch the more extended takeover of the world. And, on the other hand, by praising the Natives, Las Casas needed to practice a divide-and-conquer strategy by elevating one population to potential humanity while depriving another one of the same possibility. Theology, in the case of Las Casas, was providing a very fertile terrain for key racial constructions by arrogating to European Christianity the right to define the extension of humanity and defend its bounds.

Las Casas and Sepúlveda may have been rivals publicly but they were collaborators in the construction of a system of hierarchical racialization based on Christianity's right to define humanity and to subordinate people who lacked the characteristics that theology defined as central for the achievement of this humanity.

Indias, n.d. Eng., *A Short Account of the Destruction of the Indies* (New York: Penguin, 1992). For a discussion of relations with Africa, see Sue Peabody, "'A Nation Born to Slavery': Missionaries and Racial Discourse in Seventeen-Century French Antilles," *Social History* 38, no. 1 (2004): 116–19; and for a decolonial critique of the typology presented by Bartolomé de Las Casas, see Walter Mignolo, *The Darker Side of the Renaissance* (Ann Arbor: University of Michigan Press, 1995), 441–43.

Anti-Black Racism in Colonial Networks

Postcolonial studies, in broad terms, has argued that it was difficult to speak about the construction of race until the nascent West had gotten rid of theological discourses.[14] I would like to argue here that what is known as civilizational and eventually biological racism starting in the nineteenth century is a direct consequence of the theological formulations that emerged in the sixteenth century and that, as a consequence of this, theology has been the problem and not the solution in the racially based denial of humanity.

I would like to consider Sepúlveda and Las Casas not as rivals but as theological partners in the construction of race in modernity. Both of them agree that there are some populations who reside outside the boundaries of humanity, and both support the use of their bodies for cheap or free labor. Furthermore, both of them understand that there is only one path toward salvation and that Christianity is ultimately acting beneficially for some of these populations. Sepúlveda proposed to bring these populations forcefully into Christianity and insisted on the role of normative thinking to put these populations under surveillance, offering limited access to those who complied and extermination to those who did not. Las Casas, for his part, insisted on a higher potentiality of one of the groups to achieve a humanity that only Christianity could grant.

---

14. Postcolonial studies, largely reflecting on British imperialism, have traditionally set the beginning of modernity in the late eighteenth or beginning of the nineteenth century, with the advance in North Africa, Egypt, or India. This was the periodization proposed by Edward Said (*Orientalism* [New York: Vintage Books, 1979]) and subaltern studies. Exceptions of people drawing from the same sources who argue there is an intimate relation between colonialism and modernity starting in the sixteenth century include Stuart Hall for the black Atlantic and Ella Shohat for the Middle East and trans-Atlantic Moorish/Sephardic worlds. See Stuart Hall, *Modernity: An Introduction to Modern Societies* (New York: Blackwell, 1996); and Ella Shohat, "Taboo, Memory, and Diasporic Voices: Columbus, Palestine and Arab-Jews," in *Taboo, Memory and Diasporic Voices* (Durham, NC: Duke University Press, 2006), 201–6.

But this access still placed the privilege in the hands of the colonizer and ultimately depended on the substitution of one group's role in the division of labor by another group that would in turn be denied humanity. This is predominantly the role that the externally constituted "blacks" or "Africans" had from the beginning of modernity.

A key role for theology from the sixteenth century onward was to define humanity by exclusion. Even if it offered an inclusive format, this was used as a strategy to eliminate alternative knowledges and correct non-Christian (uncivilized, underdeveloped, undemocratic, etc.) behavior by offering restricted access to some (a small number of those given the chance to comply and who did comply) or an illusory access for the vast majority of others (including those rejected in their compliance or those who consciously or unconsciously refused to submit themselves). This primacy, this privilege to define the confines of humanity, became a key component in the development of European Christian civilization, because it allowed it not only to define the other but also to constitute itself. In the following centuries, other disciplines secularized the theological privilege, defining the bounds of humanity in ways that would have particular consequences for anti-black racism.

It is important to note that anti-black racism was not always normative. Before the fifteenth century, for example, it is difficult to trace lasting connections between blackness and slavery. Any black servants present in Europe were largely outnumbered by other Europeans, Turks, or Mongols. This is not to say that there was no contact between Europe and Africa. On the contrary, the boundaries were porous, but Africans were generally not considered "objects" of free labor. On the economic level, many merchants (Venetians, Genoese) tried to make a dent in trans-Saharan commerce, given the wealth of West Africa. In the theological political realm, the pope, resident in Avignon, was eager to establish relations with Ethiopia for reasons involving political legitimacy and self-defense. Given the inexistence of an economic world system at the time, it would not be fair to say that Africa was more highly regarded than Europe, especially when the continents were not clearly defined.

But we can safely assert that a diffuse idea of Africans seemed to be more commercially and culturally connected with other areas of the world than a very provincial Europe.[15]

Portuguese explorers slowly started to change this reality when they began to navigate along the coasts of Africa, creating narratives about African barbarism and eventually becoming a leading force in the kidnapping and enslavement of people who now started to be generally categorized as black and/or African. The economic need, the existence of mythical conceptions legitimized by theology (the myth of Ham), and the extended use of the Greco-Roman archive (Aristotle's conception of natural slavery was key for Sepúlveda) were functional to the genesis of anti-black racism that would wind up considering all Africans as part of the same group, associating them with animalizing allegories, slavery, inferiority, and defining them through the fundamental "lack" of what Europe has considered to be the minimal requisite characteristics to become human.[16]

This denial of humanity, a key theological contribution, quickly won over many supporters among the best luminaries of the Enlightenment. These intellectuals—frequently anticlerical—secularized, perpetuated, and extended the theological discourse. In eighteenth-century France, Denis Diderot accused Africans of lacking respect for human life and characterized them as cannibals. Voltaire commented on their lack of mental aptitudes and explained how "black physiology" limits their power for reasoning. In England, David Hume restricted the concept of civilization to European "white" populations and explained as natural the dominion over black populations who, by definition, lacked civilized characteristics.[17] In

---

15. Peter Mack, "Perceptions of Black Africans in the Renaissance," in *Africa and the Renaissance,* ed. Ezio Bassani and William Fagg (New York: Center for African Art, 1989), 21–26.

16. As cited in Andrew Curran, *The Anatomy of Blackness: Science and Slavery in an Age of Enlightenment* (Baltimore: Johns Hopkins University Press, 2011), 32–41.

17. Emmanuel Eze has done superb groundwork collecting these voices. See Denis Diderot, "Nègre," and David Hume, "On National Characters," in

Germany, Immanuel Kant went even further, employing the climate theories of the period. He argued that given their residency on a hot continent, Africans were unable to offer civilization any cultural achievement. For Kant, Africans were incapable of contributing to civilization or governing themselves. In a rhetoric almost identical to Sepúlveda's, Kant claimed that the lack of political, cultural, or economic ethos made them natural slaves. To paraphrase Kant, even if Africans could be trained by force, the best they could hope to achieve was servile status.[18]

But there is likely no better social informant than one of the most influential intellectuals in modernity, G. W. F. Hegel. Recent scholarship argues that a younger Hegel may have been influenced by the slave-led independence of Haiti when formulating his well-known master–slave dialectic as one that could lead to the abolition of slavery as an institution. The same sources argue that the forced decline of this liberationist movement, opposed by Euro-American powers who could not tolerate a successful slave rebellion, made Hegel discard this early approach and align himself with a more stereotypical or "dumbing" reading of Africans.[19] According to acclaimed Cameroonian theorist Achille Mbembe, these later writings made Hegel's proposal "the archetype of what would become the colonial mode of speaking about Africa" and Africans until our days.[20]

Complementing Mbembe, this colonial mode of speaking about Africa/Africans can be seen as the adaptation to an advanced modernity of the theological debate about the bounds of humanity.

Race and Enlightenment: A Reader, ed. Emmanuel Chukwudi Eze (Malden, MA: Blackwell, 1997), 29 and 30–34.

18. Immanuel Kant, "Physical Geography," in Eze, ed., *Race and Enlightenment*, 58–64. For a critical engagement see also Eze, "The Color of Reason: The Idea of 'Race in Kant's Anthropology,'" in *Postcolonial African Philosophy* (Cambridge: Blackwell, 1997), 103–40.

19. Susan Buck-Morss, "Hegel and Haiti," *Critical Inquiry* 26, no. 4 (2000), 863–64.

20. Achille Mbembe, *On the Postcolony* (Berkeley: University of California Press: 2001), 175.

In his monumental systematic explanation of world history, Hegel purposefully excludes Africa from any participation. For him Africans resided outside of history, made no contribution to universal development, and are, now using a Fanonian vocabulary, below the border of Being.[21] For Hegel, they are just "Negro hordes" who behave "with the most unthinking inhumanity."[22] It seems that the three hundred years that separate Sepúlveda from Hegel only served to reproduce and strengthen the patterns that we have defined as coloniality. From a European location an influential intellectual describes non-Europeans as living in an inhuman and perverted state given their "lack": religion (in the past), participation in history (in the present), political/economical/sexual civilizational values (in both periods). Hegel, as Sepúlveda before him, points out the need for permanent surveillance because of the risk of sedition via (and we must observe how ironic this is) "lack of respect for human life." Finally, like his predecessor, Hegel debates between the complete intractability of the "Negro character" and its "limited adaptability."[23]

The only way that the African could achieve this adaptability was through a complete submission to the designs of civilized Europe. As with Sepúlveda before him, Hegel insists that slavery is the only path to achieve this limited adaptation. As Las Casas did, he quickly recognizes that this institution is not the most charitable one. But, again following the "defender of the Indian tears," this does not prevent him from recommending slavery for Africans. Adopting a myth developed by Portuguese explorers, he explains that intra-African

---

21. On the construction of the borders of Being, see Nelson Maldonado-Torres, *Against War: Views from the Underside of Modernity* (Durham, NC: Duke University Press, 2008), 93–160.

22. Georg W. F. Hegel, *Vorlesungen über die Philosophie der Geschichte* (Berlin: Dunker & Humboldt, 1840), 116. Hugh Barr Nisbet, trans., *Lectures on the Philosophy of World History* (Cambridge: Cambridge University Press, 1975), 176.

23. Hegel, *Vorlesungen*, 116.

slavery—where one sold the other—was common and that the Africans had long grown accustomed to slavery. But he makes a clear distinction: intra-African slavery was "barbaric" because the difference between the master and slave was irrationally "arbitrary" since both were black. The slavery practiced by Europe, on the contrary, was justified by their self-evident superiority and their privileged role in history—a role that Africans "lacked." While some may protest against slavery, Hegel recalled that this was the basis of Athens, the cradle of Western culture, where only the citizens were free.[24]

Hegel is an excellent social informant concerning the development of coloniality through time, according to which a large number of groups become collectivized as one and are "altruistically enslaved" because they were defined as being outside of the bounds of humanity. Since they supposedly "lack" the characteristics that made them human, their lives do not matter. In normal circumstances, they may perish because of the hardship of labor or as a precaution to restrain their natural propensity to nonsensical violence. But this is just one side of the coin. As part of their pernicious strategy, the authors do not close off the possibility of integration since submission requires an illusory promise. And this promise of ultimate integration will be used to correct behavior, reify hierarchies, and in attempts to subdue rebellions.

I won't be the first one to denounce Hegel for reproducing a theological worldview in his philosophy of history. Here I just extend this well-known critique to argue that he has been reproducing the patterns of coloniality set by Euro-Christian theological discourse since the sixteenth century. For Hegel's system, religious from its inception, the lives of those affected by coloniality have not mattered since the sixteenth century. Theology has not been the solution. It has been the problem from the sixteenth to the nineteenth century and, as we shall see next, to the twenty-first century. And Black Lives Matter activists have responded to this challenge.

---

24. Ibid.

Black Lives Matter's Protest

The activists of Black Lives Matter understood, with intense clarity, that the right to define humanity is at the core of the problem. When they insist that the problem is the negation of humanity, they are not just denouncing a circumstantial discourse in police departments. They are confronting a longstanding pattern that describes their alleged *lack* (of soul, religion, civilization, development, etc.) as a precondition of (that excludes them from) humanity. They are protesting against a five-hundred-plus-year Euro-Christian discourse that not only arrogated to itself the right to define the bounds of humanity but also blackmailed those affected by coloniality by limiting the protest against the system to the norms of civility that constituted their inhumanity in the first place.

When officials reproducing theological discourses (from theologians to clerics and from unconsciously theologized philosophers) intervene in the protests claiming, with prophetic fervor, that they know the true meaning of humanity, they are not confronting the problem. On the contrary, they end up securing the right of religion and theology to set the conditions of humanity. So it is no surprise, therefore, when we hear these voices periodically connect two factors: the religious privilege to define humanity and the prescription that protesters should follow civil rules while confronting the negation of their humanity. This connection ignores the fact that the problem originates from the same civilization that first arrogates to itself the right to define who is and is not human and now intends to arrogate to itself the right of access by defining the conditions for its rebellious contestation. Black Lives Matter, with provocative lucidity, rejects this intervention. After insisting on the right to fight for one's humanity, the activists write:

> Many know that the black church was central to the civil rights movement, as many black male preachers became prominent civil rights leaders. This current movement has a very different relationship to the church than movements past. Black

churches and black preachers in Ferguson have been on the ground helping since the early days after Michael Brown's death. . . . But protesters patently reject any . . . theology about keeping the peace, praying copiously, or turning the other cheek. Such calls are viewed as a return to passive respectability politics.[25]

Notwithstanding different narratives about the role of religion in the civil rights movement, my intention is to interpret the stand of the activists. Religion, according to this reading, acts most times by calling for political respectability, which in the United States is a clear sign of civilization and democracy, one that has been classified by Euro-Christianity as a precondition of humanity. Religion, first, arrogated to itself the authority to define who is human and who is not. Now it also claims to know how the people whose humanity was negated should behave while rebelling. While observing the rules amounts to accepting forced inclusion in a system that negated their humanity, rejecting them—in the use of violence, etc.—will confirm their inhumanity. This is no more than the very traditional theological discourse in which discourses of civility serve to simultaneously exclude populations from humanity and subdue the rebellion against this exclusion and the system in general. As such, the rules of civilization offer no exit from one's constructed lack of humanity.

It is important to note, however, that Euro-Christianity is not the only tradition that holds this privilege nowadays. Judaism in the Global North follows a similar pattern. After having been denied their humanity for between two and five hundred years before the Holocaust, the normative Jewry led by Euro-American elites was unable to resist integration into a now normative Judeo-Christian tradition. There is always a rabbi ready to pontificate about humanity in the United States when an African American is attacked. There is

---

25. "11 Major Misconceptions about the Black Lives Matter Movement," http://blacklivesmatter.com.

always a media-savvy intellectual eager to explain the limited reach of civilization in France when Muslims fight against Islamophobia. And there is always a minister urged to emphasize the role of democratic values in Israel and limiting the right of Palestinians to rebel against their dehumanization beyond the roles of civility. Recentering in the U.S. context, a rabbi is always summoned to represent diversity. Tragically, today, he/she manifests its limitations.

Of course the permeation of this discourse goes well beyond Judeo-Christianity. In our context there is little space for full autonomy. But at this point it is important to assume one's own positionality and restrain from *punching down* communities that are currently being persecuted or simply negated. I will leave it up to critical thinkers of Muslim and Sikh communities attacked in the context of rampant Islamophobia or leading practitioners of Santería and Candomblé fighting against their invisibilization to evaluate which elements of their tradition have reproduced the problem and which ones offer an exit from it. After all, they are not yet a fixed feature of the universal interfaith community that is summoned when a racial attack takes place, as ministers with a collar or yarmulke are.

This essay does not intend to ask theological officials to desist in their support of the anti-racist movement. I am not questioning their solidarity. I am questioning the privilege that enables them to present their conception of humanity as timeless pearls of wisdom that should be applied to people who lack transcendence. I urge these discourses to recognize that their own conceptions have been constructed historically for sociopolitical reasons and how their use of civil discourses of love and humanity reproduce some of the most problematic parts of this narrative. I am even questioning the strategic usefulness of reiterating the same discourse at a time in which the victims have understood the perversity of theological privilege.

If Walter Benjamin was able to suggest that a weak messianic power was inherited from past generations, I call for a weak theological power in the construction of solidarities with the movement.[26] It

---

26. Walter Benjamin, "Über den Begriff der Geschichte," in *Walter Benja-*

is time to recognize that the disciplines of theology, ethics, unconsciously theologized philosophies, and ultimately religious studies have been part of the problem. They have not been the solution. Our contribution will be valuable only when our collaborationism is acknowledged and when we learn to learn from grassroots movements.

---

min Erzählen (Frankfurt am Main: Suhrkamp, 2007), 129. Hannah Arendt, ed., "Thesis on the Philosophy of History," in *Illuminations* (New York: Harcourt, Brace & World, 1968), 253.

CHAPTER 3

Black Exceptionalism
Anti-Blackness Supremacy in the Afterlife of Slavery

KATIE WALKER GRIMES

This chapter makes two primary claims: first, it urges theologians to exchange what I term the discourse of white privilege for the discourse of white supremacy.[1] Second, it introduces a new concept, what I term anti-blackness supremacy, in order to supplement this discourse of white supremacy. Just as white supremacy describes the fact that white people, both as groups and as individuals, possess more power than people of color, both as groups and as individuals, the phrase "anti-blackness supremacy" identifies the fact that non-black people, both as individuals and as a group, amass power because of this country's pervasive anti-blackness. Why introduce this new term? Although the discourse of white supremacy illuminates the role that power plays in racial injustice, it falsely portrays racialized evil as an injustice that falls upon all peoples of color equally and in the same way. In truth, however, only black people endure and struggle against the afterlife of slavery.

The concept anti-blackness supremacy addresses another problem in antiracist discourse: the inability to diagnose the relation

---

1. Zeus Leonardo, "The Color of Supremacy: Beyond the Discourse of 'White Privilege,'" *Educational Philosophy and Theory* 36, no. 2 (2004): 137–52.

between classism and racism without reducing one to the other. Both of these errors arise from a pervasive misunderstanding of the slave regime that has set our current racial system in motion. In truth, slavery represents not simply a mechanism of profit extraction, but a relation marked by a unique form of power that extends beyond the economic sphere. The term anti-blackness supremacy corrects both of these misperceptions, affirming both the singularity of black oppression and its fundamental connection to enslaving power, which seeks much more than economic gain.

Exchanging the Discourse of White Privilege for the Discourse of White Supremacy

Ultimately, the expression "white privilege" does not name what it purports to define. In the introduction to their groundbreaking book *Interrupting White Privilege,* Laurie Cassidy and Alex Mikulich explain that "for the purposes of this volume, we invited the reader to consider racism as 'a system by which one race maintains supremacy over another race through a set of attitudes, behaviors, social structures, ideologies, and the requisition power needed to impose them.'"[2] In a similar way, Margaret Pfeil argues, "White privilege, in general terms, functions systemically, invisibly, and without name while at the same time conferring power."[3] Indeed, as these scholars seemingly recognize, more than just privileged whiteness exists as an identity of power. Why not name it as such?

This language of white privilege also overestimates the possibility and importance of white agency and self-reform. Portraying white privilege rather than white supremacy as the ultimate evil, these scholars typically focus on ways to make white people make more

---

2. Laurie M. Cassidy and Alexander Mikulich, eds., *Interrupting White Privilege: Catholic Theologians Break the Silence* (Maryknoll, NY: Orbis Books, 2007), 2.

3. Margaret Pfeil, "The Transformative Power of the Periphery: Can a White U.S. Catholic Opt for the Poor?," in *Interrupting White Privilege,* ed. Cassidy and Mikulich, 128.

racially just choices. But if supremacy ultimately animates the evil heart of whiteness, then white power and agency represent not the solution but the problem. The expression "white supremacy" compels theologians to care less about how to persuade whites to do the right thing and more about what they need to be made to do.[4]

The white-privilege approach to racial inequality also tends to devolve into an unproductive and obfuscating comparison of individuals. I call this the "What about Oprah?" defense. This defense points to the economic prosperity, power, and acclaim enjoyed by prominent black individuals such as Oprah Winfrey, Barack Obama, or Michael Jordan as evidence that racial injustice no longer prevails.[5] More than a rhetorical strategy, this discourse actually shapes popular perception of racial reality. In response, adherents of the "white-privilege approach" attempt to avoid this individualistic understanding through extensive explanation. Despite the eloquence with which scholars remind their readers of the structural character of white privilege, this language of white privilege continues to be misunderstood.

The white-privilege approach also provides no way of attending to degrees in racial rank or differences in racial experience. This effect often occurs against the wishes of white anti-racist theologians.[6] For

---

4. Despite her embrace of the term "white supremacy," I contend that Jennifer Harvey also places too much confidence in white agency. It is not enough to describe racial evil as white supremacy; we must also recognize its corporate operation. See Jennifer Harvey, *Whiteness and Morality: Pursuing Racial Justice through Reparations and Sovereignty* (New York: Palgrave Macmillan, 2007), 41–42.

5. For recent examples of the "What about Oprah?" defense, see "No, Oprah, America Isn't Racist: Column," *USA Today*, http://www.usatoday.com; "Oprah, Obama, and the Racism Dodge," *National Review Online*, http://www.nationalreview.com; Fox Nation, "O'Reilly Clashes with Harvard Professor over Oprah: She's 'Indicting' America as a Racist Nation," FoxNation.com, (January 18, 2016), http://nation.foxnews.com; Daniel Schorr, "A New, 'Post-Racial' Political Era in America," NPR.org, http://www.npr.org.

6. Examples of this conflation abound. See, for example, Guardian music,

example, Pfeil attempts to distinguish racial injustice from other forms of injustice when she depicts "those oppressed by structures of white privilege" as "arguably the most oppressed both within the U.S. Catholic Church and in U.S. society."[7] But the framework of white privilege that she employs provides no way to justify this preference. A critical reader surely wonders what makes *white* privilege more oppressive than other forms of privilege, especially if everyone experiences different amounts and bundles of privilege.[8]

This question reflects less a misunderstanding of the concept of privilege than it does a reasonable interpretation of it. Peggy McIntosh developed her theory of white privilege based on the belief in an analogy between sexism and racism. But herein lies the problem: because of white supremacy's unique connection to the unique condition of slavery, they are not interchangeable evils. In this way, for example, wealth does not accord a black person immunity from white supremacy just as poverty does not deprive a white

---

"Madonna: Women Are the Most Marginalised Group in Society," *The Guardian*, March 12, 2015, sec. Music, http://www.theguardian.com; Nicky Woolf, "Julie Delpy on Hollywood: 'I Sometimes Wish I Were African American,'" *The Guardian*, January 22, 2016, sec. Film, http://www.theguardian.com.

7. Pfeil, "The Transformative Power," 129.

8. See, for example, a blog post in the *Huffington Post,* which argues, "I would even venture to say that a black or Hispanic gay man who exhibits the hypermasculine, alpha-male qualities that are universally prioritized in this country might be seen as more desirable than a white gay man who comes across as feminine." Tyler Curry, "The Duality of a White, Cisgender, Gay Man," *Huffington Post*, http://www.huffingtonpost.com. In a widely circulated letter, a white Jewish American male invokes the suffering of his Jewish Russian ancestors to argue against white privilege. See Tal Fortgang, "Checking My Privilege: Character as the Basis of Privilege," *The Princeton Tory,* http://theprincetontory.com. Another writer argues that "the biggest understanding of white privilege is that simply because you are white, you then *automatically* possess more privilege than someone who is black, Asian, Latino, i.e., 'nonwhite' . . . Yes, whites have differing privileges than nonwhites, but then again, I have differing privileges than many people that are white." Andy Gill, "White Privilege Is a Myth," *Patheos,* http://www.patheos.com/.

person of the power that white supremacy provides.[9] Naming the relation between race and power, the expression "white supremacy" possesses both a rhetorical effectiveness and a descriptive accuracy that the term "white privilege" lacks.[10]

But the discourse of white supremacy, while superior to that of white privilege, carries descriptive and rhetorical shortcomings of its own. It can also falsely figure "people of color" as equally and "monolithically . . . victimized" by racial evil. But as critical theorist Jared Sexton explains, anti-blackness cannot be considered analogous to racism against nonblack groups because, unlike these other forms of asymmetrical power relations, anti-blackness alone bears the imprint of black slavery.[11] Because it recognizes the singularity of the black experience, the expression "anti-blackness supremacy" in fact surpasses "white supremacy" in both rhetorical power and descriptive precision. Scholars ought to reserve "white supremacy" to designate those conditions that empower only whites over and against all peoples of color with relative uniformity.

Following George Yancey, this chapter argues that "a black/nonblack dichotomy" explains the operation of race better than the conventionally favored "white/nonwhite dichotomy."[12] Thus, even if nonblack people of color do not occupy the ontological position of "master," they enjoy immunity from the ontological position of "slave."[13] We might be tempted here to describe this reality as one of "nonblack privilege." But more than simply enjoying nonblack privilege, nonblack people accrue power over and at the expense of blackness.

---

9. Frank B. Wilderson III, *Red, White and Black: Cinema and the Structure of U.S. Antagonisms* (Durham, NC: Duke University Press, 2010), 37.

10. White Protestant ethicist Jennifer Harvey also tends to prefer the discourse of white supremacy to that of white privilege. See, for example, *Whiteness and Morality*.

11. Jared Sexton, "People-of-Color-Blindness: Notes on the Afterlife of Slavery," *Social Text* 28, no. 2 103 (June 20, 2010): 48.

12. George A. Yancey, *Who Is White?: Latinos, Asians, and the New Black/Nonblack Divide* (Boulder, CO: Lynne Rienner Publishers, 2003), 21.

13. Sexton, "People-of-Color-Blindness," 36.

I call this form of supremacy "anti-blackness" rather than "anti-black" in order to surpass the limits of individual thinking. While the hyphenated word "anti-black" draws our attention primarily to black individuals and therefore encourages the type of comparative accounting that occurs when we attempt to calculate degrees of white privilege, the more expansive term "anti-blackness" includes the black individual but also goes beyond her: it neutralizes the "What about Oprah?" defense. The term "anti-blackness" also better captures the performative character of racialized power. In this way, nonblack people perceive "blackness" as a crime of which not all black people are equally guilty.[14]

Why not just advocate for the term "anti-blackness," especially since it grows increasingly popular with black activists and theologians?[15] The term "anti-blackness" does not adequately guard against our collective tendency to reduce racial evil to displays of overt and interpersonal racial animus. Although "anti-blackness" cannot be turned into a cry of white victimization in the way the term "racism" can, it seems quite likely that it soon will give rise to a term such as "anti-whiteness." In place of the insistence that "blacks can be racists too," reactionaries likely would lament perceived occa-

---

14. Amaryah Jones-Armstrong, "Blackness and Value; Part 2: On Whiteness as Credit," *Women in Theology*, February 11, 2015, http://womenintheology.org; Amaryah Jones-Armstrong, "On the Theo-Political Vision of Macklemore; or, Why Proximity & Intimacy ≠ Solidarity," *Women in Theology*, June 16, 2013, http://womenintheology.org. See also literature scholar Yago Colás's argument about the way in which, although professional basketball players Stef Curry and Lebron James are both black, James is perceived, even if implicitly, as embodying a certain style of blackness that Curry receives credit for rejecting. See Yago Colás, "A Desire Named Steph Curry | Between the Lines," http://yagocolas.com.

15. See, for example, Sylvester Johnson, "The African American Christian Tradition," in *The Oxford Handbook of African American Theology*, ed. Katie G. Cannon and Anthony B. Pinn (New York: Oxford University Press, 2014), 71 and 77; Traci C. West, "When a White Man-God Is the Truth and the Way for Black Christians," in *Christology and Whiteness: What Would Jesus Do?*, ed. George Yancey (New York: Routledge, 2012), 116.

sions of so-called anti-whiteness. We would be right back where we started: rhetorically disempowered and descriptively unmoored. Because the expression "anti-blackness supremacy" names power as the essence of racial evil, it maintains the link between the oppression of black people and enslavement in a way the appellation "anti-blackness" cannot. It points out not just what black people endure, but also what nonblack people gain.

Defining Slavery in Order to Identify Anti-Blackness Supremacy

Linking anti-blackness supremacy to slavery alone will not illuminate its uniqueness. We misunderstand both anti-blackness and the power embodied in nonblackness because we misunderstand slavery. Contrary to prevailing notions, at its core, slavery does not constitute a condition of unpaid labor or the experience of unfreedom that comes from being owned by another human being. While slave mastership can be driven by a savage thirst for endless profit, even in the Americas, women and men owned slaves for a range of noneconomic reasons. Nor do autonomy and independence represent slavery's antithesis: many people possess "claims, powers, and privileges" over other people. For example, a wife has property rights over her husband; an owner of a professional sports team has the right to trade his star.[16]

What, then, is slavery? As Orlando Patterson clarifies in his classic study, slavery represents "the permanent, violent domination of natally alienated and generally dishonored persons."[17] The slave's relative powerlessness stems from a unique source: "it always originated (or was conceived of as having originated) as a substitute for death, usually violent death." The ideology of slavery figures the slave master not as a violent thief but as a merciful pardoner; slavery casts even newborn slaves as criminal bodies. But the slave master

---

16. Orlando Patterson, *Slavery and Social Death: A Comparative Study*, 1st ed. (Cambridge, MA: Harvard University Press, 1985), 25, 27.

17. Ibid., 13.

grants this stay of execution only as long as the ransomed captive accepts her condition of powerlessness before him. Purportedly deserving criminal death, the slave survives only through her master's power. Living only at her master's mercy, the slave purportedly owes him everything and anything: the slave exists as an infinitely fungible human surrogate.[18]

Slavery further differs from other forms of domination in that it alone renders its victims natally alienated and socially dead. Unlike immigrants, women, the proletariat, or sexual minorities, slaves

> were not allowed freely to integrate the experience of their ancestors into their lives, to inform their understanding of social reality with the inherited meanings of their natural forebears, or to anchor the living present in any conscious community of memory.[19]

Indeed, Saidiya Hartman's work reminds us that while the immigrant or refugee may leave his mother and motherland the slave alone loses them.[20] In the Americas, this natal alienation extended even to native-born, African-descended slaves, as the relationships enslaved women and men forged with each other "were never recognized as legitimate or binding." Slave couples were frequently sold away from each other, and slaves of both sexes often had to submit to sex with their master. Nor could enslaved parents keep their children's masters from selling them to another master in another part of the world.[21] Just as enslaved parents could not reliably protect their children, so enslaved children could not inherit from their parents. Denied a heritage, the slave belonged only to her master: only the master or those empowered by him could exercise rights over the slave just as the slave had obligations only to her master.[22]

---

18. Ibid., 4–5.

19. Ibid., 5.

20. Saidiya Hartman, *Lose Your Mother: A Journey along the Atlantic Slave Route* (New York: Macmillan, 2008), 103.

21. Patterson, *Slavery and Social Death*, 6.

22. Ibid., 5.

More than simply coercive as other asymmetrical power relations, slavery sustains itself through the deployment of direct violence. For example, although the capitalist certainly deploys power to coerce the proletariat into working for him, he does not drive the proletariat into his fields or sweatshops by beating or mutilating him as the slave master does.[23] Both may suffer alienation and undercompensation, but only one of them endures a life of enslavement. This is not to say that only slaves are dominated violently. Nonblack victims of white supremacy, namely, indigenous peoples and Mexican and Asian Americans, undoubtedly have endured racializing violence, but they have not been racialized as slaves.[24] The evils of settler colonialism and anti-immigrant xenophobia, for example, operate differently than slavery does. For these reasons, while other forms of asymmetrical power relations may bear a resemblance to certain aspects of the master–slave relationship, the slave suffers a reality beyond analogy.

Empowered by this more accurate understanding of slavery, we now can perceive the corporately vicious operation of anti-blackness supremacy more clearly. Today, we inhabit not the aftermath of slavery but its afterlife. Anti-blackness supremacy therefore contains three main components: first, the drive to associate blackness with slave status; second, the structural habitat that produces, sustains, and enables this association; and third, the dominating power as well as the masterly pleasure that nonblacks derive from this relation. The afterlife of slavery strives to impose social death, natal

---

23. Ibid., 4.

24. A recently published book argues that indigenous slavery was in many ways "more insidious" than the enslavement inflicted upon Africans. However, because Reséndez seems to classify all conditions of coerced labor as "slavery," he overestimates the similarity between the mechanisms of indigenous and black oppression. See Andrés Reséndez, *The Other Slavery: The Uncovered Story of Indian Enslavement in America* (New York: Houghton Mifflin Harcourt, 2016), 4. This question notwithstanding, while slavery was an event that happened in the history of indigenous peoples, it does not provide "the constitutive element . . . without which Indians would not . . . 'exist'" in the way slavery does for black people. Wilderson, *Red, White, and Black,* 10.

alienation, stigma, and direct rather than merely structural violence on black people by whatever means possible. It also attempts to manufacture blackness as an identity of dependence and ungovernability so that whiteness can continue to imagine blackness as unruly yet incapable of independence. White subjectivity sustains itself by anti-blackness supremacy.

But the afterlife of slavery comprises more than just the victories of anti-blackness. Just as enslaved women and men struggled against the antebellum forces of natal alienation and social death, so their descendants have continued this fight. The history of racialized power includes not just what white people did to black people, but what black people did for themselves.[25] As Hartman recognizes, the afterlife of slavery encompasses not just the continued attempt to associate blackness with slave status, but also the various forms of black resistance to this construction.[26] No mere tale of pure victimization, the afterlife of slavery unfolds through contestation and struggle.

In addition to honoring the agency of black Americans, this more expansive definition of the afterlife of slavery calls attention to the role that coercion must play in the struggle for racial justice. Holding both resistance and oppression in clarifying tension, we understand American history anew. Thus while abolition achieved the end of chattel slavery, it did not neutralize the drive to link slavery with blackness. It did, however, deprive unrepentant agents of anti-blackness supremacy of the most effective means by which to maintain the stigmatizing relation between blackness and slave status. In response, post-abolition anti-blackness supremacy would have to codify the sclerotic connection between blackness and slave status through other means. It found them even as it conceded to them: in the early twenty-first century, the hypersegregated black ghetto and the racialized regime of mass incarceration provide the primary means by which the afterlife of slavery is perpetuated.[27]

---

25. Patterson, *Slavery and Social Death,* 4.

26. Hartman, *Lose Your Mother.*

27. Loic Wacquant, "From Slavery to Mass Incarceration," *New Left Review* 2, no. 13 (February 2002): 41–60.

The Rhetorical Efficacy of
the Expression "Anti-Blackness Supremacy"

The discourse of anti-blackness supremacy offers several rhetorical benefits. First, the concept of anti-blackness supremacy provides scholars a more reliable way to disentangle anti-blackness from economic exploitation and marginalization. Of course, we cannot detach the pursuit of black freedom from questions of economic justice entirely. Anti-blackness has always operated as a campaign of coordinated plunder. But current categories tempt us to envision anti-blackness supremacy as just a racialized form of economic injustice.[28] Both the white privilege and white supremacy approaches to racial evil struggle to explain how impoverished white people, for example, derive racialized power at the expense of affluent black people. Liberal activists similarly tend to misidentify economic justice as the best way to combat racial inequality; their counterparts on the left occasionally succumb to the belief that racial inequality will disappear when capitalism does. Anti-blackness supremacy rooted in the European enslavement of Africans, however, preexisted capitalism; it first flourished in the late medieval monarchies of Spain and Portugal, which were neither capitalist nor neoliberal.[29] While capitalism and anti-blackness supremacy certainly have been great allies, anti-blackness supremacy surely could outlast the demise of an economic system it helped to create.[30] Anti-blackness supremacy

---

28. For several recent examples of this tendency, see Kellan Howell, "Baltimore Riots Sparked Not by Race but by Class Tensions between Police, Poor," http://www.washingtontimes.com; Chris McGreal, "Blame Poverty, Not Race, Say Ferguson's White Minority," *The Guardian*, August 23, 2014, sec. US news, http://www.theguardian.com; Lydia DePillis, "Police Union: 'We Don't Believe It's an Issue of Race. We Believe It's an Issue of Poverty,'" *Washington Post*, December 4, 2014, https://www.washingtonpost.com.

29. See Matthew Lange, James Mahoney, and Matthias vom Hau, "Colonialism and Development: A Comparative Analysis of Spanish and British Colonies," *American Journal of Sociology* 111, no. 5 (March 2006), 1416, 1421, 1422, 1436–37, and 1453.

30. Eric Eustace Williams, *Capitalism & Slavery* (Chapel Hill: Univer-

represents more than just a particularly clever way of accumulating capital and controlling the working class: it preserves the pleasures and power of racialized slavery for all those it positions as nonblack, even those who are impoverished and otherwise marginalized.[31]

Indeed anti-blackness supremacy both emerges from and helps to uphold the afterlife of slavery, and slavery comprises more than a condition of extremely uncompensated labor. For this reason, the growth of the black middle class does not necessarily signal the demise or diminishment of slavery's afterlife. To this end, the concept of anti-blackness supremacy enables scholars to diagnose the ways in which black people can experience varying levels of class exploitation yet still shoulder the weight of a common anti-blackness supremacy. Put another way, under this framework, we can recognize that a black factory worker in postwar Detroit, for example, suffers under both anti-blackness supremacy and class alienation whereas his white coworker only endures the latter.[32] Rather than obscuring the reality of class-based oppression, distinguishing it from anti-blackness supremacy makes the struggle against class exploitation both more coherent and more viable.[33]

---

sity of North Carolina Press, 1944); Edward E. Baptist, *The Half Has Never Been Told: Slavery and the Making of American Capitalism* (New York: Basic Books, 2014).

31. Nor do I deny that socialist or other anti-capitalist scholars can be simultaneously anti-racist; I claim only that anti-capitalist forms of labor organization do not necessarily overturn anti-blackness supremacy.

32. Although I define racial injustice somewhat differently than Ta-Nehisi Coates does, I believe that my analysis offers a response to the critique that my account of anti-blackness supremacy ignores or obscures class-based oppression. For an example of this critique, see Cedric Johnson, "An Open Letter to Ta-Nehisi Coates and the Liberals Who Love Him," https://www.jacobinmag.com.

33. Scholars and activists still struggle to understand how we can combat class oppression and so-called racism with equal vigor. Too often, opposition to one is perceived as and in some cases actually functions as a distraction from resisting the other because we have not yet devised a way of distinguishing one from the other.

Second, this concept enables scholars to identify which aspects of contemporary economic reality do in fact arise from the afterlife of slavery. Rather than simply analyzing how economic injustice intersects with anti-blackness supremacy, this concept highlights the way in which the contemporary economic reality carries forward or attempts to revivify the contested association between blackness and slave status. For example, while conventional analyses would tend to portray black people as more likely to experience poverty than their white counterparts, the anti-blackness supremacy approach might instead distinguish black poverty for the way it imposes a unique stigma and inflicts unique dishonor on blackness and the people who are perceived as embodying it. It might also note how we imagine black poverty as uniquely dangerous: the exploited whites of Appalachia might be economically marginalized, but they are not contained in ghettos and prisons. Black people then do not experience more of the same type of poverty that other groups experience; they alone experience anti-blackness through poverty. The concept "anti-blackness supremacy" enables scholars to uncover the ways in which our economic order, no matter what shape it takes, seeks to suture blackness's association with slave status both materially and discursively.

Third, the concept of "anti-blackness supremacy" encourages scholars to avoid lumping all people of color into a single category of racial experience. Not even the prison system impinges on all peoples of color equally. Although Latino men as a group are incarcerated more often than their white Anglo counterparts, they endure this fate much less frequently than non-Latino black men.[34] This holds even more true in the case of women: while Latina women are almost twice as likely to be incarcerated as white women, black women endure imprisonment nearly two and a half

---

34. The anti-blackness-supremacy approach also enables us to better attend to the unique violence that nonblack people of color endure. For example, native-born black people are not targeted by immigrant detention systems in the way other groups are. The prison system racializes nonwhite peoples in different ways and to different ends.

times as often as Latina women.[35] And with the exception of U.S. Americans of Laotian and Cambodian descent, Asian Americans end up in prison at lower rates than everyone else, including non-Hispanic whites. The prison system operates less as a scheme of white supremacy and more as a system of targeted anti-blackness supremacy.

What Sexton terms "people-of-color-blindness" inflicts further harm on black people. Because we conceive of the color line as cleaving between white and nonwhite, statistics pointing to the relative affluence and educational success of Asian Americans, for example, suggest to many that racism either has ceased to exist or lingers on as a faint phenomenon that can be overcome by a combination of hard work, a good culture, and strong families. Whether consciously or not, when people trumpet the high test scores and low crime rates of Asian Americans, they partake in a discourse that purports to unmask the inherent weaknesses of African Americans.[36]

This confidence in the relative uniformity of white supremacy further amplifies the ability of nonblack political projects to "allegorize themselves as revolts against slavery" or subsequent struggles for black freedom. In this way, for example, the moral authority of Martin Luther King, Jr., serves to underscore a call for immigra-

---

35. Mark T. Berg and Matt DeLisi, "The Correctional Melting Pot: Race, Ethnicity, Citizenship, and Prison Violence," *Journal of Criminal Justice* 34, no. 6 (November 2006): 632.

36. Jared Sexton, "Proprieties of Coalition: Blacks, Asians, and the Politics of Policing," *Critical Sociology* 36, no. 1 (2010): 87–108. Former speaker of the house Newt Gingrich provides an explicit example of this very common belief that not only uses the imagined experience of Asian Americans against blacks, but also ranks Hispanic people somewhere in the middle of the two groups when he stated, "for poor minorities, entrepreneurship in small business is the key to future wealth. This is understood thoroughly by most of the Asians, partially by Latinos, and to a tragically small degree by much of the American black community." "Gingrich in '93: Asians, Not Blacks, Understand 'Keys to Future Wealth,'" http://thegrio.com.

tion reform.[37] Like the white bourgeois colonists who roused their countrymen to revolution by refusing to be "slaves of King George," when the worker, nonwhite immigrant, or LGBT person of any race advocates for social and civil equality in this way, she does so on the backs of blacks.[38] Because it erroneously positions nonblack people as fighting for something they lack but black people already possess, this rhetorical strategy actually makes the case against existing anti-blackness less credible. In the afterlife of slavery, this type of unintended political blackface undermines black power.[39]

The inverse can also occur. Just as nonblack movements for justice often present themselves both implicitly and explicitly as "the new civil rights movement," so institutions can hide their uniquely severe mistreatment of black people behind their less unjust relation

---

37. See, for example, Washington Post Staff, "Full Transcript: President Obama's Speech on the 50th Anniversary of the March on Washington," *Washington Post*, August 28, 2013, https://www.washingtonpost.com.

38. Douglas R. Egerton, *Death or Liberty: African Americans and Revolutionary America* (New York: Oxford University Press, 2008), 41. Douglas R. Egerton offers a sweeping chronicle of African American history stretching from Britain's 1763 victory in the Seven Years' War to the election of slaveholder Thomas Jefferson as president in 1800. While American slavery is usually identified with antebellum cotton plantations, Egerton shows that on the eve of the Revolution it encompassed everything from wading in the South Carolina rice fields to carting goods around Manhattan to serving the households of Boston's elite. More important, he recaptures the drama of slaves, freed blacks, and white reformers fighting to make the young nation fulfill its republican slogans. Although this struggle often unfolded in the corridors of power, Egerton pays special attention to what black Americans did for themselves in these decades, and his narrative brims with compelling portraits of forgotten African American activists and rebels who battled huge odds and succeeded in finding liberty—if never equality—only in northern states. Egerton concludes that despite the real possibility of peaceful, if gradual, emancipation, the founders ultimately lacked the courage to end slavery.

39. Sexton, "People-of-Color-Blindness," 42. For more on the complex yet integral role that blackface minstrelsy has played in the history of the United States, see Eric Lott, *Love & Theft: Blackface Minstrelsy and the American Working Class* (New York: Oxford University Press, 1993).

to white Hispanics and other, non-indigenous, people of color.[40] For example, colleges and universities boast about the size of their "minority" population partially in order to draw attention from the fact that, in general, African American and Native American students are more underrepresented than other racial or ethnic groups at "elite" U.S. colleges and universities.[41] In a similar way, the federal government extends to nonblack people a disproportionate share of loans to so-called minority-owned businesses. By pretending that all people of color are the same, the federal government conceals the fact that it does not treat all peoples of color equally.[42]

Fourth, the concept of anti-blackness supremacy enables us to understand white supremacy better.[43] Even more than white supremacy empowers and preserves the purity of whites, anti-blackness supremacy feeds off the negation of blackness.[44] Put another way, prevailing modes of discourse attempt to portray Latino/as of all races as unfit for citizenship by implicitly or sometimes explicitly associating them with blackness. In this way, for example, presidential candidate Donald Trump slurred Mexican immigrants as rap-

---

40. See for example "The New Civil Rights Movement," http://www.thenewcivilrightsmovement.com.

41. "Black Students at Top Colleges: Exceptions, Not the Rule," *The Brookings Institution*, http://www.brookings.edu.

42. Tamara K. Nopper, "Minority, Black and Non-Black People of Color: 'New' Color-Blind Racism and the US Small Business Administration's Approach to Minority Business Lending in the Post-Civil Rights Era," *Critical Sociology* 37, no. 5 (2011): 651–71.

43. Importantly, the expression "anti-blackness supremacy" does not deny the distinct experiences and identities of nonblack peoples of color any more than the phrase "white supremacy" does.

44. Natasha Howard, "Black in the Non-Black Imagination: How Anti-Black Ideology Shapes Non-Black Racial Discourse" (PhD diss., University of New Mexico, 2011), 14. http://repository.umi.com. James W. Perkinson has also recognized this. See James W. Perkinson, *White Theology: Outing Supremacy in Modernity* (New York: Palgrave Macmillan, 2004), 153 and 172. See also Scot Nakagawa, "Blackness is the Fulcrum," http://www.racefiles.com.

ists, and former Speaker of the House Newt Gingrich described the Spanish spoken by immigrants from Latin America as "the language of living in a ghetto." While U.S. Americans acknowledge that rapists come in all colors, rape has long been perceived as the special sin of black men.[45] Rape still carries these racialized connotations, even if implicitly.[46] And, in the United States, only black people inhabit ghettoes.[47]

One struggles to defend Latino/a immigrants against Gingrich's accusations of blackness without indulging in anti-blackness. Responding to Gingrich's comments, Peter Zamora, the co-chair of a national organization that advocates for bilingual education, explained, "Spanish is spoken by many individuals who do not live in the ghetto." To Zamora, Gingrich's statements qualify as "hateful" not because they stigmatized the inhabitants of the United States' all-black ghettos, but because they attempted to extend that stigma onto a class of predominately nonblack Hispanics.[48] Other advocates typically argue that we ought to welcome Latin American immigrants because they are hard-working, law-abiding, humble, and family oriented. And surely they are. But this discursive strategy implies that these putatively nonblack people deserve citizenship as long as they prove themselves to be everything that anti-blackness supremacy imagines that black people are not.[49]

The concept of "anti-blackness supremacy" better enables scholars to explain how nonblack people of color are both victims of

---

45. St. Clair Drake and Horace R. Cayton, *Black Metropolis: A Study of Negro Life in a Northern City* (Chicago: University of Chicago, 2015 [orig., 1945), 132.

46. Scott Poulson-Bryant, *Hung: A Meditation on the Measure of Black Men in America*, 1st ed. (New York: Doubleday, 2005), 53 and 113.

47. Douglas Massey and Nancy Denton, *American Apartheid: Segregation and the Making of the Underclass* (Cambridge, MA: Harvard University Press, 1993), 33.

48. "Spanish-Language Ad Says Newt Gingrich Said Spanish Is the Language of the Ghetto," *@politifact*, http://www.politifact.com.

49. For an example of this discourse, see John W. Schoen, "Are Immigrants Bad for the U.S.?," TODAY.com, May 22, 2006, http://www.today.com.

white supremacy and culpable co-conspirators in anti-blackness. Nonblack people of color do not merely receive privilege passively. Like those initially unwelcome and occasionally racialized European immigrants before them, nonblack people of color typically demonstrate their suitability for citizenship or ecclesial membership by asserting their difference from the native-born descendants of black slaves.[50] As Frantz Fanon recognizes, even when groups can never fit within the prevailing parameters of whiteness, they gain admission into the category of the human "simply . . . [by] not being a nigger."[51]

Anti-Blackness Supremacy and the Field of Theology

In order to address the pernicious operation of anti-blackness supremacy, scholars both within the field of theology and without ought to resist comparing the nonblack experience to the black experience even implicitly. To this end, scholars should employ the phrase "people of color" sparingly and only when describing a condition that truly encompasses all nonwhite peoples. They should not assume that all nonwhite peoples suffer racial injustice similarly or to the same extent.

Catholic theologians in particular ought to scrutinize both their confidence in and their excitement about an allegedly approaching future in which Latino/as will outnumber whites in both society and the church. Misperceiving unsullied whiteness as our nation's anchoring injustice, Catholic theologians tend to portray this "browning of America" as the dawn of a new reality in which racial division gives way to the reconciling power of mestizaje.[52] But as theologians such as Nestor Medina, Miguel De La Torre, and

---

50. Howard, "Black in the Non-Black Imagination," 110, 112–13.

51. Wilderson, *Red, White and Black*, 37.

52. Nestor Medina, *Mestizaje: Remapping Race, Culture, and Faith in Latina/o Catholicism* (Maryknoll, NY: Orbis Books, 2009), 11, 14, and 49–51.

Michelle Gonzalez argue, while these processes may decenter whiteness, we have little reason to believe they will unseat anti-blackness.[53] Latin America itself has been structured by black slavery and its afterlife. For this reason, when people immigrate to the United States from Latin America, they do not arrive as racial innocents. Rather than defeating white supremacy, the immigration of Latin American people to the United States catalyzes a collision between systems of anti-blackness supremacy.[54] What Eduardo Bonilla-Silva terms the "Latin Americanization of race in the United States" signals not a break with the country's racial past but a new way of being what it has always been, anti-black.[55]

Plus, many Latino/as already are white; interethnic procreation as well as the expansively adaptive character of whiteness suggests that many more will be considered as such tomorrow. Besides, one does not have to be white to be anti-black.[56] Asian Americans and nonblack Latino/as desire residential distance from native-born blacks at rates that approach and sometimes even surpass those of Anglo whites.[57] Judging by their residential behavior, nonblack people place the definitive color line not between white and non-

---

53. Ibid., 11, 14, 48–51. Miguel A. De La Torre, "Masking Hispanic Racism: A Cuban Case Study," *Journal of Hispanic/Latino Theology* 6, no. 4 (1999): 57–73; Miguel A. De La Torre, "Beyond Machismo: A Cuban Case Study," *Annual of the Society of Christian Ethics* 19 (1999): 213–33; Michelle A. Gonzalez, *Afro-Cuban Theology: Religion, Race, Culture, and Identity* (Gainesville: University Press of Florida, 2011), 9.

54. Sexton, *Amalgamation Schemes*, 2.

55. Eduardo Bonilla-Silva and Karen S. Glover, "'We Are All Americans': The Latin Americanization of Race Relations in the United States," in *The Changing Terrain of Race and Ethnicity,* ed. Maria Krysan and Amanda E. Lewis (New York: Russell Sage Foundation, 2004).

56. Medina, *Mestizaje*, 11, 14, and 48–51; De La Torre, "Masking Hispanic Racism," 57–73; De La Torre, "Beyond Machismo," 213–33; Gonzalez, *Afro-Cuban Theology*, 9.

57. Camille Zubrinsky Charles, "Neighborhood Racial-Composition Preferences: Evidence from a Multiethnic Metropolis," *Social Problems* 47, no. 3 (August 1, 2000): 386.

white, but black and nonblack. We will not miscegenate or immigrate our way out of anti-blackness supremacy.[58]

Conclusion

Slavery represents a relation that is sustained by and in turn provides a distinct form of power. This power continues to operate today through the afterlife of slavery. For this reason, anti-blackness supremacy accords nonblack people not just privilege but power. Theologians who reflect on the experience of nonblack people of color and other oppressed groups must protest their marginalization and mistreatment while also accounting for these communities' empowering participation in the corporate vice of anti-blackness supremacy. Theologians and ethicists similarly ought to disentangle anti-blackness supremacy from economic injustice. In so doing, we do not elevate the fight against anti-blackness supremacy above the battle against economic evil; we instead prevent ourselves from collapsing the latter into the former and vice versa. Anti-blackness supremacy, like slavery, stands in a category of its own.

---

58. Yancey, *Who Is White?*, 3–4.

CHAPTER 4

White Supremacy and Anti-Black Logics in the Making of U.S. Catholicism

M. Shawn Copeland

Setting the Stage

Through the medieval period, the human being was conceived and defined primarily as the "religious subject of the Church";[1] in another (and more exaggerated) way being human meant being Christian. But brutal and profitable "adventures" in the Americas and Africa spawned the modern/colonial world system and consumed this identity and redefined the human as political (*read* private and secular) subject.[2] At the same time, the break with this understanding of the human being as religious or Christian allowed, accepted, even endorsed the "transformation of the indigenous peoples of the Americas/the Caribbean, together with the population group of the enslaved peoples of Africa ... into the

---

1. Sylvia Wynter, "Unsettling the Coloniality of Being/Power/Truth/Freedom: Towards the Human, After Man, Its Overrepresentation—An Argument," *CR: The New Centennial Review* 3, no. 5 (Fall 2003): 265.

2. Jacob Pandian, *Anthropology and the Western Tradition: Towards an Authentic Anthropology* (Prospect Heights: IL: Waveland Press, 1985); Walter Mignolo, *Local Histories/Global Designs: Coloniality, Subaltern Knowledges and Border Thinking* (Princeton, NJ: Princeton University Press, 2000); and Walter Mignolo, *The Darker Side of Western Modernity: Global Futures, Decolonial Options* (Durham, NC: Duke University Press, 2011).

physical referents of . . . medieval Europe's Untrue Christian Other [or] the Human Other."[3] Quite alarmingly and significantly, this deformation set the stage for the degradation of Baptism, the sacrament and mystery of human unity. Moreover, this deformation brought on the equivocation, reduction, and reification of black human beings as beasts of burden, commodities, objects of property, thus rendering blacks outside the human sphere. This devaluation of black human beings closed the door on a sacred imaginary in which Baptism called believers to live out of and to live out a new reality; moreover it opened wide the door for active U.S. Catholic institutional and individual participation in the custom, commerce, culture, and creed of slaveholding. Standing on the threshold of this open door, U.S. Catholicism exposed itself fully to white supremacy and to anti-blackness.

Considering Terms

In common sense usage, *supremacy* refers to the quality or state of having more power or authority or status than anyone else: the state of *being* supreme. In more technical usage, *white* is defined as an "achromatic color, a color without hue."[4] In Western European art and cultural aesthetics, the color white functions symbolically to represent cleanliness, to connote innocence and virginity, chastity and purity, virtue and beauty, light and intelligence. The color black, also achromatic, results from the absence or absorption of light. As the symbolic opposite of white, black serves symbolically to represent filth, to connote depravity and immorality, promiscuity and pollution, vice and ugliness, dark and ignorance. When these symbolic meanings were attached to Western European and American Christianity, they "formed and cultivated a sensitivity to color

---

3. Wynter, "Unsettling the Coloniality," 265.

4. *New Oxford American Dictionary*; along with green and blue, "white" ranks as a most common color in nature (e.g., milk, chalk, snow, clouds, limestone *appear* white).

[and] . . . created a 'backwash' of fixed impressions and attitudes difficult to efface."[5] The devil and sin were black; angels and holiness white. Over the centuries, the effect and power of such symbolism rendered the basic neutrality of color quite "irrelevant."[6] But even more disastrously, when these bifurcating symbols and their vivid meanings were fixed to human flesh, to living human beings, there arose the terms *race* and *racism*.

Race, as Lucius Outlaw observed, is one among many ways of "conceptualizing and organizing social worlds composed of persons whose differences allow for arranging them into groups that come to be called 'races.'"[7] *Racism* is a complex structural or systemic phenomenon. James Boggs offers a comprehensive definition that points up its totalizing character and intent:

Racism is systematized oppression of one race by another. In other words, the various forms of oppression within every sphere of social relations—economic exploitation, military subjugation, political subordination, cultural devaluation, psychological violation, sexual degradation, verbal abuse, etc.—together make up a whole of interacting and developing processes which operate so normally and naturally and are

5. Roger Bastide, "Color, Racism, and Christianity," in *Color and Race*, ed. John Hope Franklin (Boston: Beacon Press, 1968), 35; see also Howard Thurman, *The Luminous Darkness: A Personal Interpretation of the Anatomy of Segregation and the Ground of Hope* (Richmond, IN: Friends United Press, 1989 [orig., 1965]); Robert E. Hood, *Begrimed and Black: Christian Traditions on Blacks and Blackness* (Minneapolis: Augsburg Fortress, 1994); and Eulalio Baltzar, *The Dark Center: A Process Theology of Blackness* (New York: Paulist Press, 1973). These authors take note of *positive* meanings of blackness in apophatic theology and the Christian mystical tradition, which refer to God's splendor as overwhelming one's mental and physical senses, so that God is hidden, beyond all images and words: God is as splendid, dazzling darkness.

6. Bastide, "Color, Racism, and Christianity," 35.

7. Lucius Outlaw, "Toward a Critical Theory of 'Race,'" in *Anatomy of Racism*, ed. David Theo Goldberg (Minneapolis: University of Minnesota Press, 1990), 61.

so much a part of the existing institutions of society that the individuals involved are barely conscious of their operation.[8]

Racism goes well beyond prejudice or even bigotry and welds attitudes or feelings of superiority to the putatively legitimate and commonly sanctioned exercise of power.

White racist supremacy refers to "the nearly four-hundred-year-old system of *white-on-black oppression*" and white racial dominance originating in the "importation, subordination, and exploitation of African slaves and in the subsequent elaboration and rationalization of that oppressive system."[9] In the framework of white racist supremacy, anti-blackness connotes contemptuous or violent responses directed at black people, black culture, history, and self-presentation. *White racist supremacy* refers to (1) behaviors and actions rooted in the assumption that white people are superior to *all* other peoples in certain characteristics, traits, skills, and attributes and to (2) an ideology.[10] White supremacists ground putative white racial superiority in appeals to examples of white dominance or superiority in *history* (e.g., conquest, trans-Atlantic slave trade, lynching, apartheid) and in *contemporary* cultural (e.g., ideological, aesthetic, entertainment) and societal practices (e.g., political, economic, technological, legal), in social institutions (e.g., schools,

8. James Boggs, *Racism and the Class Struggle* (New York: Monthly Review Press, 1970), 147–48.

9. Joe R. Feagin et al., *White Racism: The Basics,* 2nd ed. (New York: Routledge, 2001), 5.

10. The critical race theory movement that emerged in legal studies in the 1980s aimed theoretical scrutiny at the idea, power, and processes of supremacist domination of thought and life by white people as a group. See Kimberlé Crenshaw et al., eds., *Critical Race Theory: The Key Writings That Formed the Movement* (New York: New Press, 1995); also Richard Delgado et al., *Critical Race Theory: An Introduction* (New York: New York University Press, 2012). As an intellectual movement, critical race theory "highlights a creative—and tension-ridden—fusion of theoretical self-reflection, formal innovation, radical politics, existential evaluation, reconstructive experimentation, and vocational anguish," in *Critical Race Theory: Key Writings,* ed. Crenshaw et al., xi.

universities, courts, hospitals, media, the Internet) and trends. As an ideology, white racist supremacy maintains that white people should direct, rule, govern, and dominate nonwhite peoples in *all* cultural, societal, and religious domains. This ideology is reinforced and expressed through behaviors and actions that coalesce in what Eduardo Bonilla-Silva labels a "white habitus, a racialized, uninterrupted socialization process that conditions and creates whites' racial taste, perceptions, feelings, and emotions and their views on racial matters."[11] White racist supremacy as an ideology and societal process secures the power of white peoples as a social group over all other groups of peoples and, as a by-product of this historical, cultural, and societal dominance, ensures certain benefits and privileges to (most) whites as individuals.

In the common-sense processes of appropriating one's culture and society, Charles Mills argues that "'whiteness' is not natural; rather infants of a certain genealogy or phenotype growing up in a racist society have to learn to be white. Correspondingly, there have always been principled and morally praiseworthy whites who have thrown off their socialization and challenged white supremacy . . . in the name of a color-blind humanity."[12] In other words, personhood has been "racially normed."[13] At the same time, inasmuch as blackness is *not* natural, black peoples or peoples of African descent must resist reduction of their personhood and struggle for their humanity, rejecting deference to what whiteness stands for and submission to caricatures of the black self. As Robert Hood declares, blacks "negated their own negation"[14] and imagined, perceived, and caressed full equality of self, of black flesh.

---

11. Eduardo Bonilla-Silva, *Racism without Racists: Color-blind Racism and the Persistence of Racial Inequality in America,* 4th ed. (Lanham, MD: Rowman & Littlefield, 2014), 152.

12. Charles Mills, *Blackness Visible: Essays on Philosophy and Race* (Ithaca, NY: Cornell University Press, 104.

13. Mills, *Blackness Visible,* 113.

14. Hood, *Begrimed and Black,* 188.

Ontological Effect of Color Symbolism

Winthrop Jordan contends that in their encounters with Africans, Europeans and white Americans did not fail to observe and remark on differences in physical appearance, in religion, and in manner of living, but "the most arresting characteristic" was the color of the Africans' skin.[15] Negative meanings of black surfaced, vibrating with connotations of filth, sin, ugliness, evil, and the devil.[16] When this color symbolism came into intense contact with a Christian theological and philosophical anthropology deeply influenced by Platonic and Aristotelian metaphysics, black flesh was devalued ontologically, and greater value was placed on the "spiritual and transcendental."[17]

> The soul was the form of the body. As form was superior to matter, giving it its essence or meaning, so the soul was superior to the body. Because of this orientation toward the soul as opposed to that of the body, the symbolism of black and white was ... related to the soul and its condition. Thus, the soul was spoken of as white when it was in a state of grace and spoken of as black when it was in a state of moral or grievous sin.[18]

European economic dominance and technological superiority confirmed and reinforced the "positive theological values attached to white skin and, conversely, the negative theological values attached to peoples with dark skins."[19] Gradually over more than three hundred years of the Atlantic slave trade, the negative meanings

---

15. Winthrop D. Jordan, *White over Black: American Attitudes toward the Negro, 1550–1812,* 2nd ed. (Chapel Hill: University of North Carolina Press, 1968), 4.

16. Ibid., 7.

17. Eulalio Baltazar, *The Dark Center: A Process Theology of Blackness* (New York: Paulist Press, 1973), 27; see also Bastide, "Color, Racism, and Christianity," 34–49; and Hood, *Begrimed and Black.*

18. Baltazar, *The Dark Center,* 27-28.

19. Ibid., 29.

of blackness were transferred and attached to black flesh, to black bodies, to black peoples. At the same time, the philosophical move from the metaphysical to the empirical shifted epistemological concerns about the object of knowledge from substances, universals, and essences to phenomena, images, and sense impressions. It was but a short step to saying that the human being is her or his appearance, or the human being is as she or he appears.[20] Black flesh, black bodies, black peoples *became* the embodiment of the sinister, the dangerous, the wicked, evil, and sin.

The racialization and devaluation of black flesh were so fixed to the black body that the very meaning of being human "was defined continually against black people and blackness."[21] Moreover, the terms and meanings, values and practices of human relating and relations, of engaging and engagement were shaped by subtle and perverse "anti-black logics"[22] that took root in cognition, language, meanings, and values, thereby reshaping nearly all practices of human encounter and engagement. Fatally, these anti-black logics have proved (and prove) resistant both to intelligibility and to critique. Thus, the normative denotation of who was (and is) human referred exclusively to white human beings, although this was expressed concretely as being white male.

The Custom, Commerce, Culture, and Creed of Slaveholding

The papal bull *Sicut Dudum*, issued by Eugene IV in 1435, was the first explicit papal condemnation of the slave trade. Four hundred years later, in 1839, Gregory XVI repeated the reproach expressed by six of his predecessors and issued the apostolic letter *In supremo apostolatus fastigio*. Gregory admonished and adjured

---

20. Ibid.

21. Rinaldo Walcott, "The Problem of the Human: Black Ontologies and 'the Coloniality of Our Being,'" in *Postcoloniality—Decoloniality—Black Critique: Joints and Fissures*, ed. Sabine Broeck and Carsten Junker (Frankfurt: Campus Verlag, 2014), 93.

22. Ibid.

all believers in Christ, of whatsoever condition, that no one here-after may dare unjustly to molest Indians, Negroes, or other men of this sort; or to spoil them of their goods; or to reduce them to slavery; or to extend help or favour to others who perpetrate such things against them; or to exercise that inhuman trade by which Negroes, as if they were not men, but mere animals, howsoever reduced into slavery, are without any distinction, contrary to the laws of justice and humanity, bought, sold, and doomed some-times to the most severe and exhausting labors.[18]

While the pope forbade any Catholic cleric or layperson to defend, publish, or teach, in public or in private, anything that supported the slave trade, nothing was said about slavery as an institution. Two more popes, Pius IX in 1866 and Leo XIII in 1888 and again 1890, would reiterate official Catholic disapproval.

Papal teaching appealed to the ideal, but Catholics living in the United States, particularly in the South, presented several dilemmas around enslavement, sex, and race. Catholics, foreign and native born, North and South, were steeped in European religious devo-tions and cultural sensibilities and relied upon a theology crafted in Europe's relatively static social order. Southern Catholics sought political and civic acceptance without surrender of religious identity and integrity. But, well before the "high tide of Catholic immigra-tion in the nineteenth century," the church had made a compromise with slavery that left some with uneasy consciences.[23]

"Slavery was the shibboleth of southern civilization. Accep-tance in the Old South," states historian Randall Miller, "meant getting right with slavery."[24] Getting right with slavery included the purchase and ownership of slaves. In the upper and lower

---

23. Randall M. Miller, "Catholics in a Protestant World: The Old South Example," in *Varieties of Southern Religious Experience*, ed. Samuel H. Hill (Baton Rouge, LA: Louisiana State University Press, 1988), 115; see also Cyprian Davis, *The History of Black Catholics in the United States* (New York: Crossroad Publishing, 1990), 35–41.

24. Miller, "Catholics in a Protestant World," 121.

South, Catholic slaveholders lived alongside their Protestant planter counterparts. Some Catholic families thrived in the South, owning slaves, achieving great wealth, professional success, and sociopolitical status.[25] Religious orders of women and men owned human property: the Carmelites, Jesuits, and Sulpicians in Maryland; Ursulines, Religious of the Sacred Heart, and Capuchins in Louisiana; the Visitation nuns in Washington, DC; Dominicans, Sisters of Charity, and Sisters of Loretto in Kentucky; the Vincentians in Missouri.[26]

Getting right with slavery also meant defending the rightness of enslavement. With conspicuous exceptions, the hierarchy failed to challenge the culture and system that legitimated, sustained, and benefited from slavery. Despite papal condemnations, Southern bishops and priests held that slavery, as a social, economic, and legal institution, was morally legitimate as long as the slaveholder's title of ownership was valid and the slave was cared for materially and spiritually.[27]

The leading moral theologian of the period was the bishop of Philadelphia, Francis Patrick Kenrick, whose *Theologia Moralis* was used in U. S. seminaries. Kenrick validated the institution of slavery by accenting respect for law. He argued

> nothing should be attempted against the law, nor anything said or done to free the slaves or to make them bear unwillingly. But the prudence and the charity of the sacred ministers should appear in their effecting that the slaves, imbued with Christian

---

25. Jon L. Wakelyn, "Catholic Elites in the Slaveholding South," in *Catholics in the Old South: Essays on Church and Culture*, ed. Randall M. Miller and Jon L. Wakelyn (Macon, GA: Mercer University Press, 1983), 211–39.

26. Davis, *The History of Black Catholics*, 35–39; R. Emmett Curran, "'Splendid Poverty': Jesuit Slaveholding in Maryland, 1805–1838," in *Catholics in the Old South*, 125–46; and Thomas Murphy, *Jesuit Slaveholding in Maryland, 1717–1838* (New York: Routledge, 2001).

27. Francis Maxwell, *Slavery and the Catholic Church* (Westminster, MD: Christian Classics, 1975), 10–12.

morals, render service to their masters, venerating God, the supreme Master of all.[28]

Bishop John England of South Carolina argued that slavery conformed to Catholic teaching and Sacred Scripture, and Bishop William Henry Elder of Mississippi sought to meet the pastoral needs of the enslaved people, even as he deemed them inferior to whites. Archbishop John Baptist Purcell of Cincinnati came out against slavery just before the Civil War. But New Orleans Archbishop Jean-Marie Odin not only suspended French-born priest Claude Pascal Maistre, when he refused to stop preaching publicly against slavery, but also put the parish he served, St. Rose of Lima, under interdict.[29] Bishops Auguste Martin of Louisiana, Augustin Verot of Florida, and John England of South Carolina, each acceded to the institution of slavery on the grounds that neither Jesus Christ nor the church condemned it.[30] Martin considered blacks dependent on whites and went so far as to pronounce slavery to be "the manifest will of God."[31]

The Vatican urged the bishops of the United States, both prior to and after Emancipation, to evangelize the enslaved and newly emancipated people, but, for the most part, their pleas fell on deaf ears. To be sure, the hierarchy in the United States was confronted with a complex pastoral situation—the needs of a growing culturally and

---

28. John Peter Marschall, "Francis Patrick Kenrick, 1851–1863: The Baltimore Years" (PhD diss., Catholic University of America, 1965), 332, cited in Richard R. Duncan, "Catholics and the Church in the Antebellum Upper South," in *Catholics in the Old South*, 76.

29. Cyprian Davis, *Henriette Delille, Servant of Slaves, Witness to the Poor* (New Orleans: Archdiocese of New Orleans/Sisters of the Holy Family, 2004), 73–75.

30. Auguste Martin was the first bishop of Louisiana (1803–1875), Augustin Verot bishop of St. Augustine in Florida (1804–1876), and John England bishop of South Carolina (1786–1842).

31. Maria Caravaglios, "A Roman Critique of Pro-Slavery Views of Bishop Martin of Natchitoches, Louisiana," *Records of the American Catholic Historical Society of Philadelphia* 83 (1972): 51, cited in Davis, *Henriette Delille,* 73.

linguistically diverse immigrant population, lay trusteeism, a short-age of clergy and religious, taxing geographic distances, breakdowns in communication, nativist attacks, and the anti-Catholic senti-ments of abolitionists.[32]

The Catholic Church in the United States, especially prior to Emancipation, faltered in its responsibility to offer a prophetic gospel witness to slaveholding society and ignored its own teach-ing regarding the dignity of all human persons and the rights of slaves. The hierarchy relegated the question of slavery to the politi-cal sphere and, Miller asserts, "yielded up its social conscience to the status quo and devoted itself to the City of God." And, further, he charged: "Even in New Orleans, where the church possessed the numbers, wealth, and prestige to withstand social and politi-cal ostracism . . . the Catholic establishment tendered no critique of Southern culture."[33] None of the "eight provincial councils held by the [hierarchy of the] American Catholic Church between 1829 and 1849 or the first Plenary Council of Baltimore held in 1832," directly addressed the problem of slavery, as Jason Wallace shows.[34]

Anti-black logics were so pervasive and so restrictive, so precise and so pleasurable[35] that they overrode the exercise of potentially legitimate authority, seized and displaced Divine Authority, thereby totalizing and fetishizing whiteness and white human beings. In

---

32. Davis, *Henriette Delille*, 73–75; see also Randall M. Miller, "The Failed Mission: The Catholic Church and Black Catholics in the Old South," in *Catholics in the Old South*, 149–70; Edward J. Misch, "The American Bish-ops and the Negro from the Civil War to the Third Plenary Council of Balti-more: 1865–1884" (PhD diss., Pontifical Gregorian University, Rome, 1968); Jamie T. Phelps, "The Mission Ecclesiology of John R. Slattery: A Study of an African American Mission of the Catholic Church in the Nineteenth Cen-tury" (PhD diss., Catholic University of America, 1989), esp. 1–146.

33. Miller, "Catholics in a Protestant World," 121, 127–28.

34. W. Jason Wallace, *Catholics, Slaveholders, and the Dilemma of Ameri-can Evangelicalism, 1835–1860* (Notre Dame, IN: University of Notre Dame Press, 2010), 119.

35. Anthony Paul Farley, "The Black Body as Fetish Object," *Oregon Law Review* 97 (1997): 461–535.

this process, anti-black logics repressed demands of conscience, obscured morality, and eclipsed ethics to induce authority and authorities to kneel before the racialized idol of whiteness. In an even more perilous, totalizing move, these authorities attempted to bleach and domesticate the Divine, to make over the Divine in their image and likeness. Thus, in adhering to the culture and custom of anti-blackness, episcopal authorities bound themselves to the idolatry of whiteness.

Black Catholic Resistance

The indifference of Catholic authorities to the care of black bodies and (black) souls neither prevented black human beings from communicating with the Divine nor drove them from that church which constitutes for them the singular way the Divine Three give their own self and life for the liberation of all. Since the Stono Rebellion[36] and, even, perhaps prior to it, God's black human creatures have improvised authenticity of life and worship in struggle in ways that were and are spiritually defiant, intellectually imaginative, culturally creative, socially interdependent—in *uncommon faithfulness*.[37]

One of the most poignant of the stories of such uncommon lived faith is that of a South Carolina settlement, now known as "Catholic Hill," in Collerton County in the diocese of Charleston. In the nineteenth century, this area was known as "Catholic Crossroads." This was the site of St. James the Greater Church, which had been established in 1833 by Bishop John England for the several slave-

---

36. John Thornton, "African Dimensions of the Stono Rebellion," *American Historical Review* 4, no. 96 (1991): 1101–13.

37. See Jamie T. Phelps, *Black and Catholic: The Challenge and Gift of Black Folk: Contributions of African American Experience and Thought to Catholic Theology* (Milwaukee, WI: Marquette University Press, 1997); Diana Hayes and Cyprian Davis, eds., *Taking Down Our Harps: Black Catholics in the United States* (Maryknoll, NY: Orbis Books, 1998); M. Shawn Copeland et al., eds., *Uncommon Faithfulness: The Black Catholic Experience* (Maryknoll, NY: Orbis Books, 2009).

holding Catholic families in the area. Fire destroyed the church building in 1856, and, roughly four years later, the Civil War was declared. The slaveholding families fled the area leaving the church buildings in disrepair, with "only a small nucleus of Catholics [left] among the blacks."[38] These black people had suffered many trials during slavery; now abandoned and forgotten, their faith would be tested by fire (1 Peter 1:6-8). Yet, Cyprian Davis writes, "Without priest, church, or sacraments the Catholic faith was kept alive [among them] over a period of forty years through the efforts of Vincent de Paul Davis, a former enslaved man who instructed the children."[39] Not until 1897 did a priest from the diocese discover this community, attend to their sacramental needs, and restore the church building.

But during that forty-year period, there had always been a "core of laymen and laywomen who taught and led the community in worship,"[40] who nourished and sustained one another in faith, who handed on what (the Tradition) they had received: "that Christ died for our sins in accordance with the scriptures, that he was buried, and that he was raised on the third day" [1 Cor 15:3-4]. Without a physical structure, a building for divine worship, through the power and grace of the Holy Spirit, these humble black people became "living stones," and they themselves were built into a house at the crossroads to welcome the risen Christ.[41]

Conclusion

The hierarchy held (and holds) interpretative and juridical power to justify geographic and spatial sequestering or segregation of black flesh and bodies. Their accommodation to anti-black logics included the establishment of segregated parishes, schools, and,

---

38. Davis, *The History of Black Catholics,* 209–10.

39. Ibid.

40. Ibid., 210.

41. I have probed this story previously, but it bears repeating in this context.

in some case, cemeteries; the denial, exclusion, and prohibition of black bodies from religious vows and from priesthood; and the proscription of black religious expressive culture and spirituality.[42] Their accommodation to these anti-black logics not only contested Catholic teaching regarding the *imago dei*, that all human beings participate in the divine likeness, not only defied the intention and effect of Baptism, but interrupted the power of Eucharist to collapse barriers of space and relation.[43]

In subtle and in crude ways, U.S. Catholicism has and continues to demonstrate contempt for God's black human creatures who share in the glory, beauty, and image of the Divine. Such contempt veers toward contempt of the Divine, toward blasphemy through enacting, even passively, such metaphysical violence. And such contempt toward black existence could set U.S. Catholicism on the path of idolatry.

---

42. See Davis, *The History of Black Catholics*; Bryan N. Massingale, *Racial Justice and the Catholic Church* (Maryknoll, NY: Orbis Books, 2010); and Diane Batts Morrow, *Persons of Color and Religious at the Same Time: The Oblate Sisters of Providence 1828–1860* (Chapel Hill: University of North Carolina Press, 2002).

43. William T. Cavanaugh, "The World in a Wafer: A Geography of the Eucharist as Resistance to Globalization," *Modern Theology* 15, no. 2 (April 1999): 194.

PART II

Black Bodies and Selves

CHAPTER 5

Sources of a Black Self?
Ethics of Authenticity in an Era of Anti-Blackness

ANDREW PREVOT

Anti-Blackness as a Threat to Black Selfhood

The discussion of anti-blackness tends to focus on violence against black bodies. Who can deny that the darkly colored bodies of African and Afro-diasporic peoples have been shackled, shipped, sold, beaten, raped, burned, hanged, mocked, banned, hosed, profiled, exploited, incarcerated, strangled, and shot—and that many of these horrors continue today with some degree of impunity and, therefore, state cooperation?[1] The analysis of such physical violence has risen together with a growing scholarly consensus that "I am my body"—or, if one likes, "I am my flesh."[2] Dissatisfied by Platonic and

---

1. See, among many citable studies, Kelly Brown Douglas, *Stand Your Ground: Black Bodies and the Justice of God* (Maryknoll, NY: Orbis Books, 2015), 48–89; and M. Shawn Copeland, *Enfleshing Freedom: Body, Race, and Being* (Minneapolis: Fortress Press, 2010), 65–78 and 110–24.

2. Hortense Spillers distinguishes body and flesh in her classic "Mama's Baby, Papa's Maybe: An American Grammar Book," in *Black, White, and in Color: Essays on American Literature and Culture* (Chicago: University of Chicago Press, 2003), 203–29, at 206. Consider also Mayra Rivera, *Poet-*

Cartesian dualisms, theorists today tend to favor phenomenological and cultural-critical accounts of the human being as constitutively corporeal. Presupposing this perspective, I argue that when black bodies are attacked, so too is black selfhood. At the same time, I contend that to understand the full scope of anti-blackness we need to think not only about violence against black bodies but also very explicitly about the ways that selfhood has been limited and denied as a possibility for black persons, both through this violence and through other means.

Countless selfhood-denying images, stories, ideas, institutions, practices, and emotions accompany blackness in this modern age. Indeed, these socially constructed linkages between blackness, on the one hand, and fear, evil, ignorance, inferiority, nothingness, unfreedom, and disposability, on the other, may seem to define "blackness" for anti-black modernity. They define it, to the extent that they do, not so much as an essence but as a web of material and symbolic connections (what Alexander Weheliye calls a "racial assemblage").[3] My claim is that these negative linkages interfere with black persons' access to an "ethics of authenticity." This is philosopher Charles Taylor's name for a modern moral ideal that allows each person to develop a meaningful sense of his or her own way of living freely as a body in relationship with others and with God. This ethics of authenticity is what I mean preliminarily by "self-hood." It is what anti-blackness threatens to strip away from black people even when it does not directly assault all of their bodies. To be a *person*, therefore someone with human rights, it is sufficient to have a living human body.[4] But to develop a sense of *self*, as I

---

ics of the Flesh (Durham, NC: Duke University Press, 2015); and Alexander Weheliye, *Habeas Viscus: Racializing Assemblages, Biopolitics, and Black Feminist Theories of the Human* (Durham, NC: Duke University Press, 2014).

3. Weheliye, *Habeas Viscus*, 46–52.

4. This idea has been crucial to mainstream Catholic bioethical recognition of the personhood of prenatal and profoundly disabled human bodies. The same moral principle demands that all black bodies be recognized as persons, regardless of any impaired selfhood that may result from anti-blackness.

use the term here, involves more than that: it means living freely in relationships as one's body.

Can we conceive an ethically authentic black self that is capable of withstanding and rising above anti-black modernity's toxic influence on the culturally disseminated and politically enforced meaning of blackness? Perhaps this must remain a *somewhat* open question. As Frantz Fanon indicates, it would be dangerous to underestimate the depths of the existential crisis that it represents. Nonetheless, with Fanon, I am convinced that we need at least to seek the possibility of such a self in order to have any realistic hope of resisting anti-blackness at its roots. The false equivalence between selfhood and whiteness must be dismantled, and a black selfhood must be envisioned that is not only distinct from a mere performance of whatever blackness is supposed to mean but also distinct from a mere interminable struggle to survive with this identity, even if that struggle is unavoidable. Black selfhood has to be more than racial conformity or racial antagonism. It has to show forth a freedom that provokes not fear but wonder and respect. A black body has to be able to mean both singularity and transcendence.

By turning toward the admittedly fraught question of the self, my intention is to point toward the depths of the anti-blackness problem that Christian ethics needs to face. Consciousness of "white privilege" and active resistance against "color blind racism" are important but insufficient measures.[5] Christian ethics needs to fight for black selfhood.[6] More specifically, I argue that the Christian tradition of theological anthropology, including especially the

---

5. These strategies are exemplified by Laurie Cassidy and Alex Mikulich, eds., *Interrupting White Privilege: Catholic Theologians Break the Silence* (Maryknoll, NY: Orbis Books, 2007).

6. For this reason, I recommend a deeper engagement with the black existential tradition, as represented, for example, by Lewis Gordon, *Existentia Africana: Understanding Africana Existential Thought* (New York: Routledge, 2000), and other works supportive of black selfhood, such as Kevin Quashie's *The Sovereignty of Quiet: Beyond Resistance in Black Culture* (New Brunswick, NJ: Rutgers University Press, 2012).

mystical awareness of God's interior presence and the spiritual practice of discerning God's individually addressed call, can contribute
powerfully to the fight for black selfhood. This tradition discloses
the possibility of a divinely grounded black self that is stronger than
even the worst ontological fabrications of anti-black modernity.
Sojourner Truth is a witness to this.

One might suggest that a simpler solution is better: why not just
promote positive associations with blackness to dethrone the negative? Recovering positive meanings drawn from the communal practices and individual achievements of black people is a crucial strategy. But there are also dangers in such a suggestion. For instance, it
may underwrite a "politics of respectability" in which black people
are asked constantly to prove their worth according to white-centric
or perhaps just overly demanding standards of cultural value.[7] This
is a cruel soteriology of works righteousness, which militates against
the hope of authenticity.

Moreover, the goal of promoting positive associations with blackness may be compromised by restrictive senses of what it takes to be
authentically and impressively black, that is, expectations for narrow forms of musical, athletic, comedic, or otherwise stereotypical
excellence. More often than not, the discourse of "black authenticity" seems to focus on black persons' supposed conformity to such
constructed meanings of blackness. Many scholars have exposed
the narrowness and insufficiency of this racially conformist way
of understanding "black authenticity,"[8] and the account of black

---

7. See E. Francis White, *Dark Continent of Our Bodies: Black Feminism
and Politics of Respectability* (Philadelphia: Temple University Press, 2001),
36–37.

8. Consider J. Martin Favor, *Authentic Blackness: The Folk in the New
Negro Renaissance* (Durham, NC: Duke University Press, 1999); E. Patrick
Johnson, *Appropriating Blackness: Performance and the Politics of Authenticity*
(Durham, NC: Duke University Press, 2003); Shelly Eversley, *The Real Negro:
The Question of Authenticity in Twentieth-Century African American Litera-
ture* (New York: Routledge, 2004); Martin Japtok and Jerry Rafiki Jenkins,
eds., *Authentic Blackness/"Real" Blackness: Essays on the Meaning of Blackness*

selfhood that I offer here also seeks to move beyond it. For black people, as for everyone, "authenticity" does not mean performing certain dubious roles assigned to their race; it means living freely in their bodies.

However, the main limitation of the strategy of attaching positive meanings to blackness is that it combats negative conceptions of blackness only within the contingent spaces of social construction in which they occur. A theological intervention in favor of black selfhood adds a transcendent vantage point that helpfully shifts the conversation. For those black persons, such as Sojourner Truth, who know themselves in relation to God, this ground of their being is irrefutable. Even when their bodies are violated or made to signify something negative, their religious faith helps them understand that they remain God's irrevocable choice and gift and dwelling place. To be sure, theology too must be recognized as one socially constructed discourse among others (and a very fallible one at that, which has often been corrupted by anti-blackness).[9] Nevertheless, theology is perhaps the one remaining discourse that allows critical distance from society's immanent frame of power/knowledge and not only from this or that formation of it. Theology's critical distance benefits the struggle for black selfhood by distinguishing it from a mere conflict of interpretations that would remain dangerously subject to the whims of capital and chance.

In my presentation of the radical depths of the problem of anti-blackness, I do ally myself to some extent with Afro-pessimist theory.[10] However, I significantly part ways with this school

---

in *Literature and Culture* (New York: Peter Lang, 2011); and John L. Jackson, Jr., *Real Black: Adventures in Racial Sincerity* (Chicago: University of Chicago Press, 2005).

9. Consider the slaveholding pseudo-Christianity analyzed by James Cone in *The Spirituals and the Blues: An Interpretation* (Maryknoll, NY: Orbis Books, 2004), 20–31.

10. I am thinking here especially of Frank B. Wilderson III's *Red, White and Black: Cinema and the Structure of U.S. Antagonisms* (Durham, NC: Duke University Press, 2010).

of thought in my Christian theological proposal. God is greater than violence. God wants to relate to black persons in their black bodies and in their individual, social, and transcendental exercise of human freedom. This divine desire is already a hidden reality, and it is accessible if we but seek it and open ourselves to it. The collective effort to transform the world accordingly remains extremely daunting. Credible support for black selfhood would require major linguistic, aesthetic, and structural changes. Human work is needed to construct different social realities. Yet there is another level at which the possibility of black selfhood has already been given by God's indomitable, indwelling love. The relationship between social construction and divine grace in the formation of black selfhood is a central question warranting further thought. To err too far in one direction invites pessimism; to err too far in the other risks idealism. Assuming one wants to avoid such extremes, what is the right proportion?

My argument for a God-given form of black selfhood proceeds in three sections. The first section argues that Charles Taylor's account of modern selfhood in *The Ethics of Authenticity* and "The Politics of Recognition" is somewhat useful but also insufficiently resistant to anti-blackness. The second section treats Frantz Fanon's *Black Skin, White Masks* as a revealing illustration of the ways that anti-blackness undermines the quest for selfhood among black persons. The final section then reads the *Narrative of Sojourner Truth* as suggesting a path forward through the complex interweavings of social construction and divine grace.

A Critical Engagement with Charles Taylor

At first glance, Taylor's philosophy may seem to exemplify the denial of black selfhood that I am trying to overcome. Performatively—that is, through his canon and his preferred problematics—he appears to align selfhood predominantly with white, male European culture. He tells a panoramic story of modern intellectual and social development that has no nonwhite protoganists (notwithstanding the North African Augustine, who functions mainly as a figure of Latin Christendom). This story makes ontological claims: it is about the conditions for the possibility of the self.[11] A few critics have resisted his eurocentrism and androcentrism,[12] two interlocking tendencies that leave the contributions of black women doubly excluded. Although there are some exceptions, such as his appreciative engagement in *A Secular Age*[13] with Nelson Mandela and Desmond Tutu and especially his treatment of race and gender in "The Politics of Recognition" (which we shall consider below), even these do not demonstrate enough rigorous attention to the ways that selfhood has been systematically imperiled for black persons or the ways that black selfhood has emerged despite all the forces conspiring against it.

Without overlooking these limitations, I contend, in harmony with Kwame Anthony Appiah,[14] that Taylor's account of an ethics of authenticity may help us think through the possibility of black selfhood in anti-black modernity. Taylor addresses certain problems that do not need to be rehashed. In particular, in *The Ethics of Authenticity*, he helpfully distinguishes his proposed model of selfhood from certain lesser analogues, such as narcissism, subjectivism, relativism, and anthropocentrism, to name but a few (2, 14, and

---

11. The fullest version of this story is found in Charles Taylor's *Sources of the Self: The Making of the Modern Identity* (Cambridge, MA: Harvard University Press, 1989).

12. See Enrique Dussel, *The Underside of Modernity: Apel, Ricoeur, Rorty, Taylor, and the Philosophy of Liberation*, trans. Eduardo Mendieta (Atlantic Highlands, NJ: Humanity, 1996), 129–59; and Susan Wolf, "Comment," in Charles Taylor, *Multiculturalism: Examining the Politics of Recognition*, ed. Amy Gutmann (Princeton, NJ: Princeton University Press, 1994), 75–85.

13. See Charles Taylor, *A Secular Age* (Cambridge, MA: Harvard University Press, 2007), 706–7.

14. See Kwame Anthony Appiah, "Identity, Authenticity, Survival: Multicultural Societies and Social Reproduction," in Taylor, *Multiculturalism*, 149–63; and Kwame Anthony Appiah, *The Ethics of Identity* (Princeton, NJ: Princeton University Press, 2005), 105–8.

68).[15] He argues that each of these deviant forms is not sufficiently relational. In addition to alienating one from others, they also disconnect one from communal structures of meaning and, in the final analysis, from any transformative openness to God (35, 40). Everything is reduced to an arbitrary "self-determining freedom" (28). In this reductive perspective, "authenticity" seems to mean living unrestrictedly how I feel like living at any given moment without any morally binding concern for others or the common good and, indeed, without any articulate sense of who I am or why I intend to do this or that. Those struggling against anti-blackness can appreciate Taylor's rejection of this socially destructive way of defining authenticity and perhaps see in it an implicit critique of harmful modes of whiteness. At the same time, this same group may be glad to have such a thin, antisocial picture of selfhood ruled out for nonwhite persons as well.

For a positive understanding of an ethics of authenticity, Taylor draws on Jean-Jacques Rousseau's idea of a "voice of nature within us" and Johann Gottfried von Herder's Romantic view that "each of us has an original way of being" (27–28). He uses these notions to suggest that modern interiority at its best is not just the site of an unfettered subjective will but rather a place in which one can conceive oneself as a participant in something mysterious and definitive. In some cases, this inner voice or individual way of being may be received and interpreted as "the call of God" (40). Taylor grants that the content of this "interior" is formed through dialogical interactions with the "exterior" (33). He understands that self-expression is not just about bringing some core identity from the inside out but also, and perhaps more truly, about using what is available on the outside to create a sense of an inside (29, 61). Nevertheless, the self, for Taylor, is no mere product of external forces. He seems to believe quite sincerely in a situated but very real freedom: a capacity to be true to oneself in relationships with others.

---

15. Charles Taylor, *The Ethics of Authenticity* (Cambridge, MA: Harvard University Press, 1991), cited parenthetically.

To some extent, Taylor appreciates that this ethics of authenticity has been difficult for black persons and other subaltern peoples, including women and the indigenous, to access (50). In "The Politics of Recognition," he cites Fanon's *Wretched of the Earth* to this effect. Fanon, he says, "argued that the major weapon of the colonizers was the imposition of their image of the colonized on the subjugated people. These latter, in order to be free, must first of all purge themselves of these depreciating self-images."[16] Taylor identifies Fanon as a key progenitor of the then-current (early 1990s) debates about "multiculturalism" in politics and the academy. Although Taylor is troubled by Fanon's support for violent means of anticolonial resistance, he does accept Fanon's point that coloniality attacks the selfhood of the colonized and then applies this logic to black persons, women, and other downtrodden groups.

The fact that Taylor engages Fanon is somewhat encouraging, but his engagement also leaves quite a lot to be desired. Taylor's main goal in this text is not to overcome anti-blackness—or, for that matter, patriarchy, colonialism, or any other form of domination. Rather, his main goal is to avoid a too procedural way of extending equal recognition to all cultures. He does not want a universal validation of all differences to occur *de jure*; he only wants particular validations to happen *de facto*, when they are warranted by discovery of concrete goods in another culture. He supports a "presumption" that there are such goods but wishes to withhold "judgment." He suggests that an affirmative judgment is possible only after a Gadamerian "fusion of horizons" yields some positive results.[17]

Taylor has good reasons to want recognition to be grounded in more than a "difference-blind" formalism and to recommend a hermeneutical approach to intercultural encounter. But to make only these points in the wake of Fanon's revelation of the violently com-

---

16. Taylor, "The Politics of Recognition," in *Multiculturalism*, 25–73, at 65.

17. Ibid., 61–73.

promised selfhood of colonized peoples betrays a way of thinking that quickly reduces to absurdity. Taylor's proposal effectively renders the conditions for the possibility of black selfhood contingent on who-knows-what-authority's decision concerning the value of black people's cultural contributions to global society. He does not seem to understand that he is asking black people to wait for certain established molders of language, imagination, and public policy in anti-black modernity to make up their minds about whether black life has any significant value, but this is what he is doing. To avoid such a ludicrous scenario, Taylor would have to admit that combatting anti-blackness and transforming society accordingly is a major priority. He would have to let the lives and deaths of black people have a greater impact on his sense of self. He would have to enter into deeper dialogue with black sources and let his moral frameworks be challenged by a fusion with their horizons. These steps would make his ethics of authenticity more credible as an *ethics*, that is, an articulation and practical embodiment of the good. They would keep his uses of "authenticity" and "the self" from appearing to signify whiteness.[18]

A Crucial Question Posed by Frantz Fanon

To appreciate the gravity of the problem of black selfhood in anti-black modernity, it is helpful to study Fanon, particularly the chapter of *Black Skin, White Masks* called "The Lived Experience of the Black Man."[19] Fanon's consciousness of self emerges in stages throughout this chapter. His first positive statement about himself is this: "I came into this world anxious to uncover the meaning of things, my soul desirous to be at the origin of the world" (89). This search for primordial meaning is, if one likes, Fanon's Herderian "original way

---

18. This critique resonates with Jared Sexton's *Amalgamation Schemes: Anti-blackness and the Critique of Multiracialism* (Minneapolis: University of Minnesota, 2008).

19. Frantz Fanon, *Black Skin, White Masks*, trans. Richard Philcox (New York: Grove, 2008), cited parenthetically.

of being," that is, his intuition of his own essence. A second positive statement focuses on his corporeality: "I know that if I want to smoke, I shall have to stretch out my right arm and grab the pack of cigarettes lying at the other end of the table. As for the matches, they are in the left drawer, and I shall have to move back a little. And I make all these moves not out of habit, but by implicit knowledge. A slow construction of my self as a body in a spatial and temporal world—such seems to be the schema" (91). His quotidian body in motion is who he is—or, rather, it is who he would be unproblematically were it not for the violent objectification of his body by others.

Sometimes this objectification occurs as a shout from a stranger: "'Dirty nigger!' or simply 'Look! A Negro!'" (89) or with more emotive content: "*Maman*, look, a Negro; I'm scared!" (91). Fanon explains the effect that this sort of experience of objectification had on his self-awareness: "As a result, the body schema, attacked in several places, collapsed, giving way to an epidermal racial schema" (92). Note that what is attacked here is not the body per se but the "body schema," that is, his sense of himself as a living body. In this moment his body means for him not life, and not selfhood, but rather an inescapable atmosphere of racial fear and judgment. It is only in such an objectified condition that he discovers his blackness and discovers it precisely in its anti-black constructs: "I cast an objective gaze over myself, discovered my blackness, my ethnic features; deafened by cannibalism, backwardness, fetishism, racial stigmas, slave traders, and above all, yes, above all, the grinning *Y a bon Banania*" (92). The weight of negative associations and the pain they cause are intense: "My body is returned to me spread-eagled, disjointed, redone, draped in mourning on this white winter's day. The Negro is an animal, the Negro is bad, the Negro is wicked, the Negro is ugly; look, a Negro ..." (93).

This "Look! A Negro!" episode has become justly iconic.[20] But

---

less often considered are the stages of Fanon's struggle for selfhood after this incident. He recounts a series of reasonable strategies for recovering a sense of self, which he, however, seems to find not entirely satisfying. He fights shrewdly against anti-blackness but is not thoroughly convinced of his victory. Each gambit leaves him feeling vulnerable in one way or another. The question that he poses for us, therefore, is this: What are the conditions for success in such a fight? One option is to suggest that the struggle itself gives sufficient meaning to black selfhood, in which case Fanon would exemplify a black ethics of authenticity precisely through his tireless search for better modes of resistance. Another option is to read Fanon's narrative as a tragic tale, in which the free sense of embodied selfhood that he desires seems always to elude him in one respect or another. A final option would be to believe that, by the end of his narrative, he has found the selfhood he was looking for. There is some merit in each of these three lines of interpretation, but Fanon does not so much leave us with an obvious answer as with the question itself. How to be black and a self?

We can distinguish four strategies attempted by Fanon: first, a defiant counter-assertion of black identity; second, an appeal to scientific reason; third, a recovery of a rich cultural history; and, fourth, an insistence on human freedom as a final criterion. As a first tactic, Fanon decides to resist anti-blackness by strongly affirming his black identity: "I made up my mind . . . to assert myself as a BLACK MAN" (95). This defiant counter-assertion is a necessary step. His body demands it of him. However, it brings him no lasting peace. He senses that, when he claims this identity, everything that he does starts to be watched and interrogated. He feels burdened by the need to disprove stereotypes. He knows that any mistake will not only cost him but also be imputed to his race. He seeks solidarity with other black people, "my brothers, Negroes like myself," but he is disappointed: "To my horror, they reject me" (96). He suggests that they do not want to be associated too closely with his blackness, preferring instead to assimilate themselves in white society.

Fanon's next recourse is to scientific reason. He is encouraged by the fact that scientists had finally "admitted that the Negro was a human being; in vivo and in vitro the Negro was identical to the white man: same morphology, same histology." He breathes a sigh of relief: "Reason was assured of victory on every level" (99). But his confidence plummets when he realizes that, despite begrudgingly granting human status to black persons, many scientists were still invested in doubting the long-term effects of racial mixture and in identifying genetic predispositions toward stereotypical racial behaviors such as cannibalism (100). In short, Fanon suspects that, despite certain gains, science will always find ways to produce racially dehumanizing scripts and give them authority. "Victory was playing cat and mouse" (99).

Rebuffed, Fanon tries a new strategy less dependent on the judgments of "reason." With other figures of the *Négritude* movement, such as Aimé Césaire and Léopold Senghor, he plunges into the rediscovered aesthetic riches of Africana culture and history. He develops a poetic sense of subjective union with the earth, the rhythms of life, and the primal origin of things. He revels in the magical or mystical quality of this return to the source, and he starts to believe that it is a much-needed contribution that black culture can make to a disenchanted modern society. But alas, as Fanon learns from Jean-Paul Sartre's *Black Orpheus*, this strategy will be easily pigeonholed as an anterior, negative phase of spirit's dialectic. Blackness will be equated with primitivism or disruption, but not with realized, mature freedom (102–16).

Fanon is on the verge of despair. He feels "like giving up" (116), but he will not. A soldier with an amputated leg tells his brother: "Get used to your color the way I got used to my stump. We are both casualties." Fanon cannot abide this advice: "I feel my soul as vast as the world, truly a soul as deep as the deepest rivers; my chest has the power to expand to infinity. I was made to give and they prescribe for me the humility of the cripple." He continues: "When I opened my eyes yesterday I saw the sky in total revulsion.

I tried to get up but the eviscerated silence surged toward me with paralyzed wings. Not responsible for my acts, at the crossroad between Nothingness and Infinity, I began to weep" (119). With these words the chapter ends. We may now insist upon a more sensitive treatment of disabled persons and their capacities to give themselves in many ways, but the more pressing question for the present argument is whether Fanon has really found a sense of self. He rebels until the end, but this rebellion leaves him caught between the extremes of all and nothing. There is no composition or composure left to him. He has lost touch with any sense of responsibility. The carefree finitude of his bodily schema is all but gone. He is reduced to tears.

The conclusion to *Black Skin, White Masks* offers one last strategy, which *may* indicate that this text is not ultimately tragic. Here Fanon emphatically refuses to be "a slave to the past" (200) and proclaims his human freedom: "There should be no attempt to fixate man, since it is his destiny to be unleashed" (205). He claims a connection with all human achievements by virtue of the fact that both they and he are fully human. He rejects the idea that, because he is black, he must limit the historical background of his selfhood to "black civilization" (201). He does not forget that as a black man he is associated in a particular way with his dehumanized black ancestors, but their experiences are not his vocation. He feels himself called to a freer form of embodied relationality: "Why not simply try to touch the other, feel the other, discover each other" (206)? This image of intimacy and freedom is, I suggest, evidence of the emergent possibility of authentic black selfhood even in anti-black modernity. Nevertheless, some may worry that Fanon risks leaving the struggle behind too soon. He does not recognize any right or duty "to demand reparations for my subjugated ancestors" (203). He strains toward the postracial: "The black man is not. No more than the white man" (206). His final word is a prayer to his body, a prayer to keep questioning: "O my body, always make me a man who questions!" (206). Has he won the fight or is he still in it?

Sojourner Truth as a Theological Model
of Black Selfhood

Sojourner Truth, born Isabella, prays not to her body but to God.[21] Like Fanon, she suffers the effects of anti-black modernity, and as a slave woman she arguably endures a more direct and intense form of this evil. Her body is violated in unspeakable ways. Her relationships are damaged and destroyed. She is afforded very little education and, for much of her life, has only a very narrow range of choices that she can make. Her existence is overdetermined by her negative social status. After being officially liberated from slavery in 1827 (when it was abolished in her home state of New York), she is still not free in any robust sense. She struggles to survive and is tempted to return to her former master. Deciding instead to make her way in the city, she quickly falls prey to other masters: misogynistic false prophets in the "kingdom of Matthias," who leave her spiritually disoriented and materially destitute. From her birth ca. 1797 until the feast of Pentecost in 1843, one might consider her all but lost. One would hardly expect that this poor, illiterate slave girl would become a great feminist abolitionist with the power to move and still crowds with her voice. The prayer life that she begins to develop as a child slowly prepares her for the extraordinary gift of self-possession that she will receive as a divine call in her adulthood. To be sure, one cannot understand her selfhood apart from the oppressive social contexts that shaped it and that it resists, but one also cannot understand her selfhood apart from its divine source. In

---

21. I rely on *Narrative of Sojourner Truth: A Bondswoman of Olden Time, with a History of Her Labors and Correspondence Drawn from Her "Book of Life"; Also, a Memorial Chapter*, ed. Nell Irvin Painter (New York: Penguin, 1998), cited parenthetically. Painter explains that Olive Gilbert composed the first edition in 1850, drawing directly from Truth's oral testimony while adding her own editorial glosses. Subsequent elements, mostly a scrapbook of clippings about Truth called "Book of Life," were added by Frances Titus to the 1875 edition. Because the reliability of these later elements is somewhat disputed, I focus on Gilbert's account.

contrast to Fanon, she provides a more explicitly theological model of black selfhood, which may help us overcome some of the antinomies that characterize his struggle.

First, let us consider the impediments to selfhood that plagued Isabella's early life. At the age of nine, she was sold at auction, together with some sheep, and made to live apart from her parents and siblings. Her new master was crueler than the first: "One Sunday morning . . . she found her master with a bundle of rods, prepared in the embers, and bound together with cords. When he had tied her hands together before her, he gave her the most cruel whipping she was ever tortured with. He whipped her till the flesh was deeply lacerated, and the blood streamed from her wounds" (18). In addition to such physical abuse, there was almost certainly sexual abuse, but Truth is reluctant to speak about the details because of "their very nature" and because she fears "they'd call me a liar! they would, indeed!" (56). She entered the world with a black female body that was, by law, not her own, and her masters beat and molested "it" (that is, her) whenever they saw fit.

Along with the mistreatment of her body, one must note the harm done to her relationships. Her forced alienation from her siblings, parents, children, and love interests was profoundly isolating. The tight-knit familial bonds that should have buoyed her sense of self were crushed by the slave trade. Her father, Bomefree, died alone and in despair (17). Her five-year-old son, Peter, who was illegally sold into slavery in the South, did not at first recognize her upon his return (36). Isabella fell in love with a slave named Robert from a nearby farm, but their relationship was forbidden. In her sight, he was beaten almost to death (24). She was forced to marry another slave, Thomas, with whom she had five children. When she fled her master's house the year she was to be emancipated, she only had one child with her, her infant daughter Sofia (28).

While enslaved, her thinking was badly distorted by the institution. She perceived her masters as gods (22). She was instructed by her mother to obey them and believed that this was the right thing to do (12). She was trained to view her body as the property of others, and for the first thirty years of her life this was the only reality she knew. When she began to have children, she even "rejoiced in being permitted to be the instrument of increasing the property of her oppressors" (25). After emancipation, she continued to suffer from distorted thinking. The clearest evidence of this comes from her involvement in the community of a dangerous charismatic figure named Matthias, who viewed himself as the embodiment of God the Father (63) and who taught Isabella that "every thing that has the smell of woman will be destroyed. Woman is the capsheaf of the abomination of desolation—full of all deviltry" (64). By the time Matthias's community collapsed, it had deprived her of the little money that she had been able to save from the meager wages her labor earned, and it left her spiritually adrift.

What hope was there that Isabella would find a way to live freely as her body in relationships with others and with God? What hope was there of true authenticity—that is, not merely conforming to negative expectations associated with her race and sex but discovering her embodied self as a singular and wondrous reality? The seeds of hope were planted by her first lessons in the art of prayer. Her mother taught her to turn to God in times of trouble (12). This petitionary practice developed in her as she grew. She eventually selected a sacred place where she would retreat to pray in solitude: "a small island in a small stream, covered with large willow shrubbery" (40). Years later, when she felt tempted to return to her former master, she was held back by a mystical vision in which "she says that God revealed himself to her, with all the suddenness of a flash of lighting, showing her, 'in the twinkling of an eye, that he was all *over*'" (44). She exclaimed: "Oh, God, I did not know you were so big" (45). Struck by the awareness of her littleness and her own moral failings (all the promises to God that she had not kept), she found herself reassured by a second vision: the apparition of a friend, whom she came to recognize as Jesus, a merciful mediator between herself and God. She perceived a "union" between herself and Jesus and found his love for her to be so personal and intimate that she felt as if it belonged exclusively to her (45).

This mystical experience of God's greatness and Jesus's loving presence in her life gave her strength and gradually transformed her self-understanding. "The sense of her nothingness, in the eyes of those with whom she contended for her rights, sometimes fell on her like a heavy weight, which nothing but her unwavering confidence in an arm which she believed to be stronger than all others combined could have raised from her sinking spirit" (47). Her feeling of being nothing was removed only by God's almighty arm. At the pivotal moment of her life, when she ceased to call herself "Isabella" and donned the new name "Sojourner Truth" as an expression of her essential identity, she was responding to a direct call from the Holy Spirit (68). After this event of pneumatological grace at Pentecost, everything changed. She began to walk about freely, wherever God directed her. She drew her sense of purpose not from slave masters or false prophets but rather from the divine truth and power that was already within her. She spoke and sang, and her voice energized disheartened communities and quieted unruly mobs (81). She became herself by becoming a visible, public witness to the full humanity of black persons and women and the God who creates and loves all human beings.

The feminist abolitionist Sojourner Truth that many readers know from the much anthologized but historically disputed "Arn't I a Woman?" speech (92) is the logical outcome of her trinitarian life of prayer. Although, like Fanon, Truth spent her life in struggle, this struggle was motivated after her conversion by a sense that God was assuredly with her. She knew that she was not nothing. Whatever lies the world perpetuated about the meaning of her body and whatever crimes it perpetrated against her body (and others like it), these had after a certain point very little power to disturb her sense of self. To be sure, early on, these lies and crimes gravely threatened her selfhood and negatively impacted her emerging theological awareness. But in her spiritual maturity she sees them clearly for what they are: malicious fictions that do not compare to the glory of God. Fanon's final criterion of human freedom is consistent with Truth's theological anthropology. I do not see a major conflict between the two.

I do believe, however, that there is something particularly notewor-thy about Truth's prayer, in contrast to Fanon's. Does it not seem to grant her a more unquestionable experience of freedom? Does it not somehow allow her both to be more comfortable in her black body and to be more attuned to the unfathomable transcendence that it shelters?

Conclusion

In this chapter, I have argued that, in order to resist anti-blackness at its roots, Christian ethics needs to affirm the possibility of black selfhood. This is no easy task. We live in a troubling age in which selfhood has been conflated with whiteness and in which blackness has been constructed in limiting and negative terms that threaten the freedom of black bodies. Without ignoring these harmful social constructions—indeed, precisely while critically analyzing and resisting them—we can also, with Sojourner Truth, contem-plate the overwhelming greatness of divine grace. Christian hope makes it possible to believe that God will be—and is already defini-tively, if imperceptibly—victorious over anti-blackness. Black self-hood is possible because God loves black people in their bodies and wants them to be free. Sojourner Truth is a powerful witness to this almighty divine desire. I have suggested that a Christian ethics of authenticity would do well to take its cues from her, with some assistance from Taylor and Fanon. Beyond racial conformity and racial antagonism, there is the hope of variously colored bodies liv-ing freely in relationships with one another. Christian ethics is not the only conceivable messenger of such a hope, but perhaps it can at least learn to speak this message and to verify it in action.

CHAPTER 6

Blackness and Anethical Performance

ASHON CRAWLEY

We always forget the labor. Labor disappears, is disappeared, into the products of exchange. We always forget the labor. The cost to produce and the compensation for the laborer are, because of this political economy, always unevenly distributed, always inequitable. This inequity is, because of Western theological and philosophical thought, necessarily racialized, gendered, and classed. To hear the sound of that inequity is what this essay attempts. To hear the crisis announced by sound, by sounding out in black, by the performance of Blackpentecostal aesthetics, is to hear the *an*ethical force of blackness. This *an*ethical performance is a critique of the crisis at the heart of Western thought, the crisis of racializing, gendering, and classing thought, and discarding the thought of the so-thought merely aesthetic flesh: the indigenous, the black, the woman, the poor. Following the work of Denise Ferreira da Silva in *Toward a Global Idea of Race*,[1] I consider how and why certain sounds are thought to be produced as racial difference. But beyond such production, I consider how to sit with and celebrate the ones who deepened into such a practice of performance, of Blackpentecostal noising, rather than renouncing such aesthetic excess in the cause of being included.

---

1. Denise Ferreira da Silva, *Toward a Global Idea of Race*, Borderlines (Minneapolis: University of Minnesota Press, 2007), 27.

The sounds I investigate vibrate out from people to whom, according to da Silva, "neither juridic universality nor self-determination applies."[2] Da Silva, in her theorizing, "seeks to understand why an ethical crisis does not ensue from the consistent, numerous, and recurrent indications that the 'others of Europe' are not comprehended by universality and self-determination, the principles governing post-Enlightenment social configurations."[3] If such ethical crises exist but are not comprehended, I contend that we can listen to the sounds emanating from zones in which the forgotten labor and exploitation that doesn't produce crises are most forcefully registered, most forcefully made evident to get a *sense*—that is, to get a feel, an aesthetic form—for what a response to such an ethics might sound like. That is, for da Silva, the ethical crisis emerges precisely by averting the ones affected by acts of violence and violation as the others of Europe.

An ethical crisis can only emerge for those that *are* subjects of juridic universality and self-determination such that the sounds made by those whose vibrations I am after here are *an*ethical injunctions against the lack of ethical crisis. They are *an*ethical injunctions against the very constitution of ethical being, of juridic universality and self-determination. They are *an*ethical injunctions against the discardability, the disposability, of the others of Europe from thought. *An*ethical insofar as they share in, without being the material of, the ethical crisis of refused comprehension. *An*ethical insofar as what is sounded out is the critique of ethics, the critique of the one, of the way to think worlds, the epistemology of Western thought—what Sylvia Wynter describes as the coloniality of being/power/truth/freedom[4]—that can produce an ethical injunction and can be ethical being.

---

2. Ibid., 9.

3. Ibid., 2.

4. Sylvia Wynter, "Unsettling the Coloniality of Being/Power/Truth/Freedom: Towards the Human, After Man, Its Overrepresentation—An Argument," *CR: The New Centennial Review* 3, no. 3 (2003): 257–337.

Vibration breaks itself off from the already, from the never having not been, from movement irreducible. Vibration announces itself as sound by such a breaking off, a breaking with. This vibratory change, this vibratory difference, is what is felt, heard. The vibratory change, what is felt and heard, is the break, the brokenness, the broken. What to make of sound as felt, heard, because of its capacity to break? This breaking, this brokenness, we might think of as the *otherwise*, the always possible plenitude of alternative modalities to organize, of alternative modes of being, of alternative ways of life. The feel and sound of vibration, its tactility and resonance, we shall call the sonic. The sonic announces the fact of ongoing vibration, some felt, some heard, always, however, moving, always abounding, always there, such that the thought of blackness, black thought, is the elaboration of the sonic capacity of the more than double, the vibratory shifting of the breaking, the broken, the vibration—the sound and feel—of otherwise possibilities.

* * *

In the movement of Helga Crane in Nella Larsen's *Quicksand*,[5] there is a demonstration of the journey of anethical being, the journey and performance of anethical possibility. Helga Crane, throughout the text, journeyed onward and onward for a place of refuge, for a place of rest and comfort. Never settled, she found herself traveling across the United States, from Tennessee to Chicago, and from Chicago to Harlem. Unsettled, she traveled to Denmark with hopes of finally being able to be at rest, stasis, the quietude of solemn existence. But she was, there as well, unsettled and left Denmark for Harlem a second time. This second move to Harlem, a chance at reprieve.

It was in the vibration, the breaking and breaking off of disruption, of the ceaseless noise and pulse of blackness, of anethical blackness, that she found—even if only momentarily—respite from the storm.

---

5. Nella Larsen, *Quicksand*, Dover Books on Literature and Drama (Mineola, NY: Dover, 2006).

[She] had opened the door and entered before she was aware that, inside, people were singing a song which she was conscious of having heard years ago—hundreds of years it seemed. Repeated over and over, she made out the words:

> ... Showers of blessings,
> Showers of blessings ...

She was conscious too of a hundred pairs of eyes upon her as she stood there, drenched, disheveled, at the door of this improvised meeting-house ... The appropriateness of the song, with its constant reference to showers, the ridiculousness of herself in such surroundings, was too much for Helga Crane's frayed nerves. She sat down on the floor, a dripping heap, and laughed and laughed and laughed. It was into a shocked silence that she laughed.

[...]

Helga too began to weep, at first silently, softly; then with great racking sobs. Her nerves were so torn, so aching, her body so wet, so cold! It was a relief to cry unrestrainedly, and she gave herself freely to soothing tears, not noticing that the groaning and sobbing of those about her had increased, unaware that the grotesque ebony figure at her side had begun gently to pat her arm to the rhythm of the singing and to croon softly: "Yes, chile, yes, chile." Nor did she notice the furtive glances that the man on her other side cast at her between his fervent shouts of "Amen!" and "Praise God for a sinner!"

She did notice, though, that the tempo, that atmosphere of the place, had changed, and gradually she ceased to weep and gave her attention to what was happening about her. . . . And as Helga watched and listened, gradually a curious influence penetrated her; she felt an echo of the weird orgy resound in her own heart; she felt herself possessed by the same madness; she too felt a brutal desire to shout and to sling herself about.[6]

---

6. Ibid., 103–5.

What does the sound, the vibrations that were gathered together in angular momentum, in angular performance, as noise and music, do to her? What does the sound allow for Helga to sink deep into, what does it make available to her as a way to think her relation to the world? What does intensity and fervor of praise and adoration, as a spoken, sung, sounded thing, do to her flesh such that she—likewise—opens herself up to praise? Stumbling into the sounds of singing, of lyrics about showers of blessings—when she felt anything but blessed by the rain—triggered the moment of laughter. But such laughter did not remain there, such laughter vibrated and broke, broken, broke off into something like a deep reservoir of intense feeling. And from such a reservoir she drew joy. She, as the saints might say, got happy. And it was the sound that made a way for such an experience, the vibration opened up a path toward some other sociality, some otherwise modality of becoming.

The refuge was there before Crane's having entered it. It was there, dwelling, in wait, a space of inhabitation and care, a space for protection and provision. It was there, waiting to embrace and she would likewise embrace. It was available for her, and for all that were there, and it was the availability of space that is of import. Stumbling into the space, the soniferous environment made a claim on her. The voices sang to her, the bodies came to her. Falling on the ground, wet, she laughed. But somewhere between laughs, her engagement became serious. Her initial posture allowed her to listen, and listening opened to experience. The sounds of people singing, praying, praising—the sounds, generally, of the inspiring and expiring of breath, inhaling and exhaling, the aestheticizing of breathing in that tight, constrained space of the storefront—produced a bass, a bottom, a foundation upon which she could be carried.

There was a resonance of the sounds, of the voices. She heard them. She inhabited them. She was, literally, covered—by sounds, by bodies—and we might say that this covering also was the refuge, at least at that temporal moment; she sought without having known it. She did not merely open up the church door but she allowed herself to be open to that which she heard, to what she felt.

It was, for her, a terrifyingly joyful experience. In the resonance, in the vibrations sounded in and out of the church space, was the trace of the *an*ethical force of black performance, of Blackpentecostal aesthetics.

What does that mean? It means that Helga Crane's peregrinations in *Quicksand* were quickened, were initiated, by the problem that announces the very possibility of ethical being, by the problem of the lack of ethical crisis that produced the racial anxiety and terror in Naxos, Tennessee. Her movements throughout the text marked the ongoing *lack* of *ethical* crisis because neither juridic universality nor self-determination applied to her or her black compatriots. Her movements remained uncomprehended—they remained nonsensical, frivolous, frantic—because they could not register as an ethical crisis, as they were not within the bounds of the category of the human. They were excluded.

Such exclusion is antithetical to the warm embrace of the storefront church, an embrace not dependent upon belief but the fact of her flesh, her being there and alive to the movements and motives of the moment. What she announces, through her journey, is the search for home, and a search for inclusion within universality and self-determination. It was only when she laughed at and broke with this desire that she felt embraced, warmly, on the floor of a storefront church. It was only, in other words, when she felt the vibration of anethical black performance, felt and opened herself up to it changing her, that she felt something of home. Helga Crane's movements that announced the problem of the possibility of ethics, of an ethical crisis, have roots in the movements against settler colonialism and anti-black racism. Her movements should be thought of as part of a trajectory of dispossession and displacement. And as part of that trajectory, we have to think about the announcement, the enunciation, of the anethical force of black performance as the ongoing disruption and critique of ethical being, of ethical becoming, of ethical crisis that cannot ensue.

* * *

Because of the Great Migration that displaced roughly six million African Americans from Southern states to urban epicenters like New York City, Chicago, and Detroit—folks moving with hopes for job and educational opportunities[7]—the sect of Christianity known as Pentecostalism rapidly spread from its mostly Southern beginnings. The modern Blackpentecostal traces one thread of its current movement to Los Angeles, 1906, and the group was noted, from its very beginning, for the sounds made during church services and prayer meetings. The *Los Angeles Times* recounted:

> Breathing strange utterances and mouthing a creed which it would seem no sane mortal could understand, the newest religious sect has started in Los Angeles. Meetings are held in a tumble-down shack on Azusa Street, near San Pedro Street, and devotees of the weird doctrine practice the most fanatical rites, preach the wildest theories and work themselves into a state of mad excitement in their peculiar zeal. Colored people and a sprinkling of whites compose the congregation, and night is made hideous in the neighborhood by the howlings of the worshippers who spend hours swaying forth and back in a nerve-racking [sic] attitude of prayer and supplication. They claim to have "the gift of tongues"; and to be able to comprehend the babel.[8]

From the very beginning of the movement, it was the sound of movement of Spirit that distinguished this group from others; not that it was the first time any religious community was known for such howlings, rantings, and babblings; it was the celebration and living into, it was the refusal of embarrassment that seems to make a difference in 1906. And this noisiness was immediately racialized, gendered, and classed. For the Los Angeles Ministerial Alliance,

---

7. Farah Jasmine Griffin, *"Who Set You Flowin'?" The African-American Migration Narrative* (New York: Oxford University Press, 1995).

8. "Weird Babel of Tongues: New Sect of Fanatics Is Breaking Loose; Wild Scene Last Night on Azusa Street; Gurgle of Wordless Talk by a Sister," *Los Angeles Times*, April 18, 1906, sec. Editorial.

the noise was such a problem that, "In June 1906, the Los Angeles Ministerial Association attempted to silence [William] Seymour and the [Azusa Street] revival. It filed a complaint with the Los Angeles Police Department against the 'negro revival' (thus injecting race into the complaint) on the grounds that it was disturbing the peace. The police investigated the charges and decided against their request because it was located in an industrial, not residential, section of the city."[9] The "disturbing of the peace" needs further consideration. And that because *peace* shares with *ethical being* in that the desire for, the claim about, peace would come to mark the ones that are, and produce, European thought.

The disturbance of peace is a disturbance produced by the others of Europe, and such a disturbance marks the crisis of the ethical zone and field, the zone of black being, of black becoming, of Blackpentecostal aesthetics. Disturbing the peace is the noisiness of blackness, of black being, of Blackpentecostal aesthetics. This disturbance of peace has been considered noise because of its refusal to adhere to Western musical harmonics: "Some of the most distinctive sounds made by slaves were not easily categorized, being neither speech nor music but more howl or shout,"[10] and "African American vocal music sounded dissonant to many whites not only because of its harsh, impassioned, or gravelly tonalities, but also because slave singers inflected the pitches of notes 'in ways quite foreign to regular melodic practice in Western art music,'"[11] such that we have to consider the weird babel of tongues as an enactment of the *an*ethical force of black performance, opening up a way to consider the vibrations of the ones that have been excluded from the zone of the human, from the zone of man, from the zone of the ones to which

---

9. Gastón Espinosa, *William J. Seymour and the Origins of Global Pentecostalism: A Biography and Documentary History* (Durham, NC: Duke University Press, 2014), 66.

10. Shane White and Graham White, *The Sounds of Slavery: Discover African American History through Songs, Sermons, and Speech* (Boston: Beacon Press, 2005), xvii.

11. Ibid., 30.

juridic universality and self-determination apply. Such vibration is coded as against the possibility of peace because there is no possibility to produce ethics from that mode of inhabitation, the zone of the purportedly socially dead.[12]

Moving outward from Los Angeles, I want to consider the dynamics of urban spatial organization through discussing two kinds of religious cultural zones found in these urban epicenters: the storefront and the cathedral. Sociologist E. Franklin Frazier in *The Negro Church in America* placed the then-fledgling Holiness/Pentecostal religious movement under the heading "Negro Cults in the City."[13] And this not simply because the Holiness/Pentecostal movement allowed for women clergy and child preachers, and not simply because of the aesthetic practices of loud dancing, clapping, and speaking in tongues, but also because of the architectural spaces in which many of these believers worshiped: storefront churches. He discussed the Holiness/Pentecostal movement, with its "Jackleg" preachers, under the heading of "Negro Cults in the City." Because of these dilapidated, nonstandard religious spaces, the religious movement itself was thought to be improper and a development from the zone of the proletariat into the black bourgeoisie.

Religious spaces are within the crosshairs and trappings of economic logics. Storefront church buildings are evidence of a general theological ideology that allows for any space to be sacrilized and made holy. Storefront churches democratize the concept of what can be used as instrument and implement of divine call and encounter, such that even those discarded as tattered and indecorous spaces are recuperable. Susan Buck-Morss, in an essay titled "Aesthetics and Anaesthetics: Walter Benjamin's Artwork Essay Reconsidered," discusses the etymology of the word "aesthetics" and its relation to the

---

12. For an extended meditation on the concept of "social death," see Orlando Patterson, *Slavery and Social Death : A Comparative Study* (Cambridge, MA: Harvard University Press, 1982).

13. Edward Franklin Frazier, *The Negro Church in America*, Sourcebooks in Negro History (New York: Schocken Books, 1974).

forms of cognition: taste, touch, smell, sight, sound. Aesthetics, she says, are related to a mode of cognition that is unacculturated, that is previous—or what I here say is *vestibular*—to culture because the senses "maintain an uncivilized and uncivilizable trace, a core resistance to cultural domestication" and "their immediate purpose is to serve instinctual needs—for warmth, nourishment, safety, sociability," a biological concern.[14] It is the resistance to acculturation that is of critical importance. It is a resistance that exists previous to encounter.

Blackpentecostal churches generally, and storefront churches particularly, are modes of marronage, of marooning, of stealthily moving toward a different rhythm and the creation of radically new epistemological centers. We can look to the emergence of maroon communities during the antebellum period in the Suriname River in South America, or those who took up dwelling in the South Carolina/Georgia interior border, or those who lived in the cypress swamps in Louisiana.[15] These communities "secreted" themselves from local plantations, creating radically different modes of life, radically different modes of sociality. These communities were vestibular to culture, they stood on the outside, in the narthex, awaiting—but refusing—culture, since culture conceptually denotes having been trained, ordered, systematized to normative function and form.

Maroons, once secreted into communes in which they would dwell, tilled land, grew food, cleaned pots, etched spoons, built dwellings, birthed and cared for children. They created a form of life that could sustain. But importantly, the threat of violence from the outside world was always there, so the preparation of the ground, of traps, of food, was always infused with a preparation for possible encounter. Preparation, readiness, practice for encounter, was of

---

14. Susan Buck-Morss, "Aesthetics and Anaesthetics: Walter Benjamin's Artwork Essay Reconsidered," *October* 62 (October 1, 1992): 6.

15. Timothy James Lockley, *Maroon Communities in South Carolina: A Documentary Record* (Columbia, SC: University of South Carolina Press, 2009).

necessity an aesthetic, *a*theological-*a*philosophical practice. It was a way to study the swamp, to survey the interior, to know when to let go and to recede into the background. It was to be prepared for the surprise of encounter. This way of life was apposite the ethical life but against ethical being. This way of life, marronage, is *an*ethical black performance.

Marronage, then, was a gathering of social thought. It had to be done with others, *together*, the refusal of Enlightenment thought (what Immanuel Kant says is man's ability to escape self-incurred minority, man's ability to think alone for himself). Storefront churches, like maroon communities, are places where thought happens, where thought prompts engagement in the world. This is not to valorize the conditions, such as poverty, which create the need for storefront churches. Rather, this is to assert that storefront churches are *likewise* places of study, places of life. But Blackpentecostals did not only remain in these often-uncelebrated temples. White flight made other possibilities possible.

In 1972—the same year that Motown closed their Detroit operations, two years before Detroit elected its first black mayor—Bailey Temple Church of God in Christ, a Blackpentecostal congregation founded in 1926 by John Seth and wife, Anna J. Bailey, relocated to the former Adat Shalom synagogue in the University District of Detroit, Michigan. Detroit had been through much political, material, and social upheaval with rebellions grounded in desire for economic equity, rebellion contending against police power and abusive authority. Whites had become increasingly uncomfortable with the movement of black people into formerly segregated, red-line-zoned areas. Though white flight began as early as the 1950s, it was not until after the 1967 rebellions that a major movement of white people relocated to the suburbs,[16] such that by 1972, the Adat Shalom synagogue was available for use. Bailey Cathedral answered such a call.

---

16. Dan Georgakas, Marvin Surkin, and foreword by Manning Marable, *Detroit: I Do Mind Dying: A Study in Urban Revolution*, rev. ed. (Cambridge, MA: South End Press, 1999).

Bailey Cathedral would eventually become, in 1979, the location where one of the most important Blackpentecostal music albums— the Clark Sisters' "Is My Living in Vain"[17]—would be recorded. The album is most noted for the sound of the sisters' signature harmonies and Elbernita "Twinkie" Clark's skilled musicianship on the Hammond B-3 organ. What I want to argue, more generally then, is that the movement of Bailey Temple from a home basement to storefront beginning in 1926 to a former synagogue in 1972 is a general move that lots of Blackpentecostal churches made because of white flight in various urban centers: Newark, Brooklyn, Detroit. And I want to further insist that such a movement shares in that which Nella Larsen fictionalized of Helga Crane. That is, the movement of Bailey Cathedral to the former synagogue because of white flight occasions the sound of black performance, of *an*ethical being.

I contend that what eventually gets thought to be the signature sound of Blackpentecostalism has much to do with what I call *architecclesial* possibilities. That is, there is a way that architecture of buildings informs what is heard therein. This point remains to be elaborated. Consistent with how storefronts were made sacred through intention, Blackpentecostals also utilized these former synagogues in similarly sacred ways. What was desired was an encounter, a holy encounter, and any space could make such possible.

With the Clark Sisters' recording, one hears the density of the space when there is abandonment and reanimation of sound, when there is the leaving and arrival, the breaking away from and coming back to of instruments to transform such force of testimony, song, shout, happiness, dance into otherwise modality, otherwise feel. It was the black symphonic, the sounding out together of the ecology of gathering black being, blackness as becoming, as a force of critique and *an*ethical demand upon the world. What one hears in the density of the space made through these prayer meetings is the sound of love, the sound of radical welcome beckoning the margin to join in; the sound of radical hospitality.

---

17. The Dynamic Clark Sisters, *Is My Living in Vain*, audio CD (SBME Special Mkts., 1991).

To return to the beginning and da Silva's concerns regarding the lack of juridic universality and self-determination as possibilities for racialized others of Europe, I want to consider how Bailey Cathedral emerged as a space with the sound of Blackpentecostalism because of white flight, because of the exodus after the uprisings in Detroit in 1967 and after. I want to ask the question of ethics that undergirds the production of sound in a particular spatiotemporality. What is heard, in the Bailey Cathedral recording of the Clark Sisters, for example, is "blackness" that is produced "as radically distinct from the kind of subject presumed in the ethical principles governing modern social configurations."[18] This radically distinct existence of blackness is through the nonconvergence of black being and the ethical terrain and horizon, through the impossibility of blackness producing the ethical because the ethical emerges from the coloniality of being/power/truth/freedom. And a sonics attends such a modern social configuration. Thus, the *an*ethical force of black performance. That which is heard in the Clark Sisters' recording, what is heard in the arpeggio and chord change, in the growling bass notes and the pedal, is the *an*ethical injunction and charge against the evacuation of the city, the *an*ethics of otherwise possibility.

We know, for example, that Detroit was known for its sound, the Motown Sound. Buried within such a concept was the concept of a Motor City, a city that was home to Chrysler, Ford, and others. As such, labor, political economy, is attendant to the Motown Sound. I am interested in thinking through the problem for ethics that raciality produces, the problem for ethics of racial fantasy and flight, of class differentiation and hierarchy, that produced the demand for anethical performance, anethical black aesthetic practice, as a response:

> The rebuilding of the center of Detroit [beginning in 1967 as a response to the rebellion there] proposed by the New Detroit Committee would mean that eventually the blacks,

---

18. Da Silva, *Toward a Global Idea of Race*, 9.

Appalachians, and students who inhabited the area between the riverfront commercial center and the Wayne State University area would be removed to make room for a revitalized core city repopulated by middle- and upper-class representatives of the city's various racial and ethnic groups.[19]

And:

In the first six years of the New Detroit Committee's existence, the quality of life in the city deteriorated to a new low. The industrial workers who made up more than 35 percent of the population were the hardest hit. They found that the New Detroit meant working longer and faster and paying higher taxes in exchange for diminishing city services and for wage gains more than outpaced by inflation ... Black workers continued to hold the most arduous, dangerous, and unhealthy jobs. Their moves toward job improvement, union office, and shop floor reform were resisted by the company, the unions, and even their fellow workers. The black population also bore much more of the burden of curtailed public services, especially the nearly nonexistent public transit and a school system on the verge of bankruptcy.[20]

That these measures to suppress the upheaval produced by black radical social organization signals the lack of ethical crisis, and that there is a sound that we might find that metaphorizes and makes felt, known, the lack of juridic universality and self-determination through *an*ethical performance is important. The music of the Blackpentecostal church in places like Detroit, in otherwise worlds, elaborates the fact of the crisis of juridic universality and self-determination, being unable to, failing to, account for the lives of those that are cast as otherwise than European. White flight is movement predicated upon settler colonial logics, predicated upon the assumption that there is always land available to be inhabited

---

19. Georgakas and Surkin, *Detroit*, 3.
20. Ibid., 3–4.

and that such inhabitation through displacement and appropriative measures does not in the white imagination produce a crisis or concept of failure. That the land was worked by enslaved people, land that was stolen and thus veils the labor of indigenous people, means that the *an*ethical force elaborated in the sonic sociality to which I attend is about the ongoing nature of displacement, dispossession, and misrecognition. Forgotten labor.

CHAPTER 7

The Haunting of Lynching Spectacles
An Ethics of Response

ELIAS ORTEGA-APONTE

We live in a country where Americans assimilate corpses in their daily comings and goings. Dead blacks are a part of normal life here. Dying in ship hulls, tossed into the Atlantic, hanging from trees, beaten, shot in churches, gunned down by the police, or warehoused in prisons: Historically, there is no quotidian without the enslaved, chained, or dead black body to gaze upon or to hear about or to position a self against.[1]

Introduction

Our responses to injustice reveal our commitments and values, as well as the "kind of country" we are willing to live in. To respond is not to be primarily motivated from within our own motivations—though how our motivations align with ends that we deem as ethical and justified is a necessary consideration. To respond is to act out of a sense of accountability in the presence of others and to satisfy the moral demands that their being before us raises in their particular context, because of the circumstances. But how are we moved

---

1. Claudia Rankine, "The Condition of Black Life Is One of Mourning," in *The Fire This Time: A New Generation Speaks about Race*, ed. Jesmyn Ward (New York: Scribner, 2016), 147.

to respond? Is it a matter of physical proximity, when the gaze of another makes demands on us? Are we responsible to communal others? Do strangers also make moral demands on us, as those to whom we are tied by filial bonds? The Christian tradition has put forth a rich banquet from which to nourish the moral imagination that stretches us to think of bonds of ethical responsibility for the sake of a justice-making kingdom to come where the sin of injustice will be no more.

A central feature of American society is the perniciousness of anti-black racism. From its beginning, the routine denigration, often unto death, of black bodies has been a cornerstone shaping the American social landscape. As Claudia Rankine makes mournfully clear, the killing of black bodies is a normal state of affairs. In spite of strides made in the civil arena recognizing the political protection of blacks, the moral worth of black subjects is not guaranteed. Under the hegemony of white supremacy black life can be taken at any moment, without the need to give reason, and without accountability. The black body seems not to demand an ethical response.

One need only be attentive to the news, and there, one will see broken black bodies. For those committed to the Christian faith it is imperative to decry the sinful transubstantiation of black living bodies into dead flesh. A response is demanded from us. Will we respond with concern, care, and a commitment to address ourselves as participants, filled with pathos, moved by the suffering of others? Would we turn our faces away so as to ignore the interrogation of another's face and its demand for justice? Would we ultimately choose to regard one another with disdain?

An ethics of response reveals a commitment, beyond normative claims, to a critical consideration of particular situations, to those surrounding particular agents and their bodies in relation to structures, histories, and others. In this essay, I am concerned with how we think about and respond to the increased practices of "lynching" black bodies in social media platforms. Videos capturing violence against black bodies are shared as witnesses of tragedy as well as artifacts of debates, as contested evidence. In such instances, we see how the suffering of black subjects is not often a matter of ethical regard but instead perceived as a justified response to the wrong-headed question mentioned by Rankine: "What kind of savages are they?" In this essay I will first discuss a speech delivered by Huey Newton at Boston College. This speech raises themes I wish to pick up in the second part of this essay, pertaining to how we respond to what I call "neo-lynchings," that is, the making of black suffering the stuff of social media spectacle, and the sinister ways in which black suffering enters as a good to be exchanged in the media economy.

Huey Newton's Speech at Boston College

On November 18, 1970, the minister of defense and co-founder of the Black Panthers Party for Self-Defense (BPP) took the Roberts Center stage at Boston College.[2] To the three-thousand-plus crowd in attendance that evening Newton explained that the 10-Point Platform was neither a revolutionary nor reformist project. It was a survival platform. He explained: "We feel that we, the people, are threatened with genocide because racism and fascism is [sic] rampant. Not only in this country, but throughout the world." In his analysis repression and blatant disregard for the well-being, health, and flourishing of communities of color at home and abroad were logical outgrowths of Western-style capitalist modes of production and the political systems that support them. The platform in and of itself, Newton warned, was not a revolutionary solution to the problem. Because for Newton "revolutions are made of sterner stuff." To many in attendance, then, this position went against the grain of how the BPP's actions were, and often continue to be, understood. "The people," Newton concluded, "make revolution, and only the

---

2. Newton's transcript of this speech, "Let Us Hold High the Banner of Intercommunalism and the Invincible Thoughts of Huey P. Newton, Minister of Defense and Supreme Commander of the Black Panther Party," can be accessed at http://www.itsabouttimebpp.com.

people." Anyone, then, can be a revolutionary if they struggle for the people.

For close to two hours that evening, Newton guided the crowd through an ideological tour of the BPP's mission. He weaved a Marxist-Leninist framework to illuminate the conditions of those living under colonial/imperialist regimes in general and of those black peoples at the margins of society in particular. The sufferings of colonial nations and blacks shared one root cause—racism-infused capitalism with fascist tendencies. He chided the dream of black capitalism as a solution considering it to be as destructive as white capitalism. Capitalist predatory predilections run counter to the aspirations of communal flourishing. The wealth capitalism brought to one community has syphoned life from another. Can black freedom be achieved through a clear-cut, Marxist, progress-infused historical materialism? If ever the oppressed and colonized peoples of the world reach a capitalist production developed enough, and one in which they sufficiently controlled the means of production, perhaps it may be enough to move into a communist utopia. But Newton's tempered hope propelled him to be satisfied with proposing that the best we can hope for is to

> linger with *Revolutionary Intercommunalism* until such time that we can wash away bourgeois thought, until such time that we can wash away racism and reactionary thinking, until such time that people are not attached to their nation as a peasant is attached to the soil. Until such time that people can gain their sanity and develop a culture that is "essentially human," that will serve the people instead of serving some god.

What I take as key in Newton's speech is the suspicion that a political agenda embedded within the logic of capitalist exchange, and the political systems arising out of this particular social organization, will necessarily devolve into a system of control in which the "goods" of one group of people will be syphoned for the benefit of another. And more than an extraction of resources, there will be a pillaging of their lives and bodies in the name of a reified "greater good" and "democracy." I sense that the media economy in which images, videos, and photographs enter into the process of user consumption may also exhibit the same predatory predilections as the economy of exchange. In this case, however, it is the cheapening of black suffering and the devaluing of claims for justice for black lives, while giving greater credence to the white gaze and white supremacist ways of explaining events of violence against black bodies, that characterize the dynamics of exchange.

Newton's speech was not passively received but critically engaged by a mostly black audience. Paul Dillon's reporting in the student newspaper, *The Heights*, on November 30, 1970, made it clear that the responses were varied.[3] Long before intellectuals traded "Fuck you's"[4] as we saw last summer in social media, "Fuck you Marx, Fuck you Lenin" were heard at Boston College. Members of the audience questioned the tenor of intellectual sophistry presented by Newton. In their minds, their everyday conditions, ironically the conditions Newton sought to speak about, were not clearly, certainly not plainly, addressed by Newton. In a way, it could be argued, their voices were left out of a conversation when their bodies were constantly on the line.

This gave me a moment of pause. Earlier in the article, Dillon had reported that during the waiting time for Newton's arrival, "a black woman left the anonymity of the benches and shouted to the crowd not to be afraid, to stand up and be proud. Her exhortations were the focus of attention until Newton entered." This woman is also referred to at a later point in the article as one entering into an exchange with Newton, pushing him to clarify his ideas, to divest from purchase in Western modes of thinking, to strive to communicate with the people in an authentic and comprehensible way—without fancy words. However, apparently, this woman's mention

---

3. *The Heights* 51, no. 11.

4. Here I am referring to the blog exchanges between Hamid Dabashi and Slavoj Žižek. For Dabashi's posts see "Fuck You Žižek," https://www. zedbooks.net. For Žižek, see Slavoj Žižek, "A Reply to My Critics," http:// thephilosophicalsalon.com.

of God as site of power was the straw that made her credibility collapse. (Why?) We don't have much information to make an informed judgment. In fact, Dillon did not take the care to pen her name, even as he was clearly focused on her interactions with the crowd and Newton—such a common, and unjustified, failure to recognize the full subjectivity and agency of women while centering a male hero.

It is significant to me that over four decades have passed and a different group of scholars and community members are gathered to carry on "the same conversation." Why is anti-black racism so pernicious in the white liberal imagination? As Claudia Rankine has so aptly put into words, to live while black is to live in a condition of mourning: "Though the white liberal imagination likes to feel temporarily bad about black suffering, there really is no mode of empathy that can replicate the daily strain of knowing that as a black person you can be killed for simply being black."[5] An all-too-common occurrence yesterday and today, part of the everydayness of living while black, the possibility of joy is always threatened. A black body, man, woman, or child, subjected to abuse—far too often, abuse unto death. To add insult to injury, the perpetrators of violence against black bodies will be white bodies who will be deemed to be acting out of personal safety, or justifiably scared to the point that taking a black life was reasonable, at times even celebrated. Unlike times past, in which to witness the lynching of a black body required being *there,* present in close proximity, or at least being the recipient of a gruesome memento, a photograph or a postcard, our current technosocial life brings the act straight to our mobile devices and personal computers. The last breath of a black life captured by digital technology, shared, debated, justice having been denied, and exchanged in an economy grown accustomed to cashing in on black suffering as a spectacle. How can a Christian ethics respond to this?

---

5. Rankine, "The Condition of Black Life," 145–46.

Anti-Black Racism and H. Richard Niebuhr's Christian Ethics of Response

Even as my commitment to the Christian tradition has undergone transformations over the years, I am bound to Christianity and to the liberationist imagination of the prophetic black and brown tradition that it has nurtured and sustained. I owe a debt of life gratitude to those who responded to my enfleshment, motivated by a deep understanding of living inspired by the Christian message. In a very literal way, as a child of color growing up working class, a step ahead of poverty for most of my life, it was sitting in the church bench's corner, instead of the street corner, that kept me and some of my peers alive—tenuously and fragilely alive—by keeping us focused on the hope of a better tomorrow. It was the push toward holiness in my pentecostal upbringing that drew a circle of protection as friends' figures were drawn with chalk on pavements across the streets of my childhood, every corner a potential site of mourning. But at that time, the holiness language did not provide an explanation of the nature of structural oppression nor of the blatant disregard for black and brown lives. It was personal sin, and not systemic oppression, surveillance, policing, and marginalization of community, that was deemed responsible for our dead ones. I admit that I still struggle to firm up my position regarding the possibility of Christian ethics—would it strive for a personal ethics, or would it seek communal well-being? The conundrum I seek to untangle is this: how can Christian ethics influence habits of mind, habits of seeing, practices of touching that deal death to black bodies? It should be clear from my writing so far that I turn toward an ethics of response akin to that developed by H. Richard Niebuhr.

For Niebuhr, responsibility as a symbol of the moral life aims to help us understand ourselves in action. We act toward a purpose, toward an end, and in a variety of relationships with others, each one with a particular demand upon us. According to Niebuhr, central to our moral acts is that at every moment of decision, we ask ourselves, "what is going on?" In asking this question, we are searching for a fitting action. In *The Responsible Self*, Niebuhr understands responsibility as comprised of the following four elements—first, response: we respond to actions upon us; second, interpretation: we search for understanding of what has happened to us and how we are to respond faithfully to the question "What shall I do?"; third, accountability: we respond in anticipation to our actions, to our responses; and, fourth, social solidarity: we are responsible insofar as we are continually participating in a community. In the ethical framework of Niebuhr, community is understood in an expansive sense, including not only those whom we know but the stranger as well. This is made clear in the special place Niebuhr gives to our collective responses to suffering. For Niebuhr, "it is in the response to suffering that many and perhaps all men and women, individually and in their groups, define themselves, take on character, develop an ethos." Furthermore, how communities and individuals respond to suffering is motivated out "of their interpretation of what is happening to them as well as of the actions upon them."[6]

Niebuhr's ethics takes into account the singularity of the ethical encounter and how agents, whether as individuals or communities, respond in each encounter. In this way, Christian ethics is tasked with the accountability to respond to the suffering of others by interpreting the events of the day and in so doing live the content of their character. I find in this model of ethics as responsibility a tool to engage the outright transmutation of living bodies unto dead flesh and the circulation of such events via digital tools in an economy created by participation.[7]

Spectacles of Violence: Democracy's Disposables

There is a connection between the democratic nature of society and the current state of violence against black bodies. Put more

---

6. H. Richard Niebuhr, *The Responsible Self: An Essay in Christian Moral Philosophy* (Louisville, KY: Westminster John Knox Press, 1999), 60–65.

7. Mary Chayko, in *Superconnected: The Internet, Digital Media, & Techno-Social Life* (Thousand Oaks, CA: Sage Publications, 2017), says that "a participatory culture is also an economy in which content, goods, time, effort, and money are, to one degree or another, shared, exchanged and spent" (69).

starkly, the preservation of the ethos of democracy in the United States and abroad, as argued by Newton in his Boston College speech, relies on spectacles of violence in which black bodies are routinely mutilated and displayed for the consumption of the white liberal imagination. It may very well be that the aspiration for a full democratic inclusion of blacks will be an impossibility within the bounds of the current existing democracy as long as the political recognition of black lives does not also include moral recognition of their worth. The rise of the digital commons, that fractured enlargement of the public sphere where issues are debated, opinions exchanged, data collected and explained, gifs and memes created, alchemically transforming expression, because an image is a thousand words, has opened yet another dimension in which the debates about the "mattering" of black life continue. How does black life matter? What are the possibilities of black embodiment? Do the increase in broadband and the speed of information open other possibilities for black safety? Or does the digital commons become another site where the lynching of black bodies can be not only exposed, but circulated, re-created, debated, and dismissed, and eventually archived as yet another bit of compressed information in the cloud? And yet, if *the condition of black life is one of mourning* the digital commons is an extension of Emmett's open casket. Now no longer the remains are exposed, but the "shot-by-shot," the choke until breathless, cries for empathy ignored, the bodies of children dragged against pavements, slammed against school floors, homeless hogtied and thrown into police cars as officers chat amicably. And yet, these images and videos play not the role of durable witness to injustice but as fodder for debate. To the white gaze, there must have been some wrong committed, or a prior incident to justify the killing, or, well, you never know—for black people, black s(kin) folk, this is another burial ground in which we mourn our dead in the struggle for a justice tardy in coming.

In the age of social media, a moment in history in which events, news, information, and opinions hit us like information bombs, in constant streams of factoids, parodic skits presenting news items, news outlets masquerading as late night shows through their incongruous messages, instead of a song for a movement, what has captured our collective attention is a hashtag—#BlackLivesMatter/#BLM. These characters express an assertion of a reality that, judging by the states of affairs, is not self-evident, that of the dignity of black lives. Black lives remain excluded from the protection granted to other lives, particularly white lives; black lives may be taken, caged, or snuffed out routinely without consequence and with the expectation of acceptance and acquiescence from communities of color. It is as though it were enough to fear the embodiment of a black life in order to respond to it justifiably with violence. Time and again, over the last few years we have seen events along these lines: a white person kills a person of color and whether the evidence points to unnecessary use of force or not is not the question. In spite of what remains as testimony in digital form, the white liberal imagination is more inclined to believe that there must be reason enough to justify such a death; something must have prompted such a tragic end, even if viewers are not privy to those events, and even if only based on conjectures. The message for people of color is clear: the mattering of our lives is not a given. The waters of our national lives continue to be muddied by displays of violence against colored bodies. And the gap between justice demanded and justice given continues to widen.

Charles Cobb Jr., in *This Nonviolent Stuff'll Get You Killed*, writes that "experience taught then and teaches now that blacks should never underestimate the level of violence that could be brought against them by white authority, and that they should never overestimate the prospects for receiving understanding and support from white people."[8] At any given moment, colored folks can expect violence while also assuming that support will not be easily forthcoming or at least not with the necessary impetus to change

---

8. Charles E. Cobb, Jr., *This Nonviolent Stuff'll Get You Killed: How Guns Made the Civil Rights Movement Possible* (New York: Basic Books, 2014), 76–77.

social realities. Although not a poem written with Ferguson or New York or New Orleans or Minnesota or Baltimore or countless other recent locations of anti-black violence in mind, Pamela Mordecai's poem "This Is the Way" to my mind aptly captures the sentiment of the moment; at the very least, it captures the ways in which communities of color feel and live with the disposability of their lives. Below, the first stanza:

> Monday. This is the way we wash our clothes.
> Whites on this side for they need special care.
> Put the darks yonder in a separate pile.
> Sort coloureds—light, not-so-light, darkish over here,
> each shade in its right place as the hymn says.
> White in the water first as it behooves,
> gentled in Ivory flakes with temperate scrub,
> then set on coral stones to profit from the sun's
> abundant coin. Now and then, on tougher stains, rub
> with brown soap and a tip of Adam's ale
> till blemishes erased, garments gleam clean.
> Coloureds get shift according as they pale.
> Darks last, slapped on the beating stone, hung on the fence.
> To coddle drugging clothes don't make no sense.[9]

This stanza encapsulates the devaluing of black lives in a society structured by the sin of anti-black racism. A society that seeks a place for each shade of blackness, of browness, by separating it from whiteness, and in so doing sets in motion the racial projects of white supremacy.[10] To this we could add the attribution of guilt and disposability attached to black bodies and the heightening of these in

---

9. Pamela Mordecai, *Subversive Sonnets: Poems* (Toronto: TSAR Publications, 2012).

10. My reading of racial projects is informed by Michael Omi and Howard Winant, *Racial Formation in the United States: From the 1960s to the 1990s* (New York: Routledge, 1994), in conjunction with Achille Mbembe, "Necropolitics," *Public Culture* 15, no. 1 (2003): 11–40.

digital environments. Treatment is accorded not by merit of character but by shade. James Baldwin puts it as follows:

> If one really wishes to know how justice is administered in a country, one does not question the policemen, the lawyers, the judges, or the protected members of the middle class. One goes to the unprotected—those, precisely, who need the law's protection most!—and listens to their testimony. Ask any Mexican, any Puerto Rican, any black man, any poor person— ask the wretched how they fare in the halls of justice, and then you will know, not whether or not the country is just, but whether or not it has any love for justice, or any concept of it.[11]

With mounting evidence that, as it pertains to black lives, our country lacks love for justice, and perhaps even a concept of it—and in spite of the often-heralded progress in terms of race relations— the legacy of slavery, racial segregation, and lynching still bears their pernicious influence in our present. Below, I present a piece of political satire by artist A. B. Frost, published at the time in which the nation was abandoning the failed project of Reconstruction. In this piece, the living out of Southern chivalry is displayed as the fear unto death against black lives. This satirical image powerfully depicts what Danez Smith writes in his poem "Alternate Names for Black Boys": a black boy is a "monster until proven ghost" and "guilty until proven dead." Frost's image displays the racist fear that shapes the white liberal imagination—fear that makes clear white supremacy's inability to cede power. In the face of this fear, there is no safety, not even for a child.

Today this anti-black strain in democracy shapes the spectacle of neo-lynching in digital environments. And it demands a faithful response in the face of ongoing suffering. Digital environments and the violence perpetuated in them should not be taught as separated from enfleshed social interactions but as part of the physical

---

11. James Baldwin, *No Name in the Street* (New York: Vintage, 1972), 149.

"In Self-Defense,"
cartoonist: A. B. Frost,
Harper's Weekly, October 28, 1876

environment. This is not to deny that digital environments have opened new dimensions of how we understand issues of, for example, privacy and bullying, which call for careful consideration of the digital as a very specific sort of environment in which particular kinds of actions are possible. Nevertheless, in spite of their particularity, digital environments, as Mary Chayko writes, "are so fully enmeshed with the physical world that one need not even be online to feel the impact. . . . Technology can be so deeply integrated with so many aspects of life that it is almost as though the tech has seeped inside the person, cyborg-style."[12] Furthermore, interacting in digital environments also means that the field of actions of the social world will continue into the digital arena and give rise, as Chayko theorizes, to a "participatory culture in which members of the public take active part in the creation and consumption of their cultural

---

12. Chayko, *Superconnected*, 67.

products," and in so doing giving rise to an economy where goods are exchanged.[13]

An Ethics of Response to Neo-Lynching Spectacles

An ethics of response informed by H. Richard Niebuhr must understand that the unfolding of responsibility, and our concern for the suffering of others, now takes place in a technosocial environment where the extension of digital technologies is not a separate dimension of the social world but a component of it. In this technosocial world we must pay attention to the ways in which power also circulates through these e-landscapes, as well as the nature and impact of our responses in the face of the challenges that are arising.[14] When we take seriously the task of theorizing the unfolding of agency in digitally mediated environments, and understand that technological developments are "enmeshed with the physical world" in ways that increasingly expand the field of action of humanity, then we should work toward deepening our understandings of how forms of violence enacted in the physical world can be extended into the digital. It is this enmeshment of the physical and the digital that gives raise to the possibility of what I here term "neo-lynching."

At the center of this task is the need to critically engage the circulation of videos and images that depict violence against black bodies. These images, videos, and bits of data are circulated in digital environments in an orchestration that pits black suffering against the white liberal gaze—that is, the historical and enduring witness of black lives afflicted by the violence of white supremacy and the white liberal gaze that cannot empathize with this witness but seeks ways to explain it away. In the circulation of these images and videos as data to be debated, what would have been private affairs, or events witnessed only by bystanders, now become social (albeit virtual) happenings. Thus, a hyperreal public sphere is created where

---

13. Ibid., 69.

14. See Christian Fuchs, *Social Media: A Critical Introduction* (Los Angeles: Sage Publications, 2014), chs. 1 and 3.

some agents have little control over the circulation of materials but bear the burden of not only being victims but also having to relive the painful events over and over again. Compounding this harm is one's exposure to the voices of acquaintances and strangers in debates gone viral over what "actually" happened. That is to say that due to increasing technological mediation, social reality now is open to dissection, interpretation, and even re-created in ways we could not have fathomed before the rise of digital environments that never sleep and are distributed through a plurality of networks, with and without our knowledge or consent. In this way the terror experienced by black lives in the social world now extends to the digital.

I take neo-lynching spectacles to be comprised of two aspects. First, there are those captured moments in which we, as spectators, are given first row seats at the last breath of a person of color dying at the hands of white supremacy. And, second, more than just witnessing, one also faces the possibility of entering into social media debates with known ones and strangers in which attributions are made, events are reframed, and the visual contested, while deferring, and even ignoring, the incarnate suffering of the victims and victims' loved ones. Such neo-lynching spectacles are also real death-dealing acts, and, as a result, extend the victim's suffering, and of their loved ones, to digital environments. Digital spaces increasingly are being shaped by this process in which the dignity of black life and suffering can be contested because of the ways in which their civil existence can be negated and their lives made superfluous.

Central to my conceptualization of neo-lynchings is the work of Koritha Mitchell. Mitchell says that lynching "as an anti-black form of political terrorism was a distinctly post emancipation phenomenon." This form of political terrorism became possible, Mitchell explains, because whereas during slavery the death of a slave would constitute a financial loss for white slave holders "once blacks were no longer chattel, there was no incentive to avoid killing them." Furthermore, Mitchell, commenting on the racism explicit in the American theater, says that, as an extension of social drama "the

American stage would prove as suitable for killing African Americans as for portraying them in dehumanizing ways." She points out the contrast created by black-authored lynching plays. These plays presented mob violence more as a crime against households than against bodies, and in them the audience is given glimpses of home spaces. The audience sees the suffering of widows and children, but physical violence may not be depicted. In this way, the black-authored lynching plays suggest that "the brutality continues long after a corpse would have deteriorated."[15] Colin Dayan also follows this line of thought. For her the enduring of brutality even after the corpse's return to the dust from whence it came is possible because of the rendering of black lives as superfluous and the ease with which they may be stripped of civic worth to perpetuate the white national imaginary of belonging and citizenship, and ultimately be deemed not worthy of empathy.[16]

To Mitchell and Dayan, I would add that the history of punishable bodies, real and virtual, also requires that we trace the mobilization of "moral panic" as a trigger for securitization.[17] In order to activate moral panic, a discourse of "insecurities" has to rise to the fore—this is also behind notions of the disposability of black lives after the emancipation period. It is the fear that a society will become unsafe that leads to attempts to punish and control other bodies that do not present the understanding of the polis of the hegemonic segments of society. The activation of moral panic gave rise to racialized forms of punishment starting from the periods of slavery and

---

15. Koritha Mitchell, "Black-Authored Lynching Drama's Challenge to Theater History," in *Black Performance Theory,* ed. Thomas F. DeFrantz and Anita Gonzalez (Durham, NC: Duke University Press, 2014), 87 and 89.

16. Colin Dayan has shown how racialized bodies can be denied civil and biological existence and can remain suspect even in death. Dayan argues that "the negation of civil existence requires that a person be made 'superfluous.' To be made superfluous is to be outside the pale of human empathy." See Colin Dayan, *The Law Is a White Dog: How Legal Rituals Make and Unmake Persons* (Princeton, NJ: Princeton University Press, 2011), 72.

17. For my use of moral panic and insecurities, see Sean P. Hier, *Moral Panic and the Politics of Anxiety* (New York: Routledge, 2011).

Western expansion. In the technosocial world, moral panics also extend to digital environments. Just as A. B. Frost depicted in his political cartoon, in digital environments white fears can also spell black deaths through the activation of moral panics. Calls for justice for lives lost are responded to with force and brutality. '

What Marx said of capitalism, that it continually transforms its existence and shape in order to continue its rule over economic life and the lives of workers, is also true about racist dynamics of domination. They morph, take new shapes, more creative practices, novel institutional forms, more procedural forms of justice that give impressions of heightened professionalization and thus, of being more just, all along leaving a trail of victims. In digital environments, neo-lynching practices are but one more evolution of our nation's chattel-slavery past embedded in geopolitics of the subjection and terror of black bodies.

I wonder how an ethics of response in our time can make us ready to respond to those who are putting their lives on the line. In fact, what kind of resources does it provide, not only to those reaching for comfort, but also to those who are having the kinds of conversation that make it possible to offer an explicit "yes" to the question: "So are you telling me that you are ready to put your life on the line . . . ?" In order to be effective in the face of the extension of the political terrorism experienced by black lives into digital environments, an ethics of response needs to see itself, to echo Huey Newton, as a survival program. After all, survival is necessary and essential to any revolution. But in the meantime, how are we to act in ways that contribute to laying the groundwork for a revolution?

The paradigm of an ethics of response as described above requires that we give an answer to the question: "What is going on?" As we respond to actions upon us, we need to offer an interpretation of the states of affairs and be accountable for our responses in acts of social solidarity. In this light, what is happening in the extension of the political terror of lynching to neo-lynching in the digital environments? More importantly, how do we respond to the compounding of suffering in communities of color as the white liberal gaze has no love for justice and no capacity for empathy? To respond faithfully and to strive for social solidarity with the hopes of alleviating suffering demands critical attention to the extensions of political terrorism of lynching into digital environments. It requires the questioning of how we engage in the economics created by the participatory culture in social media. Because in this economy not all transactions are monetized but may instead take the shape of content creation, how we contribute to the "goods" in the process of exchange can either compound suffering or be real acts of solidarity.

I am hopeful that the liberation of black (s)kin folk will be a reality one day. But my hope is tempered by the reality of grief, the knowledge that between my utopian hope that my children's children will be singing the songs of black and brown liberation and the present moment lies a road of grief and mourning that might be recorded, shared, and debated, but seldom believed.

PART III

Black Loves

CHAPTER 8

Eldridge Cleaver, George Jackson, and the Ethics of Love

VINCENT W. LLOYD

The two great books of the Black Power movement were love stories. These were the books that circulated the most widely, reaching hundreds of thousands of Americans, books that set out the ideas and aesthetic that would succeed Martin Luther King, Jr., and define blackness in American culture. Stokely Carmichael was the movement's most talented orator, and images of Huey Newton and Angela Davis became iconic, but Eldridge Cleaver's *Soul on Ice* (1968) and George Jackson's *Soledad Brother* (1970) were the movement's outstanding texts. Today these books are occasionally mentioned but rarely read. Cleaver and Jackson are seen as problematic products of their moment, suffering from unchecked machismo, unqualified rejection of their civil rights movement precursors, and a dogmatic embrace of communism, particularly Maoism. Overdetermined by these associations, the literariness, idiosyncrasies, and essential theme of Cleaver's and Jackson's books are forgotten. That theme is love: how it goes wrong, how it can be turned right, and what an ethics of black love looks like.

While these two love stories have passed into obscurity, in recent years black love has emerged as the moral heart of racial justice movements. "The project that we are building," writes Black Lives

Matter co-founder Alicia Garza, "is a love note to our folks."[1] She defines "black love" as "building community and solidarity," overcoming the legacy of slavery and racial injustice to cultivate affection across intra-racial differences, including class, gender, sexuality, region, and age.[2] This justice-oriented account of black love has been percolating among black intellectuals, developing beyond the apparent opposition between King's liberal love and black power's radical rejection of it, in rage. Over the past two decades, the feminist bell hooks has argued that the radical self-assertion of black power must be coupled with the vision of harmonious community put forward by King in an expansive conception of self-love in, and as, black community.[3] Jennifer Nash has tracked the centrality of black love-politics in black feminism over the past half century: "Love acted as a *doing*, a call for a labor of the self, an appeal for transcending the self, a strategy for remaking the public sphere, a plea to unleash the radical imagination, and a critique of the state's blindness to the violence it inflicts and enables."[4]

By revisiting Cleaver's and Jackson's writings as love stories, offering accounts of black love, we find a quite different way of thinking about black love than we find circulating in black activist and

---

1. Alicia Garza, "A Love Note to Our People," *n+1*, https://nplus onemag.com. Garza also suggests, "For us as women who are organizers, there's a way in which our hearts connect to each other and to a real deep love for our people." Garza's Twitter handle for a time was Love God Herself.

2. Alicia Garza, "We Gon' Be Alright: Black Love, Black Resistance and Black Liberation," Truthout, http://www.truth-out.org.

3. bell hooks, "Love as the Practice of Freedom," in *Outlaw Culture: Resisting Representations* (New York: Routledge, 1994), 243–50. See also James Cone, *Martin and Malcolm and America: A Dream or a Nightmare* (Maryknoll, NY: Orbis Books, 1991).

4. Jennifer Nash, "Practicing Love: Black Feminism, Love-Politics, and Post Intersectionality," *Meridians* 11, no. 2 (2011): 19. Nash positions such a love politics as a preferable alternative to the identity politics into which intersectionality may descend. The other important figure, whose cultural stock has recently soared, is James Baldwin. See the centrality of love in *The Fire Next Time* (New York: Dial Press, 1963).

intellectual communities today. What emerges is a more *theological* account of love. Rather than seeing the Christian-driven civil rights movement transforming into a secular, Marxist-oriented black power movement, and the two synthesizing into the vaguely spiritual black love talk of today, I suggest reading the black power movement as deepening the civil rights movement's theological engagement even when explicitly Christian language is absent, and I worry that black love talk as it circulates today is a hollow parody of the theological.[5] Turning to Cleaver's and Jackson's accounts of love not only deepens black political-theological reflection, it also challenges Christian ethical reflection on love that often continues to take King as an exemplary theorist of Christian love.[6] Cleaver and Jackson attend to the effects of systemic injustice on love, complicating the picture of a Christian love ethics as offering a path from disordered to rightly ordered love. For Cleaver and Jackson, that path is not just difficult to traverse; it is interrupted by a gorge that requires a radical reorientation—a conversion—to leap beyond.

There are major obstacles to appreciating the insights of Cleaver's and Jackson's texts. Each was written while its author was incarcerated, and to reach publication each had to pass under the eyes of a prison censor.[7] Each encourages a sense of immediacy, in part through using the epistolary form, and yet each is carefully crafted, not only by Cleaver and Jackson but also by a network of editors and publishers whose interests and politics differed significantly from those of the authors. Each does include problematic language and ideas that reflect the specificity of the historical moment when they

---

5. I develop this argument more broadly in Vincent W. Lloyd, *Religion of the Field Negro: On Black Secularism and Black Theology* (New York: Fordham University Press, 2017).

6. For example, Eric Gregory, *Politics and the Order of Love: An Augustinian Ethic of Democratic Citizenship* (Chicago: University of Chicago Press, 2008); Timothy P. Jackson, *Political* Agape: *Christian Love and Liberal Democracy* (Grand Rapids, MI: Eerdmans, 2015).

7. It is possible that some of the material in these texts was smuggled out, rather than sent through regular correspondence, so avoided censorship.

were written, but rather than dwelling on these as limitations of the texts that must be repudiated, the pages that follow will focus on the texts' overarching moral visions.[8] Finally, there is the elephant in the room, the reason the content of these texts is often ignored: both are stories of black men describing their embrace of radical black politics while at the same time falling in love with their white lawyers. Readers usually focus exclusively on the radical politics, confused and frustrated by the love stories. What if we understand the texts' depictions of politics and love as inextricably intertwined?

Disordered Love

Eldridge Cleaver and George Jackson occupy privileged positions in the pantheon of black power revolutionaries. Both were incarcerated in California at the age of eighteen—Cleaver on a marijuana charge, Jackson for stealing $70 from a gas station—developed radical politics while in prison, and reached a huge audience beyond prison walls. Cleaver was eventually released, became the Minister of Information of the Black Panther Party, moved to exile in Algeria, split with party leadership, converted to evangelical Christianity, returned to the United States to serve a prison sentence, converted to Mormonism, and spent his last days holding court at Berkeley cafes.[9] Jackson, whose prison sentence was indefinite,

---

8. For example, in contrast to Huey Newton's embrace of the gay liberation movement, Cleaver associated homosexuality with child molestation (as well as grotesque capitalism). See Eldridge Cleaver, *Soul on Ice* (New York: McGraw-Hill, 1967), 106. Further references to this text are parenthetical. Jared Sexton offers a particularly sophisticated argument that Cleaver's views on sexuality are intertwined with, and compromise, his political project as a whole: see "Race, Sexuality, and Political Struggle: Reading *Soul on Ice*," *Social Justice* 30, no. 2 (2003): 28–41.

9. Cleaver published an account of his exile and his first religious conversion in *Soul on Fire* (Waco, TX: Word Books, 1978). On Cleaver's Mormonism, see Newell G. Bringhurst, "Eldridge Cleaver's Passage through Mormonism," *Journal of Mormon History* 28, no. 1 (2002): 80–110. For a

never saw freedom. He was appointed a field marshal of the Black Panther Party; in August 1970 his younger brother Jonathan was killed while attempting to free him, and a year later George Jackson himself was killed by prison guards during an alleged escape attempt.[10] Cleaver's prison writings first attracted attention when they were featured in the left-wing Catholic magazine *Ramparts*, and *Soul on Ice* consists of some of this cultural criticism, excerpts from letters to his attorney Beverly Axelrod, and Cleaver's own early musings on race relations composed before he had found an audience.[11] Jackson was already a figure of great public interest, one of the three "Soledad Brothers" charged with murdering a white prison guard in a widely publicized case, when the collection of letters to his parents, brother, and friends was published. Both were organic intellectuals, reading as widely as possible and critically analyzing anti-black racism. Both argued that the American prison stands in continuity with American slavery and segregation. For them, racial injustice was not accurately described as a public policy issue calling for policy fixes, or even fixable with new social norms. Racial injustice was so deeply entrenched that a radical reconfiguration of social, and especially economic, arrangements would be necessary before justice could prevail.[12] By telling their distinctive love stories,

---

biographical overview, see Melanie Margaret Kask, "Soul Mates: The Prison Letters of Eldridge Cleaver and Beverly Axelrod" (PhD diss., University of California, 2003).

10. See Dan Berger, *Captive Nation: Black Prison Organizing in the Civil Rights Era* (Chapel Hill: University of North Carolina Press, 2014), ch. 3.

11. Cleaver first met Axelrod when he was looking for a lawyer to persuade the prison authorities to allow him to submit a book manuscript, then titled "White Woman/Black Man" (the title of the final section of *Soul on Ice*) for publication.

12. Jackson describes himself as "born a slave in a captive society," adding that "Capture, imprisonment, is the closest to being dead that one is likely to experience in this life." See *Soledad Brother: The Prison Letters of George Jackson* (Chicago: Lawrence Hill Books, 1994), 4 and 14. Further references to this text are parenthetical. These themes are picked up from Jackson's writings and elaborated into a general theory of anti-black racism by Frank Wilderson

Cleaver and Jackson showed how anti-black racism is sustained by a perversion of the desires of both blacks and whites, with disordered love at the individual level (both romantic love as well as love of worldly things and ideas) resulting from and contributing to unjust social arrangements.

For a time, Eldridge Cleaver was confined to the prison psychiatric ward. The staff wanted him to discuss his relationship with his parents. Cleaver wanted to talk about racial injustice. Eventually he learned that the only way to return to the general population of the prison was to stop talking about racism, but Cleaver knew it was racism that had caused his nervous breakdown. The breakdown happened when he saw a picture of the white woman who was said to have flirted with Emmett Till, precipitating Till's widely publicized lynching. "While looking at the picture, I felt that little tension in the center of my chest I experience when a woman appeals to me. I was disgusted and angry with myself" (23). Two days later, Cleaver's mental health was in a state of total collapse. From the perspective of the white prison psychiatrists, mental health was related to rightly ordered loves; that right ordering began in childhood with the parents and then continued as loves extended out into the world, to other individuals, to objects, and to ideas. Cleaver argues that such an approach ignores the way that anti-black racism casts a shadow over all affect, and over libidinal desire in particular, for both blacks and whites. The racial order shapes what we are able to feel and how we feel; all other factors that form us, even our parents, take a secondary role. Much of *Soul on Ice* consists of developing an account of just how racism disorders love, offering an explanation for his reaction to that picture of a white woman—all in the context of professing his own love for his white lawyer.

Cleaver, who had spent time in the Nation of Islam, read widely in Marxism, and was clearly influenced by Nietzsche, developed an idiosyncratic theory that blended racial and economic analysis. Modernity requires society's elites to use their minds, not their

---

in *Red, White, and Black: Cinema and the Structure of U.S. Antagonisms* (Durham, NC: Duke University Press, 2010).

bodies, so elites celebrate those activities associated with the intellect and denigrate physical activities. On Cleaver's account, the distinction between elites and manual laborers maps on to the racial divide: elites are white and so associate whiteness with the intellect and blackness with physicality. Not all whites are elite, but because whiteness is associated with the elite, middling whites are all the more eager to identify themselves with the intellect and distance themselves from the body. This dualistic set of associations both undergirds anti-black racism and has harmful effects on relations between the sexes, Cleaver argues. Women are placed in impossible positions. White women, as white, must reject all that is associated with the body; white men who, according to the racial order, are supposed to desire white women have their desire thwarted by white women's rejection of their own bodies. Black women embrace their bodies and desire social advancement or security so would naturally pair off with white men, if it were not for the social prohibition on miscegenation. Similarly, white women look to black men when they desire sensuality that is not repressed by white men's (racially motivated) rejection of physicality.[13]

On Cleaver's account, the affective distortions of the racial order are most dramatic in the case of the black man. Because the black woman has been systematically denigrated, reduced to the status of an animal, and because the white woman holds the promise of social advancement and serves as a symbol of freedom, desire for (and self-protective aversion from) the white woman pervades black male life and loves. Because of this, Cleaver considers the white woman demonic: "The Ogre had its claws buried in the core of my being and refused to let go" (19). Her effects are "like a cancer eating my heart out and devouring my brain" (149). Before any other ethical or political formation can happen, Cleaver finds it necessary to "repudiate The Ogre, root it out of my heart" (19). His mental breakdown offers the opportunity to do that—but the prison psychiatrist does not allow it, forcing Cleaver to speak only

---

13. Michele Wallace develops a related schema in *Black Macho and the Myth of the Superwoman* (New York: Dial Press, 1979).

of his parents, leaving the fundamental social-psychological problem intact. On my reading, Cleaver argues that the specific case of
racialized erotic desire is at the root of a more general disordering of
loves caused by American racism. The only options Cleaver thinks
he has are to follow the rules, guided by alien affect, or to rebel.
When he was briefly released from prison, Cleaver began raping
white women. As he later observes, the form rebellion can take is
itself shaped by the racial order: his desire to rape white women was
an evil result of an evil system rather than a means to achieve liberation from that system.

Cleaver argues that love, at its best, involves a complicated join-
ing of equals, but this is absolutely impossible when race and class
have already shaped how we see ourselves and others. The love that
we encounter in this world, the racialized world, is not really love
at all in the sense that its shape is given by the world, not by the
self—and so it does not point beyond the self. Jackson develops a
similar point when he writes that his father has never displayed "*real*
sensitivity, affection, or sentiment" (240). Jackson does not offer an
equally elaborate analysis of entangled racial and class dynamics,
but he does argue that whites and elites "have reduced all life to
a very dull formula" with the result that "all natural feelings have
been lost" (40). In general terms, Jackson asserts, elites are anxious
about surprises, so they create abstractions through which to understand the world, and then they confuse those abstractions for the
world itself. The world they live in is supposedly entirely legible by
reason; feeling is superfluous and distracting. Jackson would likely
endorse the more specific claim that, for the smooth functioning of
the modern, capitalist order, there must be regularity and predict-
ability—including in the affective domain, in the domain of loves.[14]
Moreover, affect circulating among a group, for example, the love of
blacks for other blacks, has the potential to complicate this atom-

---

14. For a more elaborate account of the way capitalism shapes the order
of love, see Lauren Berlant, *Cruel Optimism* (Durham, NC: Duke University
Press, 2011).

ized order and so must be discouraged. Humans naturally love those who are like themselves, so the racial-capitalist order must actively discourage black-directed love (41).

Both Cleaver and Jackson present themselves as militant atheists. However, what they mean by atheism involves a rejection of all that is associated with the racial order, and institutionalized Christianity is associated with that order. For them, Christ-like love as it was taught by the preachers they encountered means love shaped by the racial order. Cleaver illustrates this vividly when he describes his youthful Catholicism: "I chose the Catholic Church because all the Negroes and Mexicans went there. The whites went to the Protestant chapel" (40). The juvenile prison where Cleaver was then housed required attendance at a religious service, so Catholic he became. Jackson had a similar youthful experience with Catholicism: he "sang in the choir because they made me," but his main church activity was stealing wine (3). For Jackson, Christianity was just another abstraction that was taken too literally by whites. At its best, religion could be used practically by blacks, and Jackson harangued against those blacks who took useless religious doctrine too seriously. For Cleaver, the desire to worship Mary and Jesus, imagined as white, and the desire for salvation through them, is clearly a product of the disordering of black loves by the racial order. He could hardly be more explicit on this point: he writes that "during coition and at the moment of her orgasm, the black woman, in the first throes of her spasm, shouts out the name of Jesus. 'Oh, Jesus, I'm coming!'" (157). Whether or not we agree with the specifics of the analysis here, it certainly seems to be the right sort of analysis: seeking out and challenging idolatrous reductions of the wholly other to the racial order.

Learning to Love

Christian ethicists agree with Cleaver and Jackson that human love is disordered and that disordered love is closely tied with injustice. Cleaver and Jackson can help sharpen Christian ethical reflection on the question of how love can become more rightly ordered.[15] The prison psychiatrist Cleaver mentions presents one, characteristically secular route: reflection on formative childhood experiences. Christian ethicists are necessarily more open to additional sources of moral formation: community, new experiences, introspection, and of course revelation. Yet many Christian ethicists (for whom King is often a paradigm) present the ordering of love as a quantitative task, suggesting that loves can be more or less rightly ordered on a continuous path to the divine. For example, Edward Vacek's important study of Christian love describes this process as a "gradual conversion to coresponsibility," and he writes of growth in love involving repeated cycles of frustration, reformation, harmony, and new frustration. Gradually, the individual's loves become more closely aligned with God's loves, expanding to include more aspects of the world.[16] Eric Gregory develops an Augustinian account of human beings as, ontologically, "bundles of loves." However, "in a fallen world," these loves "are disordered, misdirected, and disproportionate."[17] They point in all different directions, as it were, leading to spiritual and moral chaos; Christian faith gradually restores order—in an aesthetic sense, closer to beauty than rigidity—to these loves, and so to ourselves. On Gregory's account, King realizes that the United States is "in need of refreshment through active practices of love."[18] Segregation contributed to the disordering of loves; the civil rights movement contributed to the right ordering of loves—all presented as if on a quantitative scale. Rather than conversion from disordered to rightly ordered loves, Gregory

---

15. This question has received relatively little attention in Christian ethical analysis of love, perhaps because it is largely ignored in Gene Outka's seminal *Agape: An Ethical Analysis* (New Haven, CT: Yale University Press, 1972).

16. Edward Collins Vacek, S.J., *Love, Human and Divine: The Heart of Christian Ethics* (Washington, DC: Georgetown University Press, 1994), 146–47.

17. Gregory, *Politics and the Order of Love*, 20–21.

18. Ibid., 192. Gregory also addresses the role of love in the thought of Gustavo Gutiérrez, focusing on neighbor love rather than on ideology as distorting love.

writes of "an education in loving rightly," a "spiritual therapy" that incrementally improves the ordering of loves.[19]

In contrast, Cleaver and Jackson hold that however much work of moral formation happens, unless anti-black racism is addressed loves will remain fundamentally disordered. In other words, there must first be a qualitative rather than a quantitative shift in the ordering of loves, given the shadow that anti-black racism casts over our social world. The question, then, is what it looks like to address anti-black racism in moral formation, a daunting task when anti-black racism is understood to be so deeply rooted and so pervasive. While Cleaver and Jackson do not write in explicitly Christian or even spiritual terms, they describe this transformation in a way that sounds like conversion, a dramatic turning away from one way of understanding and living in the world and toward another way. Cleaver and Jackson describe this process, but they also perform it in their books, showing readers how the authors' own loves—both romantically and more broadly—take a new shape as they undertake something like a conversion.

When Cleaver first went to prison, he "was in love with" marijuana (18). During his initial stint in prison, Cleaver became a rebel, trying to extract his mind from the racial order by fighting directly against whiteness—first white ideas and white gods, in prison, and then through rape of white women when he was released.[20] "I became an extreme iconoclast. Any affirmative assertion made by anyone around me became a target for tirades and criticism and denunciation" (19). The racial order seemed ubiquitous and suffocating; his only option was to say no and strike out. When he entered prison again, he realized that this anger at whiteness was

---

19. Ibid., 274.

20. Cleaver notoriously describes "practicing" rape on black women before he moved on to raping white women (*Soul on Ice*, 26). Both he later understands to be examples of his rage against the racial order, which shapes the desires of all, not just whites. Jackson similarly went through an initial moment of pure resistance: "What I do feel is the urge to resist, resist, and never stop resisting" (*Soledad Brother*, 126).

insufficient. He still remained under the gravitational pull of the racial order. He felt that something was amiss: not that he was guilty for breaking the law but that the act of rape reflected, rather than overcame, disorder. Cleaver suffered another breakdown— "my whole fragile moral structure seemed to collapse, completely shattered"—but this time he did not end up in the care of white psychiatrists. He immersed himself in reflection, social analysis, and cultural criticism, which held the promise of allowing Cleaver "to save myself" (27). His task was not unlike that of the white psychiatrist, but he acknowledged the way racism cast a shadow over his desires: "I had to seek out the truth and unravel the snarled web of my motivations" (27). Despite Cleaver's sharp rejection of religious ideas, he is comfortable describing this practice as a path to "salvation" (29).

For Cleaver, this capacity for critical analysis and reflection has as its prerequisite an initial moment of hatred directed against the racial order in all of its forms. Critical analysis without that hatred would just lead to a quantitative improvement in the ordering of loves—which is really no improvement at all as it is still in the shadow of anti-black racism, and all in that shadow is fundamentally disordered. The critical capacities might tackle the questions whites were discussing among themselves, such as questions about the logistics of desegregation or, earlier, how to end slavery, concealing the deeper problem, that slavery and segregation are part of a grossly unjust racial order. To seriously consider those debates between white liberals and white conservatives is to be drawn into the orbit of that racial order, allowing it to further shape, to further disorder, one's loves. The effect of that initial hatred is to make everything—facts, reasons, affects—seem contingent, changeable, in need of change. It is the emotional equivalent of the intellectual project of genealogy. Radically new possibilities open once the hold of the current order of things loosens. In theological terms, we must first reject father and mother, son and daughter, all that shapes our affective world, before we become open to eschatological possibilities (see Matthew 10:37).

While Cleaver focuses on the role of hatred during this initial phase of conversion, Jackson focuses on ascetic practices. "I must rid myself of all sentiment and remove all possibility of love," he declares (38). What precisely these practices involve Jackson does not detail for his readers, other than the occasional mention of calisthenics. Their effect, however, he is explicit about: "My mind is fast becoming clear and I am slowly harnessing my emotions" (112). First, Jackson is purged of all loves so that new loves, rightly ordered, might then develop. While Jackson charged that his father could never *really* feel anything, his father *falsely* felt: his affect was ordered by anti-black racism. Jackson is suggesting that those false feelings must be purged before true feelings (that is, rightly ordered loves) are able to develop.

Jackson describes his conversion process as involving not only new ideas but also, even more so, a new way of approaching ideas. "I have completely arrested the susceptibility to think in theoretical terms," he asserts (38). Loosening the affective hold that abstractions have on him, Jackson is able to focus on what matters and what works in the real world, not the world as imagined by whites. This openness allows for a continual process of discovery, of world and self, rather than a perpetual repetition of the same—that is, rather than a perpetual regurgitation of the thoughts and desires of elites. At times Jackson (and Cleaver) seem to embrace an excessive confidence in the self, a valorization of the self made possible by the demonization of the world.[21] In fact, both Jackson and Cleaver hold that loves must be ordered by a principle that is neither found in the world nor found in the self. They must be ordered in anticipation of something wholly other: the revolution, the complete overturning of the social order. "Believe me, there is a better life," Jackson intones (76). This is the ultimate aim of the affective conversion Jackson recommends. With loves transformed so that they become harmoniously ordered in light of the revolution, the self is

---

21. Consider Jackson's conclusion, "I place no one and nothing above myself" (88) or, more dramatically, "Any woman I may have when I get out . . . must let me retrain her mind" (116).

entirely shaped by anticipation of that moment. "I have completely retrained myself and my thinking to the point now that I think and dream of one thing only, 24 hours of each day. I have no habits, no ego, no name, no face" (122). This makes clear the sense in which Jackson fully embraces his self—insofar as that self is constituted by an other that is reducible neither to the world nor the self. Given the limited content attributed to revolution, and given Jackson's insistence that there is no clear path from here to there, it is hard not to read this as a theological point.

The result of this commitment to what is effectively an eschatological event is to allow worldly loves to be understood as necessarily imperfect. It is only after the revolution that it will be possible for all loves to be perfectly ordered. In this world, today, Jackson and Cleaver must negotiate between the powerful gravitational pull of the racial order, effecting everything and everyone in the world, and a commitment to that which is beyond the racial order. It is in this light that we should read the form of their books. In the sequence of love letters, Jackson and Cleaver offer a pedagogy of desire, inviting the reader to reflect on how the author's ordering of loves improves, and continually reminding the reader that the author is still far from achieving rightly ordered loves. However, post-conversion, having turned their backs on the racial order, Jackson and Cleaver now have loves that are improving quantitatively, steadily moving in the direction of the eschatological. Yet the distance from the eschaton persists, and Cleaver and Jackson remain painfully aware of it—indeed, the resemblance between their beloveds and the white women of their preconversion fantasies makes it impossible to ignore.

Cleaver is clearly aware of the ways that his love toward his white lawyer may be led astray. "Of all the dangers we share, probably the greatest comes from our fantasizing about each other. Are we making each other up? We have no way of testing the reality of it" (137). On the one hand, Cleaver is referring to the physical constraints imposed by his incarceration that prevent cohabitation; on the other, the prison, like the racial order as a whole, encourages fantasy and prevents "testing the reality"—since all loves remain fundamentally disordered. Cleaver's love language focuses on anticipation and possibility; the love of which he writes is in the future rather than the present. "What an awesome thing it is to feel oneself on the verge of ... really knowing another person" (137). Once again, the nominal obstacle is the prison walls, but the real obstacle is the prerevolutionary, or pre-eschatological, context. It is only in the future that true knowledge of a lover, and of all things, will be possible.

Where Cleaver's love is directed only at his white lawyer, Jackson's first love letters were sent to his family, then he opens himself to romance with his white lawyer, then he spreads his love more broadly, with multiple correspondents (including, famously, Angela Davis). Like Cleaver, he worries about distortion and fantasy. "I am uneasy thinking that you may be attracted to the tragedy of me," he writes to a black woman friend (271). Jackson at times scolds his parents, tells them that they do not listen carefully enough to him, that their love is still ordered by anti-blackness, and at times praises them for seeing the world in light of the revolution. "Though I care about your feelings I care more for your well-being," he tells his mother in one letter (45). While Jackson himself often displays remarkable self-confidence, after Jonathan's death he realizes that he had related to his mother wrongly, that she had, in fact, formed Jonathan to resist the racial order. In short, the right ordering of loves is an ongoing process for both Cleaver and Jackson, but that process cannot begin until a radical break with the racial order is made.

Black Love Ethics

In describing his total commitment to the revolution, Jackson explains how love between two individuals (such as the love that forms the frame of his book's narrative) might be possible. "I feel no love, no tenderness, for anyone who does not think as I do," he asserts (122).[22] Jackson does not think that it is legitimate to love

---

22. The epistemic hubris implicit in such sentiments is never satisfactorily addressed by Jackson (or Cleaver). How can he be sure he is rightly oriented

anyone because of facts about them, or for who they are. (Cleaver would likely agree.) He only believes it is legitimate to love someone when that person also allows her loves to be ordered in light of the revolution. In fact, the right response to anyone who does not view themselves in this way, the right response to anyone who allows his or her loves to be ordered by the current racial regime, is hatred—in Christian terms, hatred of blasphemes.[23] Jackson describes his ideal mate as all *uti*, no *frui*: "The only woman that I could ever accept is one who would be willing to live out of a flight bag, sleep in a coal car ... own nothing, not solely because she loved me, but because she loved the principle, the revolution, the people" (227). In other words, romantic love is possible when all loves are rightly ordered, arranged not by the racial regime but in light of a future moment of total transformation.

Cleaver dedicates *Soul on Ice* to his white lawyer with the words, "To Beverly, with whom I share the ultimate love" (viii). According to Cleaver, Beverly Axelrod is "a rebel, a revolutionary who is alienated fundamentally from the *status quo*, probably with as great an intensity, conviction, and irretrievability as I am alienated from it" (32). As was the case with Jackson, for Cleaver love between two individuals is only possible when that love is subordinate to the love both share for something else, for the revolution, salvation. The lawyers who Cleaver and Jackson loved were both immersed in the black liberation movement, even though they were white. (In fact, both were Jews with relatively dark complexions, and at least Axelrod, whose law office was in an all-black neighborhood in San

---

toward the wholly other? Any criterion would seem to make the other—the revolution, God—not quite so *wholly* other, and so suggest idolatry.

23. What Cleaver revisits during his second period of incarceration is the question of how this hatred is to be put in practice, not whether this hatred is legitimate. He no longer believes rape is a proper way of acting on this hatred, and he generally moves toward Jackson's embrace of ascetic practices. This hatred of sinners might be contrasted with, to oversimplify, Christian hatred of sin coupled with love of sinners. But in Cleaver's view, as I reconstruct it, there is no way of seeing or knowing the sinner behind the sin, given the epistemological limitations that racism imposes on us—so we are left only to hate.

Francisco and whose law partner was black, was sometimes confused for an African American herself.[24]) Whiteness and blackness only hopelessly distort desire if affections have not been disciplined in light of the revolution.

This account of *ultimate* love, directed beyond the world and constitutive of the converted self, this account of love that is theological in everything but name, sharply distinguishes the ethics of love embraced by Cleaver and Jackson from the accounts of love circulating in black activist and intellectual circles, on the one hand, and in Christian ethics circles, on the other. In contrast to both, Cleaver and Jackson recognize the radical otherness of the ultimate object of their loves. They never try to describe it; they never paint a picture of "beloved community." Words are inadequate for what it is; it is only the effects of such love that we can observe. It has three components: first, a radical break with the racial order; second, practices of moral formation that attempt to sustain a way of life orthogonal to that order; third, perpetual self-criticism directed at the ways the racial order continues to shape our loves. Cleaver and Jackson are in a privileged position: the prison cell, and the position of racialized minority. From these spaces of confinement and marginalization, the limits of other approaches to the ethics of love become all too apparent. The gradual attunement of love, becoming progressively more just, sounds absurd when there is a metal door (or the barrier of race) between you and the person (or aspects of the world) with whom you are supposed to become attuned.

By the time *Soul on Ice* was published, Cleaver's relationship with Beverly Axelrod had disintegrated—he had fallen in love with the black activist Kathleen Neal, a decade younger than Axelrod, whom he would go on to marry—but he chose not to change the book's dedication. The "ultimate love" remains, and it continues to shape both of their lives, even if their lives have moved apart. Axelrod, who had been a leading light in the Bay Area political scene, was broken by the end of her relationship with Cleaver. She retreated from public life, spending some time in the Caribbean before returning

24. See Kask, "Soul Mates," though Cleaver knew she was white.

to activist work outside of the public spotlight. Cleaver promised her a quarter of the royalties from *Soul on Ice*, but he stopped paying her; she sued but never received the funds. Cleaver's split with Black Panther leadership over their degree of militancy—the Bay Area leadership was focusing on community organizing, Cleaver in Algeria wanted immediate, violent uprising—accelerated the party's downward spiral. George Jackson's lawyer, Fay Stender, fared worse. On some accounts, Jackson had asked her to smuggle weapons into his prison, and when she refused, he found a new lawyer. Nine years after Jackson's death, his political associates, seeking revenge, invaded Stender's home and shot her, leaving her paralyzed. Unable to find relief from the pain, a few months later she would commit suicide.

Are these reasons to question the love ethic put forward by Cleaver and Jackson? Or are these further reminders of just how far our world is from that eschatological moment when all loves will be rightly ordered? It is hard to say: we are, after all, dealing with literary texts, necessarily partial and polished, not biography. It could have been that no one was quite so committed to the revolution as they purported to be, the pulls of the racial order and mundane pressures overcoming the anticipation of a time beyond. It could have been Cleaver's and Jackson's publishers that molded their words into the form of love stories, a genre so familiar to American audiences. Even if that were so, even if the relationships between Cleaver and Jackson and those they loved remained primarily at the level of fantasy, the ethics of love they develop remains instructive. It offers a framework that can be filled in with various specific practices of renunciation, moral formation, and self-criticism. Whatever the details may be, this framework, this theology, offers a reminder of just how pervasive anti-blackness is, and it motivates us to think and live beyond our familiar ideas and feelings, to explore how we might be affectively shaped by an orientation to the radically other.

Finally, a curious feature of the love expressed in the writings of Cleaver and Jackson is its focus on the mundane.[25] In part, this was

---

25. While this is more present in Jackson's book than Cleaver's, see the

necessitated by the genre. In prison, there were practical measures to be considered, shoes, food, books, Christmas gifts, and updates on family. "I got the nuts and cake today, thanks, socks and handkerchiefs also," Jackson writes (42). In the next letter, he scolds his mother for sending him a card depicting white people. "I guess she just can't perceive that I don't want anything to do with her white god" (42). Critique and everyday affection coexist. This practical care and concern for family are the foundation on which the possibilities for conversion and critique are built, but it is a foundation that never disappears, even once Cleaver and Jackson have been radicalized. Perhaps it is in these practical matters, in the responsiveness to those with whom we find ourselves in relation, that we see a counterpoint to the conversion-focused account of love at the center of Cleaver's and Jackson's narratives. Perhaps this represents something analogous to natural rather than revealed religion, a tendency for selfless concern and affection beginning with family and extending to others, a tendency that is repressed when we are gripped by abstractions sold to us by elites. Perhaps such natural loves offer a necessary counterbalance to the revealed, a check on the epistemic hubris entailed when one believes oneself to be responding to the wholly other. Such natural love remains when illusions ring hollow, when the prison walls remind us of the mundane.

---

critical edition of Cleaver's letters in Kask, "Soul Mates."

CHAPTER 9

Facing Pecola
Anti-Black Sexism and a Womanist Soteriologic of Black Girl Disrespectability

EBONI MARSHALL TURMAN

"I don't think us feel old at all. I think this is the youngest we ever felt. Amen."[1] These are the concluding words of prayer uttered by Alice Walker's renowned protagonist, Celie, in the Broadway production of *The Color Purple*. Having traced the life, love, and troubles of a battered and abused adolescent black girl in the twentieth-century American South through her staggeringly painful though self-redemptive journey to middle-age womanhood, as the story-line draws to a close Celie utters these words, "I think this is the youngest we ever felt," to convey the feelings of joy, wonder, and innocence that mark the moment of reunion with her beloved sister, Nettie. After having been estranged by force for decades, the monologue that accompanies Celie and Nettie's unexpected sisterly restoration as adult women reveals an irreconcilable absurdity of black womanhood that offers initial cause for this meditation, namely, what black feminist scholar Monique W. Morris has identified as the malleability of black girlhood and black womanhood that not only subjects "Black girls to . . . aspersive representations of black women," but even more, compels black girls, under the age of

---

1. *The Color Purple*, Broadway production, August 2016.

eighteen, through a gender racialized project of age compression, to be women, or at least to be "womanish"—rationalizing, emoting, acting and being acted upon as adult women before fully approximating womanhood.[2]

Womanist theology and ethics have appropriated the "womanist" designation as first defined in Walker's 1983 *In Search of Our Mothers' Gardens: Womanist Prose* for the task of black women's religious and theological reflection in order to faithfully attend to the distinct epistemes—those ways of knowing, being, and doing—that both distinguish and circumscribe the lives and spiritual witness of black women. What womanist theological inquiry has done less of is explore the inherent continuity between the lived realities of black womanhood and black girlhood, especially in relationship to the hegemonic imagination of white patriarchy and its concomitant misogynoir, both of which have historically looted black girlhood and coerced the absurd interchangeability of black women and girls in ways that make sense of Maria Stewart's mid-nineteenth-century reflection on black women's stages of life that concedes, "most of our color have dragged out a miserable existence . . . from cradle to grave."[3]

While recognizing the certainty of the diversity of black girls' experiences asserted, for example, in bell hooks's *Bone Black: Memories of Girlhood*, this chapter presupposes moral continuity between black girlhood and black womanhood and thus endeavors to begin uncovering a genealogy of black women's suffering that "didn't just growed" but that emerges out of a precise and unscrupulous historical denigration of black girls in the United States.[4] Building

---

2. Monique W. Morris, *Pushout: The Criminalization of Black Girls in Schools* (New York: New Press, 2016), 34.

3. Nazera Sadiq Wright, "Maria W. Stewart's 'The First Stage of Life': Black Girlhood in the Repository of Religion and Literature, and of Science and Art," in *MELUS: Society for the Study of Multi-Ethnic Literature in the US*, 40, no. 3 (2015): 152. See also Nazera Sadiq Wright, *Black Girlhood in the Nineteenth Century* (Urbana: University of Illinois Press, 2016).

4. Emilie M. Townes, *Womanist Ethics and the Cultural Production of Evil* (New York: Palgrave Macmillan, 2006), 139–58.

on Emilie M. Townes's treatment of "Topsy as pickaninny" in her groundbreaking ethical investigation of memory and malevolent imagination, this chapter embraces Topsy-as-counternarrative to locate the ethical origins of black women's suffering in an initial subjection and erasure of black girlhood that manifests in both church and society, and resonates with Celie's paradoxical mid-life confession in prayer, "this is the youngest we ever felt." Following Joyce Ladner's pioneering work in black girlhood studies, which persuasively contend that black girls are "socialized into womanhood as early as seven or eight years old," this paper casts this reality as a moral problem by critically asking why girlhood is so often denied to black girls, while also attending theologically to the ways in which many black girls renounce and resist this brazen contradiction.

To be sure, the intergenerational character of the first part of Walker's four-part definition that asserts its derivation,

> From the black folk expression of mothers to female children, "You acting womanish," i.e. like a woman. Usually referring to outrageous, audacious, courageous or willful behavior. Wanting to know more and in greater depth than is considered "good" for one. Interested in grown-up doings. Acting grown up. Being grown up. Interchangeable with another black folk expression: "You trying to be grown." Responsible. In charge. *Serious.*[5]

appears, at first glance, to affirm and celebrate this "womanish" black girl reality that incubates the radical subjectivity required of black women to brave a house wherein, as black feminist Akasha Gloria Hull surmised, all the women are white and all the blacks are men.[6] This paper, however, is careful to distinguish between what the definition uncovers as voluntary desire (i.e. *wanting* to know more"),

---

5. Alice Walker, *In Search of Our Mothers' Gardens: Womanist Prose* (New York: Mariner Press, 2003), xi.

6. See Akasha (Gloria T.) Hull et al., *All the Women Are White, All the Blacks Are Men, But Some of Us Are Brave: Black Women's Studies* (New York: Feminist Press, 1982).

intellectual sophistication (i.e. *interested* in grown-up doings), play ("*acting* grown-up"), the *attempt* toward ontic presuppositions of black womanhood ("*trying* to be grown") as indicated above, and the external coercion of black girl self-dispossession that is propelled by a normative revulsion for the embodied interdigitation of subjugated social indices, namely, race, gender, class, sexuality, and generation that typically guides the moral compass of the arbiters of power. It acknowledges such aggressive compulsion as a form of gender-racialized moral paedocide, that is, the social and moral slaughter of black girls as structural and systemic evil that is too often also intimately enacted as individual sin.

In making such a moral claim, this chapter begins with an examination of the textures of black girls' social and moral crucifixion by focusing on their respective criminalization and demonization at the hands of anti-black state-sanctioned and anti-black church-sanctioned gender terror. An exploration of the nature of suffering in the lives of black girls will follow and assert black girlhood as a theological problem to which the Black Church must be held accountable. The constructive edge of the paper finally contends that the disrespectability attributed to black girls is in fact a responseable and deeply embodied soteriologic. In other words, black girl disrespectability functions as its own enfleshment of a salvific *logos* toward the end of black girl redemptive self-love.

Black Girl Blue

Sixteen-year-old Ashlyn Avery—assaulted by police and arrested for falling asleep in class while reading *Huckleberry Finn*. Seventeen-year-old Marché Taylor—arrested for resisting "being barred from prom for wearing a dress that was considered too revealing."[7] Seventeen-year-old Pleajhia Mervin—assaulted by police and arrested for refusing to pick up a piece of cake that she had dropped on the cafeteria floor. Six-year-old Desre'e Watson—arrested for throwing a tantrum in her kindergarten class. Seven-year-old

---

7. Morris, *Pushout*, 3.

Michelle Mitchell—arrested for fighting on the school bus. Seven-year-old Aiyana Mo'Nay Stanley-Jones—shot and killed by Officer Joseph Weekley while sleeping in the home of her paternal grand-mother. These are the names of just a few black girls who have been publicly crucified by the staggering escalation of the criminaliza-tion of black girls in the U.S. public education industrial complex, specifically, and the concurrent rise, at least in terms of visibility, of anti-black state-sanctioned sexist, heterosexist, and transphobic violences, more generally.[8]

In February 2015 the African American Policy Forum (AAPF), a Columbia University–based think tank oriented toward dismant-ling structural inequality through the propagation of intersectional analyses, frameworks, and strategies that combat racial and gender injustice, released a groundbreaking study on the issue of the ever-growing criminalization of black girls. Titled, "Black Girls Matter: Pushed Out, Overpoliced, and Underprotected,"[9] the study uncov-ers the debilitating social and political trends that disproportion-ately affect the flourishing of black girls in the public square. Circu-lated on the heels of President Barack H. Obama's widely celebrated launch of "My Brother's Keeper," the White House initiative aimed at empowering "boys and young men of color" who face "dispro-portionate challenges and obstacles to success," the AAPF's "Black Girls Matter" garnered considerable attention as, with empirical precision, its deliberate focus on black girls' lives pressed beyond the absurdity of twenty-first-century gender hierarchies to challenge the metanarrative of male exceptionalism and its culture of exclu-sion that renders black girls invisible—even on Facebook Live—and, in so doing, implicitly asserts that black girls do not matter.

Morris employs the AAPF's study in *Pushout: The Criminaliza-tion of Black Girls in Schools* to deepen her analysis of the complex-

---

8. Ibid.

9. http://www.aapf.org/ourmission; For the full report, see also "Black Girls Matter: Pushed Out, Overpoliced, and Underprotected," http://static1.squarespace.com.

ity of black girls' marginalization that results in a disproportionate school-to-confinement pathway for black girls in relationship to nonblack girls. While only constituting 16 percent of the female student population, black girls make up close to "one-third of all girls referred to law enforcement and more than one-third of . . . female school-based arrests." Morris contends that the "mark of double jeopardy," namely, black girls' racial and gender subordination, fuels their "pushout."[10] Combined with the marginalized economic, sexual, and generational realities that disproportionately distinguish the lives of black girls, such double jeopardy is intensified by an insidious pentagonal social subjugation. As noted above, the hostility and aversion that condemn the intersection of race, gender, class, sexual, and generational subordinate realities provoke "policies, practices, and consciousness" that promote "[black girl] invisibility . . . and [facilitate her] criminalization."[11] Accordingly, Morris uncovers how the varieties of intersectional social subjectivity position black girlhood within a "taxonomy of deviance" that imagines and brands her as bad, loud, defiant, irate, insubordinate, disrespectful, uncooperative, uncontrollable, and thus the antithesis of the protected and racially specific category "girl."[12]

Such caricatures of black girls sometimes are based on behavioral distinctions that arise no doubt from the specificity of social location and context. But they are also and too often attributed to them because of a fabricated complementarity between black girl aesthetics and oppressive racial-gender tropes that objectify and strip black girls of their girlhood. At times, caricature performs as a messy "third way" that exists somewhere between the "sometimes true" of black girl behavior and the "true-true" of racial-gender tropes that oppress in ways that resonate with the ethical "almost-

---

10. Morris, *Pushout*, 3.

11. Ibid., 23–24.

12. Michael A. Rembis, *Defining Deviance: Sex, Science, and Delinquent Girls, 1890–1960* (Urbana, IL: University of Illinois Press, 2013), 6. See also Morris, *Pushout*, 11.

ness" that, echoing Gramsci's meditations on hegemony, Townes asserts as a viable counternarrative. We will return to this later as we engage in thinking christically about black girl disrespectability. Suffice it to say for now that the black female child and/or adolescent subject is "not-girl" insofar as she is perceived as "radical other" in relationship to meta-assessments of "girlhood," those social and moral calculations that almost always imply white girl, or "Becky with the good hair,"[13] who is fictively constituted as respectable, kindly, and penetrable via physical and emotional vulnerabilities that are real and yet simultaneously not true, though consistent with the dubiety of white women's tears and the defective logics of Victorian domesticity. Black girl defiance is of the ever-calcifying white supremacist gendered-racial order that designates her loud, outrageous, and courageous "misbehaving" body as illicit and criminal. It presupposes her subjection to exclusionary technologies of racialized gender terror that surveil and contain.[14]

In accordance with literary analysis as black womanist ethical method, the weight of black girls' flesh and blood subjection to technologies of discipline can readily be found in the literary enunciation of black girls' social crucifixion. In reflecting on the impetus behind her classic *The Bluest Eye*, Toni Morrison insists that the black female child is society's "most vulnerable member." Pronouncing the "woundedness" and estrangement of her novel's protagonist, Pecola Breedlove, Morrison attempts to uncover what she identifies as the social and domestic aggression that injures "young [black] girls" who are subject to the "damaging forces . . . of youth, gender, and race."[15] Facing Pecola, the elusive

---

13. Diana Gordon et al., "Sorry." Beyoncé Knowles. *Lemonade*, 2016.

14. Morris, *Pushout*, 70. Morris argues that "willful defiance" is an actual, though controversial, disciplinary category used to identify black girl confrontation with and complication of teacher's ability to manage the classroom. It is used as a catchall category to suspend and punish black girls even though they present no threat to themselves or others.

15. Toni Morrison, *The Bluest Eye* (New York: Vintage Books, 2007), xi.

nature of black girlhood especially in its encounter with white male antipathy is palpable:

> She looks up at him and sees the vacuum where curiosity ought to lodge. And something more. The total absence of human recognition—the glazed separateness. She does not know what keeps his glance suspended. Perhaps because he is grown, or a man, and she a . . . girl. But she has seen interest, disgust, even anger in grown male eyes. Yet this vacuum is not new to her. It has an edge; somewhere in the bottom lid is the distaste. She has seen it lurking in the eyes of all white people. So. The distaste must be for her, her blackness. . . . And it is the blackness that accounts for, that creates, the vacuum edged with distaste in white eyes.[16]

It is precisely the racial-gender coordination of "her blackness" that lends itself to racialized gender terrorism, or what has been identified above as the social and moral crucifixion of black girls. The sort of violence that locates its dynamism in "her blackness" can be found beyond the assumed simplicity of the schoolyard and the imagined interior lives of the oppressed. As revealed in the experience of Dajerria Becton, who was fourteen years old at the time of her state-sanctioned assault at a pool party in a predominantly white neighborhood to which she and other black youth had been invited, the physical dispossession of black girlhood is an imperial design such that it can happen anywhere and nowhere at all insofar as "everywhere is its domain."[17] Here I am reminded of the wisdom of Ms. Sophia's counsel, "a girl child ain't safe in a house [or church or world] full of men." In the case of Dajerria Becton, however, the Free Thought Project reported that a resident of the Craig Ranch North Community in McKinney, Texas, where the incident occurred, called in a disturbance to the McKinney Police Depart-

---

16. Ibid., 48–49.

17. Michael Hardt and Antonio Negri, *Empire* (Cambridge, MA: Harvard University Press, 2000), 189.

ment upon noticing multiple black youth "who do not live in the area or have permission to be there" in and/or near the community pool.[18] Morris explains at length:

> "Call my mama!" This was the cry of fourteen-year-old Dejerria Becton, who in the summer of 2015 was thrown to the ground as well as physically and verbally assaulted by [police] after she refused to leave her friends at the mercy of . . . law enforcement officer[s] in McKinney, TX. A video, which later went viral, showed [Corporal Eric] Casebolt pushing Dejerria's face into the ground as she, a slight-framed, barefoot, bikini-clad teenager who presented no physical threat or danger—screamed for someone to call her mother for help. The video showed Casebolt grinding his knee into her bare skin and restraining her by placing the full weight of his body onto hers.[19]

The visibility of Becton's experience exposes a state-sanctioned menace to black girlhood, and black youth broadly construed. Close review of video of the incident shows that prior to Becton's assault a group of black adolescent girls was standing by as police aggressively rounded up several of their black male peers while relatively disregarding the comparable presence of white youth, male and female. As the girls prepared to walk away after having been instructed by the police to do so an animated verbal exchange between the girls and the police ensued. From the video, it appears that as Becton, "slight-framed, barefoot, and bikini-clad," walked away from the dispute, she realized that she was walking by herself in the opposite direction of her girlfriends. As she turned to change her course and catch up with her friends who were walking the other way, Corporal Casebolt physically accosted her and violently pulled her to the ground in a manner more consonant with a defensive response to a threatening adult offender, though even then still questionable. In an instant Becton's

---

18. Police statement at "Pool Party Turns Violent When Police Show Up and Assault and Nearly Shoot Multiple Teens," http://thefreethought project.com.

19. Morris, *Pushout*, 1.

"weekend pool party" girlhood evaporates as her willful adolescent behavior is perceived by the dysconscious racism of state power, which is almost always synonymous with white power, as criminal activity, and *"her blackness"* condemned as ground zero for the performance of anti-black girl rage and brutality that defies modern concepts of reasonable postwar child-adult interactions.[20]

Interestingly enough, in *No Mercy Here: Gender, Punishment, and the Making of Jim Crow Modernity*, Sarah Haley argues that historically the criminal legal system has "crafted, reinforced, and required black female deviance" in order to justify the extension of "structures of captivity."[21] Echoing Hortense Spillers, Haley further contends that the "gendered logics of punishment," its "systems of terror and structures of . . . subordination," perceive the black female subject as "the principal point of passage between the human and the non-human world . . . the route by which the dominant modes decided the distinction between humanity and 'other.'"[22] When read in tandem with childhood studies that assert the flexibility of "ideology at the conjunction of childhood and innocence," classifying black children, black girls in particular for our purposes here, as "unfeeling, noninnocent, nonchildren," a precise connection may be drawn between how racialized gendered logics of punishment position the black girl as "not-girl" in the effort to naturalize and justify anti-black paedocidal politics that cast black children into contemporary scenes of subjection.[23] Becton's repeated cry of "Call

---

20. See Hugh Cunningham, *The Invention of Childhood* (New York: BBC Books, 2006). For further treatment of "dysconscious racism," see also Anna Duane and Annette Ruth Appell, *The Children's Table: Childhood Studies and the Humanities* (Athens: University of Georgia Press, 2013).

21. Sarah Haley, *No Mercy Here: Gender, Punishment, and the Making of Jim Crow Modernity* (Chapel Hill: University of North Carolina Press, 2016), 3.

22. Ibid., 5–6. See also Hortense J. Spillers, *Black, White, and in Color: Essays on American Literature and Culture* (Chicago: University of Chicago Press, 2003), 155.

23. Robin Bernstein, *Racial Innocence: Performing American Childhood from Slavery to Civil Rights* (New York: New York University Press, 2011), 33.

my mama!" however, stands in stark contrast to her abjection and palpably reveals the actuality of black girlhood in contradistinction to the perception of her adolescent girl body as adult threat at best, and bestial female at worst.

Lest we mistakenly think that black girls' crucifixion is unique to the public square, it must be noted that the moral crucifixion of black girls is consistently evident in the Black Church as well. It should be noted that black churches are not homogenous and not every black church is circumscribed by sexual-gender injustice that targets black girls, although I would argue that too many are. As I have indicated elsewhere, my use of "the Black Church" as a rhetorical device does not endeavor to minimize the significant varieties of denominational polity and communal praxis that guide the ecclesial practice of Christian persons and communities of African descent in the United States. It rather signifies the historical continuity and expression of black Christian faith that is no greater than the sum of its varied parts. Accordingly, "the Black Church" does not only refer to the seven primary historically black Christian denominations—African Methodist Episcopal (AME), African Methodist Episcopal Zion (AMEZ), Christian Methodist Episcopal (CME), Church of God in Christ (COGIC), National Baptist Convention of America (NBCA), National Baptist Convention, USA, Inc. (NBC), and the Progressive National Baptist Convention, Inc. (PNBC). It also includes those smaller historically black denominations like the Sanctified Church (also known as the Church of God), the United Holy Church of America, and the Fire Baptized Holiness Church of God of the Americas, in addition to those primarily black congregations in historically white majoritized denominations, and multicultural nondenominational churches whose liturgical expressions are primarily guided by the norms of African American preaching and worship traditions.[24]

Although in the past ten to fifteen years the Black Church has

---

24. See Stacey Floyd-Thomas and Juan Floyd-Thomas, *Black Church Studies: An Introduction* (Nashville, TN: Abingdon Press, 2007).

seen a remarkable uptick in the number of women in pastoral and/ or ministerial leadership positions, as is evidenced by black women's disproportionate misrepresentation or rather their relative absence, to be more precise, from the highest levels of Afro-ecclesial leadership when compared to the church's majority female constituency, a large proportion of black churches continue to prohibit black women from exercising the arts and gifts of ministry from the pulpit. In fact, in recounting this Black Church reality I distinctly remember my own experience. As a licensed and ordained minister in the National Baptist Convention, USA, as well as a theological educator, I have been instructed to address congregations from the floor while the platform of black male ministers ascended toward the sacred desk. The masculine erection of the pulpit, that notably defies Black Church origins as slave religion, begets the sort of sexual-gender discrimination that regularly excludes women from ordained ministry and restricts them to lay service—like teaching in the Sunday School, singing in the choir, answering the phones, and cooking in the kitchen—all of which are, no doubt, significant service that often constitutes the principle viability of a congregation, and concretely serves at least two of the three tables of an ordained, though typically male, diaconate. Nevertheless, sexism in the black church does not commence in adulthood, when and if one approximates sacred consciousness and the courage to affirm call. To the contrary, the effects of sexual-gender discrimination in the Black Church begin taking hold in childhood wherein girls are often conditioned into a gendered variation of Duboisian double-consciousness that functions as sacralized schizophrenia, "two souls, two thoughts, two unreconciled strivings, two warring ideals" in one black woman-child's body, that is concurrently both "image of God" and "female subject to men," echoing an Augustinian designation of women as "special symbol[s] of evil" and Thomistic regard for women as "defective and misbegotten"; indeed, in the alleged safety of the Black Church one ever feels her twoness.[25]

---

25. See W. E. B. DuBois, *The Souls of Black Folk,* ed. Brent Hayes Edwards (New York: Oxford University Press, 2007), 8; Thomas Aquinas, *Summa*

As I note in my forthcoming book, *Black Women's Burden: Sexism, Sacred Witness, and Transforming the Moral Life of the Black Church*, strong arguments can be made about the effects that the invisibilization and marginalization of black women in the church have on black girls, as well as the paralyzing theological trauma that accompanies preaching misogyny from the pulpit in ways that insult, shame, and spiritually wound. These sorts of hostile and discriminating liturgical practices have been notably recognized in, for example, the Reverend Jamal Harrison Bryant's impertinent reprimand of disloyal "hoes" in his now infamous sermon, "I'm My Enemy's Worst Nightmare," preached at the Empowerment Temple AME Church in Baltimore, Maryland, where he is senior pastor. Surprisingly, even the contemporary black social gospeler, the Reverend Calvin O. Butts III, and the homiletical association he made between Hosea's "whore" and the "Lenox Avenue ho" in a sermon delivered at the historic Abyssinian Baptist Church in Harlem where he is senior pastor is likewise hermeneutically slothful and deeply problematic. Similarly, Juanita Bynum's recent viral soliloquy concerning the necessity of black women's combining their "ho" with God's "ly" toward the approximation of divine "holiness" is one example of the ways in which black women participate in their own subjection through the performance of patriarchy in drag. The corresponding demonization of black girls' bodies in the Black Church, however, is equally intriguing insofar as it situates their bodies, apart from their practices, on the moral fault line of "not-girl." In this way the Black Church, as a "supportive institution" that is party to what womanist systematic theologian Kelly Brown Douglas asserts as the "white cultural attack" and what black feminist anti-colonial geographer Katherine McKittrick identifies as state-sanctioned human geographies that displace and

---

Theologiae, 1.92.1; and M. Shawn Copeland, "Freedom, Emancipation, and Deliverance: Toward a Theology of Freedom," in *Full of Hope: Critical Social Perspectives on Theology*, ed. Magdala Thompson (Mahwah, NJ: Paulist Press, 2003), 41–73.

dispossess, targets not only what black girls do, but also who black girls inherently are.[26]

For black girls, then, there is seemingly no escape. While in the public square, both the schools and the streets, negation of black girlhood functions as a pathway toward the subhuman criminal, literally dragging black girls to prone positions where, as we have seen with Dajerria Becton and even Shakara, the sixteen-year-old black girl known only by her first name, who in October 2015 was assaulted and dragged from her math class by school police at Spring Valley High School in Columbia, South Carolina, they can also be incapacitated and sat upon by the arbiters of power as if inanimate objects. At the same time, in the Black Church the negation of black girlhood functions as a pathway toward her objectification not so much as subhuman but as "sinner." One way that black girlhood is pilfered in the Black Church is through the prioritization of what I have discussed elsewhere as the "cover-up"—literally lap scarves, turtlenecks, and hose (but this time pantyhose)—that police the bodies of women and girls so they will not, primarily, awaken the wanton passions of cis/het-in-public clergy and churchmen who are, due to the malformed privilege of patriarchy, presumed incapable of regulating their own wills to power. The "cover-up" also underscores a theologically deformed Platonism most often attributed to Pauline influences that imparts a fundamental and particular enfleshed deviance to black bodies.[27] Because black girls inhabit the

---

26. For further treatment of the Black Church as a "supportive institution," see Marcia Y. Riggs, *Plenty Good Room: Women Versus Male Power in the Black Church* (Eugene, OR: Wipf & Stock, 2008). See also Katherine McKittrick, *Demonic Grounds: Black Women and the Cartographies of Struggle* (Minneapolis: University of Minnesota Press, 2006), 9.

27. See Eboni Marshall Turman, "Black & Blue: Uncovering the Ecclesial Cover-Up of Black Women's Bodies through a Womanist Reimagining of the Doctrine of the Incarnation," in *Reimagining with Christian Doctrines: Responding to Global Gender Injustices*, ed. Grace Ji-Sun Kim and Jenny Daggers (New York: Palgrave Pivot, 2014). See also Kelly Brown Douglas, *What's Faith Got to Do with It: Black Bodies/Christian Souls* (Maryknoll, NY: Orbis Books, 2005).

potential lasciviousness typically reserved for black women, as has been observed in the bizarre and fanatical public infatuation with First Lady Michelle Obama's body and has cast it as varied spectacle based on the myth of black female bodily deviance, black girls' bodies must be covered up in ways that approximate an illusory and thus impossible respectability, one that black girls and black women can never really possess because they are not white. In other words, Pecola's bluest eye eludes black girls, even as it is peddled as a violent liturgical racial-gender self-loathing, what Morrison asserts as the "internalization of assumptions of immutable inferiority originating in an outside gaze," that colors and condemns too many black churches.[28]

Black Girl Joy and Pain

The despoiling of black girls' lives through their moral and social crucifixion in church and society is a theological problem. It is rooted in a systemic and structural objectification of life that, while caricaturing black girls as some amalgamation of subhuman sinner, alienates them from "the ways and the will of God" through physical and ecclesial violence that criminalizes and literally condemns them, in some instances, to hellfire and damnation via sexist liturgical practices or at least hell on earth, at school, and at the swimming pool.[29] To be sure, the theological production of black female juvenile deviance is part of a "broader constitution of Jim Crow modernity premised upon the devaluation of black life broadly" speaking, which is why liberationist theological trends contend that theological inquiry apart from historical and sociological analysis is inadequate and futile at best.[30] Even "traditional" white trinitarian commitments would affirm Karl Rahner's stimulating axiom which contends irrevocable continuity between the economic and imma-

---

28. Morrison, *The Bluest Eye*, xi.

29. Kelly Brown Douglas, *Sexuality and the Black Church: A Womanist Perspective* (Maryknoll, NY: Orbis Books, 1999), 194–95.

30. Haley, *No Mercy Here*, 3.

nent trinity, namely, that God and the world are bound together.[31] Thus, the brilliance of, for instance, Kelly Brown Douglas's theological treatment of state-sanctioned violence against black bodies in her *Stand Your Ground: Black Bodies and the Justice of God* is indisputable. She carefully traces the phenomenon of the "guilty black body" in the United States, that is, the criminal and sinful non-white body, to the Anglo-Saxon chauvinism on which the grand mythos and theology of American exceptionalism is based, the kind that formerly "made a liturgy out of its history" of "planting a colony . . . for the glory of God" on top of indigenous people, and the kind that contemporarily propels trumped-up and violence-laden claims that propose to "make America great again." Brown Douglas is tracing the peculiarity of how the theology of the "guilty black body," at work in both church and society, takes root with exacting social consequences for black youth.[32]

This strange fruit of the white Christian imagination that emerges from its prevailing theology of triumphalism and its concomitant mythos of white exceptionalism has historically been transmitted in the particularity of designating the black child as nonchild, that is, as "pickaninny." For our purposes here, the pickaninny is a "subhuman black" girl void of innocence who, as queer cultural historian Robin Bernstein advances, merrily accepts or even invites violence precisely because of her presumed inability to feel pain.[33] Although the word pickaninny is derived from the Portuguese word *pequenino*, meaning "small child," its usage can be traced back to the seventeenth-century pejorative reference to any child of African descent. Interestingly enough, by the nineteenth century it mainly referred to "black children in the US and Britain" as well as to nonblack "aboriginal children of the Americas, Australia, and New Zealand" who, as children of color, were absorbed into

---

31. See Linn Tonstad, *God and Difference: The Trinity, Sexuality, and the Transformation of Finitude* (New York: Routledge, 2016).

32. Kelly Brown Douglas, *Stand Your Ground: Black Bodies and the Justice of God* (Maryknoll, NY: Orbis Books, 2015), 25.

33. Bernstein, *Racial Innocence*, 34

blackness according to the logics of black-white dyadic hierarchies. While the pickaninny was a routine caricature of black children throughout American slavocracy and well into the early twentieth century, it must be observed that she has not vanished and, in fact, not only continues to embellish the kitchenware and mantelpieces of many twenty-first-century homes but also tragically continues to guide social interactions with black youth in church and society. Bernstein explains that the pickaninny, the juvenile "childlike Negro" stripped of her childhood as she is simultaneously "always-already" an African American adult, is typically characterized as dark-skinned with exaggerated facial features. Bernstein further clarifies that the pickaninny is almost always represented as the target for an animal attack:

> Pickaninnies often wear ragged clothes (which suggest parental neglect) and are sometimes partially or fully naked. Genitals or buttocks are often exposed, and not infrequently targeted for attack by animals.... When threatened, [pickaninnies] might ignore danger...when attacked they might laugh ... but, in either case, they never experience or express pain or sustain wounds.... The absence of pain unifies the construction of the pickaninny.[34]

Bernstein also contends that some pickaninnies, like the Cottolene girl, were depicted as "clean, well-dressed, and engaged in domestic chores" in ways that could imply an adorable childlikeness that was never to be mistaken for innocence or even humanness.[35] As William Cowper Brann notes, "there is probably nothing on earth 'cuter' than a nigger baby; but, like other varieties in the genus 'coon," ... they are not...valuable additions to society."[36]

The pickaninny is rooted in a Christian imagination propelled by white exceptionalism that, as Kelly Brown Douglas contends,

---

34. Ibid.
35. Ibid.
36. See Bernstein's discussion of William Cowper Brann, ibid., 35.

guides America's grand narrative.[37] The image of the noninnocent, nonchild, black female juvenile subject in church and society proves to be its own sinful brand of Christian sadomasochism that requires pain as not-pain but as that which necessarily precedes the eternal pleasure of the joy of salvation.[38] In other words, black girl pain must be reconfigured as not-pain insofar as it feeds another's pleasure, namely, the invention of white superiority and male exceptionalism. Black girl pain, to which Bernstein alludes in her treatment of the precarious erasure of black childhood, is not pain insofar as it functions as a sort of surrogate mechanism of salvific pleasure for those who aspire to approximate normative power. It is this Williamsian surrogacy that ennobles Christians to sing on Sundays, "at the cross, at the cross, where I first saw the light and the burdens of my heart rolled away." Christo-ethically configured, it is feasible to suggest that, in a real sense, black girls are too often on that cross, wounded for [our] transgressions and bruised for [our] iniquities (Isaiah 53:5). On the one hand, this peculiarly Christian ethic of black girl social and moral crucifixion continues to designate black girls as ragged criminals deserving of state-sanctioned and state-sponsored violence, as well as the carceral ethics of disciplinary exclusion as has been witnessed in the public square. On the other hand, black girls are paradoxically deemed blameworthily adorable, that is, as sinfully cute, in ways that approximate visual aesthetics of respectability for the purpose of Sunday School, choir, and junior usher, without the revaluation and disavowal of demonizing moral claims compelled and undergirded by Afro-ecclesial practice and polity that performs contemporarily, in opposition to its theological and ethical origins, as its own evil massa in blackface. As Morrison's Pecola Breedlove fictively indicates, as well as my more recent public access work, "Fight-

---

37. See Douglas, *Stand Your Ground*, 3–47.

38. Beverly Wildung Harrison and Carter Heyward, "Pain and Pleasure: Avoiding the Confusions of Christian Tradition in Feminist Theory," in *Sexuality & the Sacred: Sources for Theological Reflection*, ed. Marvin Ellison & Kelly Brown Douglas (Louisville, KY: Westminster John Knox, 2010), 165–82.

ing for Amy," on intracommunal black girl violence, the nature of black girl suffering is so insidious that it often engenders sarcophagic, that is, self-cannibalizing practices of self-loathing that compel black girls to destroy themselves and others who look like them based on their caricature as criminal and sinner that is just not true.

Black Girls Rock

Given such daunting realities, in an effort to push back against the theological ghettoization of black girls to a contemporized calvary, M. Shawn Copeland's womanist theology of suffering asserted in her "Wading through Many Sorrows: Toward a Theology of Suffering in a Womanist Perspective" is particularly instructive.[39] In relationship to the social redemption of black girls, Copeland's contention that black women do not drown, but rather wade through many sorrows, indicates that even in the face of the unspeakability of black women's suffering movement persists in the interior and exterior lives of black women in ways that keep them afloat amid the heaviness of suffering. The tradition of Black Church hymnody might speculate about such resilience by pointing toward what the Black Church psalmist Lucie Eddie Campbell, born a slave in Mississippi before becoming the music director for the new National Baptist Convention in 1916, identified as that "something within that holdeth the reins; something within I cannot explain."[40] Or as I note elsewhere, Copeland's "wading" black woman may be the explicable and embodied evidence of a womanist Christology, which contends an inconceivable a priori "isness" at work in the lives of black women, one that mediates between the materiality of *kata*

---

39. See M. Shawn Copeland, "Wading through Many Sorrows: Toward a Theology of Suffering in a Womanist Perspective," in *Womanist Theological Ethics: A Reader*, ed. Katie G. Cannon, Emilie M. Townes, et al. (Louisville, KY: Westminster John Knox, 2001), 135–54.

40. "Something Within" is a well-known hymn that is sung in many African American churches. For full text lyrics, see "Preachers and Teachers Would Make Their Appeal," http://www.hymnary.org.

sarka realities (the sufferings of this world) and the reality of Jesus as the *en sarki* first word (logos).[41] As such, black women not only wade through sorrows. Insofar as they are positioned in relationship to the redemptive authority of the life of Jesus who suffers and yet comes again, as much as black women suffer they too survive.

Consequently, black women can be imagined as ethically inhabiting the redemptive both/and christic *almostness* that makes room for the claim of black women as *homoousios* with Christ as to his ethical identity.[42] Black women thus participate as wading protagonists in deeply embodied self-redemptive action that is consistent with womanist ethical methodology which identifies a black slave girl announcing, "I am walking to Canada . . . and taking you and a bunch of other slaves with me." It is similarly aligned with the womanist biblical interpretive framework and theological imagination that is found in Delores S. Williams's Hagaritic emphasis wherein Hagar, an African slave woman, liberates herself. In other words, a womanist soteriologic contends that there are some things black women must do for themselves.

In her recent book *Shapeshifters: Black Girls and the Choreography of Citizenship*, black feminist sociologist Aimee Meredith Cox identifies dance and poetry as social choreographies that homeless black girls engage to critique the illegibility of black girl citizenship that is undergirded by their categorization as "unworthy" and "disrespectable," the "not-girl." Cox further interrogates how black girls employ creative and strategic methods or what she characterizes as "choreography of citizenship" to disrupt social hierarchies and prescriptive narratives that marginalize them.[43] A black womanist theoethics echoes the criticality of Cox's inquiry concerning black

---

41. For a womanist treatment of the Pauline *en sarki/kata sarka* distinction, see Eboni Marshall Turman, *Toward a Womanist Ethic of Incarnation: Black Bodies, the Black Church, and the Council of Chalcedon* (New York: Palgrave Macmillan, 2013), 39–58.

42. Ibid. See also Townes, *Womanist Ethics*, 79–110.

43. Aimee Meredith Cox, *Shapeshifters: Black Girls and the Choreography of Citizenship* (Durham, NC: Duke University Press, 2015), xi–xix.

girl survival by asking: what are black girls doing with their bodies that is indicative of a self-redemptivity that reclaims the girlhood that has been stolen, pilfered, and stripped from them by and/or according to crucifying social realities?

The notion of black girl self-redemption or what has been identified here as a burgeoning womanist soteriologic of black girl disrespectability is particularly discernible when assessing the physical assault of fourteen-year-old Dajerria Becton. As she is attacked by the white male police officer, Becton is loud, willful, courageous, and consistent in her cries of "Call my mama!" As such, her behavior in the presence of law enforcement might be characterized as disrespectable, especially by those who foreground matters of compliance and propriety in the face of anti-black state-sanctioned violence. Thinking christologically, Becton's cries echo Jesus as he hanged from the cross and called out to the first person of the Trinity amid the approximation of his death at the hands of the Roman Empire. In Jesus's "Eloi, eloi lama sabachthani," Becton's fear reverberates as she, literally bearing the weight of white supremacy and white patriarchalism as the police officer burrows his knees into her bare back, calls out for her mother, the first person to know her.

"Call my mama!" It is an ontic proclamation. In its simplicity it asserts three critical concepts for the continued elaboration of a womanist soteriologic. In the first place, the black female juvenile subject typically cast as pickaninny, criminal, subhuman, subject to attack, and unable to feel pain, the "not girl" or "not child," in the very act of crying for mama—an ontic proclamation, that is a verbal articulation of being-ness—asserts her own "girlhood/childhood" in opposition to dominant narratives of black girl dispossession. Becton thus embodies a womanish "I am" even as the arbiters of power say and perform as if "I am not." As ontic proclamation, "Call my mama!" further clarifies that black girls resist in motley ways. In this instance Becton is not just acted upon but talks back to her oppressor and to the community of voyeurs. In doing so, she instigates a generational remix on Copeland's "wading through sorrows." In this millennial moment on the spectrum of the black freedom movement, we find black girls "talking back" to oppression with fierce precision. Such "talking back" is not only based on verbal comment but is also propelled by an articulating body that speaks concurrently. As Becton pounds her fists into the ground in one instance, and repeatedly claps her hands in another, her body performs its own choreography of wounded citizenship that does much more than wade.

Finally, Becton's resistance presupposes that there is theological value in disrespectability. First theorized by black feminist sociologist Brittney Cooper in her "Disrespectability Politics: On Jay-Z's Bitch, Beyoncé's 'Fly' Ass, and Black Girl Blue," the politics of disrespectability are defined as those strategies and acts that black women and girls employ where they live between the "diss" of social and moral crucifixion and the "respect" that they seek. A black feminist-womanist perspective finds continuity between Cooper's assessment of disrespectability in relationship to popular culture and the disrespectability of Jesus's birth in the poverty of a barn and his death as a slave on the cross, that is, the ordinary dis- of the world and the respect that Christ's *adventus* commands. Accordingly, such "disrespectful" strategies and acts that are normatively characterized as "bad, loud, defiant, irate, insubordinate ... uncooperative, uncontrollable, unladylike, and sinful" are to the contrary, integral for a black womanist soteriologic of black girl disrespectability which claims that "the bad, loud, defiant, irate, insubordinate, uncooperative, unladylike" is a core mandate of black womanist redemption and response-ability. Black girl disrespectability functions as a vector of black womanist virtue in church, academy, and society in ways that serve as a salvific word made flesh for black women and black girls as they carry and clap back at the sins of the world.

In conclusion, the fact of the matter is that black girls are dying at the intersection of social crosses in the street and moral crosses in the church. In reading Toni Morrison's Pecola Breedlove through Alice Walker's staged Celie, that is, in praxeologically reading the lives and life chances of black women and girls together, a womanist soteriologic of black girl disrespectability intends to compel

womanist ecclesial praxis that awakens the church to the signifi-
cance of the earthly redemption of black women and girls in ways
that are consistent with the authority of black soteriologies of liberation. The intergenerational, intracommunal mandate of womanist thought compels black women to hear Becton's cry, "Call my
mama!," and the cries of black girls, in relationship to the relative
and respectable silence of women in black churches in response to
racial-gender paedocide.

Following christologically, the silence of the first person in
response to Jesus's crying out with a loud voice might be appealed
to as regulative for the church in the face of black death. It shows up
as an ethic of "we don't talk about *that* at church." Moreover, it is
gospeled that in the face of black death, or, in view of the imminent
death of the body that defies the established normativity of the arbiters of the status quo, the first person may very well have been silent
in the face of suffering. Williams has already proffered, "God is partial and discriminating." But the church, which, as James Cone contends, harbors the contemporary manifestation of the saving signifi-
cance of the Black Christ in the historicity of the world, ought not
be. The church must respond to the denigration of black girls that
strips them of their childhood—making them old to the point of
death, while they are yet young—with a resounding "Hell no!" that
echoes the proto-womanist wisdom of Walker's Ms. Sophia and a
fight that endures. God very well may be silent, but what will we
say to these things? Black girls are being crucified every day. Yet it
is written that in the face of crucifixion, "the veil of the temple was
rent in twain from the top to the bottom; and the earth shook, and
the rocks split, and the tombs broke open, and many bodies of the
saints that slept arose" (Matthew 27:51-52). Stay woke.

CHAPTER 10

The Erotic Life of Anti-Blackness
Police Sexual Violation of Black Bodies

BRYAN N. MASSINGALE

Sex is never simply a sensual experience between two bodies but is also an encounter between social beings endowed with collective memory.[1]

Sex is the whispered subtext in spoken racial discourse. Sex is the sometimes silent message contained in racial slurs, ethnic stereotypes, national imaginings, and international relations. *Although the sexual meanings associated with ethnicity may be understated, they should never be underestimated.*[2]

The noted African American essayist James Weldon Johnson asserted the following concerning U.S. race relations: "At the core of the heart of the race problem is the sex problem."[3] He thus succinctly

---

1. Mara Viveros Vigoya, "Sexuality and Desire in Racialised Contexts," in *Understanding Global Sexualities: New Frontiers,* ed. Peter Aggleton et al. (London: Taylor and Francis, 2013), 219, explicating Roger Bastide.

2. Joane Nagel, *Race, Ethnicity and Sexuality: Intimate Intersections, Forbidden Frontiers* (New York: Oxford University Press, 2003), 2 (emphasis added).

3. Cited in Charles Herbert Stember, *Sexual Racism: The Emotional*

described the deep sexual subtext that pervades U.S. racial discourse and practices. In other words, conversations about race inevitably are also conversations about sex.

Almost every marginalized or outcast group has its sexuality maligned and stigmatized by the socially dominant or privileged. The denigration of a despised group's sexuality is part of the apparatus of oppression. Therefore, deconstructing systems of oppression, like racism, also must entail the deconstruction of "deep-level investments in sexualized and even eroticized assumptions [and practices] of dominance and submission."[4] That is to say, effective struggle against anti-black racism requires engagement with its sexualized expressions and manifestations.

In plain speech, sex matters in pursuing racial justice. Racial conflicts, hatreds, and antagonisms have been enacted and are still expressed, in no small measure, through sexual relationships and behaviors (e.g., sexual objectification, exclusion or avoidance, violence, abuse, and/or exploitation).

This essay is part of a larger current project tentatively titled "Race, Sex, and the Catholic Church." In it, I explore the intersections between racial injustice, sexuality, and religious faith. This project takes seriously the deeply sexual subtext of U.S. racism and thus explores the "complicated intermarriage between racialized boundaries as sexual and sexualized borders as raced."[5] Moreover, it also will examine how Catholic practices both reflected and reinforced pervasive race-based sexual beliefs about African Americans and other persons of color. My goal is to set the stage for developing an anti-racist sexual ethics. A central question of this project is: What happens to Catholic sexual ethics if it takes

---

Barrier to an Integrated Society (New York: Elsevier Scientific Publishing, 1976), ix.

4. Laurel C. Schneider, "What Race Is Your Sex?," in *Queer Religion: LGBT Movements and Queering Religion*, vol. 2, ed. Donald L. Boisvert and Jay Emerson Johnson (Santa Barbara, CA: Praeger, 2012), 138.

5. Zillah R. Eisentein, *Hatreds: Racialized and Sexualized Conflicts in the 21st Century* (New York: Routledge, 1996), 14.

racialization and racism as serious factors in human sexual relationships?

This essay, which is an exploration of anti-black sexual violence and, more specifically, anti-black sexual violation perpetrated by police officers, is a small part of that project. I begin by defining "racialized sexuality" and "sexual racism." I then examine a particular instance of sexual racism, namely, racist sexualized police misconduct. The sexual meanings of these encounters is then clarified by an excursus into the realm of racist Internet pornography. The paper concludes by noting the silence of Catholic sexual ethics in addressing sexual racism, and how a trinitarian-inspired healthy eroticism might inform more adequate ethical reflection and praxis.

Defining "Racialized Sexuality" and "Sexual Racism"

There are a variety of terms used by authors to describe and discuss the complicated nexus between racialization and sexuality. I here describe my usage of these terms.

By "racialized sexuality" I mean *sexual desires, fantasies, prohibitions, aversions, ascriptions, descriptions, depictions, stereotypes, and/or beliefs based upon a person's or group's racial or ethnic identity.* With very little reflection, examples come readily to mind. For instance, the pervasive beliefs that black men are well endowed; black women are sexually promiscuous; Asian women are sexually submissive; Latinos/as are passionate or "hot blooded" lovers; black men are sexual aggressors or rapists; white women are pure and chaste; white and Asian men are not well endowed. Racialized sexuality is also evident in phrases or aphorisms such as "jungle fever," "once you go black, you never go back," and "the blacker (or darker) the berry, the sweeter the juice." That such beliefs and phrases are readily familiar testifies to the reality that *our sexuality is deeply racialized and cannot be fully understood apart from our assigned racial identities.* Racial and ethnic identity not only affects a person or social group's sexual self-understanding but also how they view the sexuality of other racial or ethnic groups.

Racialized sexuality is not inherently problematic from an ethical perspective. That is, it need not always be a negative factor in human relationships. At times, it can have a benign character. However, racialized sexuality is often deployed to the end of *sexual(ized) racism* when such ascriptions or beliefs are used to justify or maintain racial inequality and social injustice. That is, *racialized sexuality becomes sexual racism* when race-based sexual beliefs and stereotypes are used as a pretext or justification for social exclusion, inequality, subjugation, control, denigration, and inferiority. For example, racialized sexuality becomes sexual racism when race-based sexual beliefs or stereotypes become the basis for negative public policies (e.g., the sexual subtext present in welfare or immigration debates; the practice of forced sterilizations of poor black women; and the sexual subtext present in the infamous Tuskegee syphilis experiments, where a people deemed sexually irresponsible were deliberately infected with and then left untreated for a sexually transmitted infection).[6]

Thus, John D'Emilio and Estelle B. Freedman helpfully describe sexual racism as "the [race-based] propagandized denigration of sexuality . . . to perpetuate social inequality."[7] Sexual racism, then, can be understood as a subset of the broader category of sexual injustice, that is, attacking or denigrating a group's sexuality to establish or justify social hierarchy, inferiority, or exclusion.

There is widespread awareness of race-based sexual myths and stereotypes. What often passes unnoticed, however, is (1) how cen-

---

6. Studies of the infamous Tuskegee experiments, where African American men were injected with the syphilis virus and left untreated long after effective treatments were developed, abound. For a study that notes the sexual subtext of these experiments, see James H. Jones, *Bad Blood: The Tuskegee Syphilis Experiment,* rev. ed. (New York: Free Press, 1993). For an examination that situates this tragic event within the broader context of medical abuse inflicted on African Americans, see Harriet A. Washington, *Medical Apartheid: The Dark History of Medical Experimentation on African Americans from Colonial Times to the Present* (New York: Anchor Books, 2006).

7. John D'Emilio and Estelle B. Freedman, *Intimate Matters: A History of Sexuality in America* (New York: Harper & Row, 1988), 105–6.

tral they are for U.S. race relations and the maintenance of white (male) supremacy; (2) their enduring power and pervasiveness; and (3) the role of faith communities and religious practices in justifying and maintaining sexual racism, specifically, their roles in policing racialized sexual borders.

Sexual Racism: A Tool of Racial Dominance and Humiliation

Unfortunately, sexualized violence is a constant in U.S. racial and ethnic relationships. Sexual violation, denigration, and humiliation have been staple features in the arsenal of white supremacy, used to manifest and reinforce the superior status of whites in general—and white men specifically—and the inferior status of people of color. Race-based sexual violence has been constant from the days of slavery, through the lynchings of black men and the coerced sexual relationships with black women domestics during Jim Crow, and even into the present.[8] I now consider a contemporary instance of race-based sexual violence and violation, namely, the sexual abuse perpetrated by police officers upon African Americans—what in more sanitized accounts may be called sexual police misconduct.

Sexual Violation and Humiliation by Law Enforcement

The sexual humiliation of people of color at the hands of police officers acting under the cloak of law and public authority is far from being isolated, episodic, or sporadic. Rather, it is so recurring that it must be considered a key expression of white supremacist practice. For example, Toni Morrison provides a graphic account of the sexual humiliation of black chain gang prisoners in the Jim Crow South by their wardens in her acclaimed novel *Beloved*. One also notes the depiction of a black woman's public digital rape by a white police officer in the 2005 Oscar-winning film *Crash*. Yet

---

8. For a comprehensive presentation of this history and its present-day effects, see Patricia Hill Collins, *Black Sexual Politics: African Americans, Gender, and the New Racism* (New York: Routledge, 2004).

there are nonfictional events that are part of the historical record, such as the public strip searches of Black Panther Party members in 1970s Chicago[9] and the horrific sodomizing of a Haitian immigrant, Abner Louima, in a New York City police station in 1997.[10] Three more recent instances of race-based sexual police violence and humiliation attest to the continuing need to ethically interrogate this reality.

(1) *Recent (2013) strip searches and invasive public rectal cavity invasions of black men in Milwaukee.* I cite here from an account provided by the local paper, the *Milwaukee Journal Sentinel:*

> Five black men filed federal suits against eight white Milwaukee police officers accused of conducting or permitting illegal strip searches. Five white officers are accused of using their fingers to probe the men's rectal and genital areas without probable cause; two others watched and did nothing to stop the abuse; one police captain is being charged with failing to supervise and suspend the officers involved. . . . Plaintiffs Jerrold Ezell (25) and Anthony Pettis (23) charged that officers stormed into their friend's house without a warrant in November 2011 and then shoved two bare fingers into each man's rectum without pausing to put on gloves or wash their hands. "It wasn't right—to just come into the house and stick his fingers into us," Enzell said, his voice trailing off. Pettis estimated he'd been rectally probed about 30 times, and said he didn't believe the officers when they said they were searching

---

9. For a history of the Black Panther Party that treats the lengths and tactics employed by public authorities to crush this movement, see Joshua Bloom and Waldo E. Martin, Jr., *Black against Empire: The History and Politics of the Black Panther Party* (Berkeley: University of California Press, 2013).

10. For an incisive analysis of this event, see Carlyle Van Thompson, "White Police Penetrating, Probing, and Playing in the Black Man's Ass: The Sadistic Sodomizing of Abner Louima," in Carlyle Van Thompson, *Eating the Black Body: Miscegenation as Sexual Consumption in African American Literature and Culture* (New York: Peter Lang, 2006), 145–65.

for drugs. "I think it is a powertrip, man," Pettis said. "Race plays a role in it, too."[11]

"Race plays a role in it, too." Undoubtedly, for while it is not impossible for white men to be sexually violated by law enforcement, there is no documented instance of a white man being so sexually abused and humiliated by white—or black—Milwaukee police officers.

More disturbing is the fact that these two young black men are only the tip of the iceberg. In all, five Milwaukee police officers, all white men, were indicted on multiple charges of illegal strip and rectal searches of at least thirteen victims, all black men. Most disturbing is that the allegations against the purported ring leader of these crimes were known to police commanders for at least five years prior to any legal action being taken against him. The lead prosecutor stated,

> "I know Michael Vagnini [the worst perpetrator] understood the sexual undertones of what was going on," Assistant District Attorney Miriam Falk said. "It was intended to degrade and humiliate them, and that's what makes it a sexual assault." She said while Vagnini may not have obtained sexual gratification from penetrating his victims' anuses, the victims felt violated nonetheless.

Yet as part of a plea deal, prosecutors agreed to drop the sexual assault charges since Vagnini agreed to plead no contest

---

11. *Milwaukee Journal Sentinel*, "Strip Search Victims Speak of Helpless Humiliation," (July 11, 2013), http://archive.jsonline.com. In another interview, Pettis further described his excruciating sexual assaults: "I feel humiliated," said Pettis. "It's like I just want this to end. This ain't right." Pettis said police followed and stopped him as many as thirty times, doing similar illegal searches on the streets. "Every time they would see me, pull me over, pull my pants down, my boxers—he would stick two fingers inside me," said Pettis." See Fox6, "Civil Suit Filed against MPD for Illegal Cavity Searches" (July 11, 2013), http://fox6now.com.

to four felony charges and four misdemeanors. Vagnini will no longer have to register as a sex offender.[12]

(2) *Unlawful strip searches by the Baltimore Police Department.* In the aftermath of the 2015 death of an unarmed black man, Freddie Grey, while in police custody, the U.S. Department of Justice (DOJ) conducted an investigation of the Baltimore Police Department (BPD). Among its many findings of concern was what the DOJ called a "pattern" of unconstitutional strip searches on the part of police officers.[13] The DOJ determined that "BPD officers frequently ignore" the constitutional requirements for legal strip searches, noting that the BPD in the past five years "has faced multiple lawsuits and more than 60 complaints alleging unlawful strip searches."

The investigation provided detailed accounts of several such incidents. One involved the public strip search of a black woman following a routine traffic stop for a missing headlight. "Officers ordered the woman to exit her vehicle, remove her clothes and stand on the sidewalk to be searched. . . . Finding no weapons or contraband around the woman's chest, the officer then pulled down the woman's under-

---

12. Police State USA, "Officer Who Forced Dozens of Anal Cavity Searches for Fun Gets Only Two Years in Prison" (December 28, 2013), http://www.policestateusa.com.

13. It is noteworthy that the Department of Justice (DOJ) has a specific understanding of the phrase "pattern or practice" of misconduct: "The finding of a pattern or practice of unlawful conduct within a law enforcement agency does not mean that most officers violate the law. Nor does a pattern or practice reflect that a certain number of officers have violated the law or that the number of unlawful acts have reached a particular threshold. . . . Rather, *the touchstone is whether the unlawful conduct appears more typical than isolated or aberrant.* A pattern or practice exists where *the conduct appears to be part of the usual practice, whether officially sanctioned by policy or otherwise.*" Thus a "pattern or practice" is "more than the mere occurrence of isolated or 'accidental' or 'sporadic'" acts. A "pattern or practice" must be a *"regular rather than the unusual practice."* (Note the parallels to what theological ethicists call "social or structural sin.") See DOJ, "Newark Police Department—Findings Report" (July 22, 2014), www.justice.gov, quoting *International Brotherhood of Teamsters v. United States*, 431 U.S. 324 (emphases added).

wear and searched her anal cavity." This search "occurred in full view of the street" notwithstanding the fact that there was no indication that the woman "had committed a criminal offense or possessed concealed contraband." Finding no evidence of wrongdoing, the woman was released with only an order to repair her headlight.

The DOJ also discussed another case where a black teenage boy was subjected to two public strip searches in the winter of 2016 by the same officer. "The officer . . . pulled down his pants and boxer shorts and strip-searched him in full view of the street and his girlfriend." After the teenager filed a detailed complaint with the BPD over the incident, "the same officer approached [the teen] near a McDonald's restaurant in his neighborhood, pushed the teenager against a wall, pulled down his pants and grabbed his genitals. The officer filed no charges against the teenager in the second incident, which the teenager believes was done in retaliation for filing a complaint about the first strip search." Citing this event, one local activist declared, "What that officer did is not just violate a body, but he injured a spirit, a soul, a psyche. And that (young boy) will not easily forget what happened to him, in public with his girlfriend. It's hard to really put gravity and weight to that type of offense."[14]

The consistency of such sexual humiliation and degradation at the hands of police is confirmed again by other instances cited in the official report, including one of an African American man who was searched by an officer several days in a row, "including 'undoing his pants' and searching his 'hindquarters' on a public street. When the strip search did not find contraband, the officer told the man to leave the area and warned that the officer would search him again every time he returned." The DOJ thus concluded that sexual humiliation by law enforcement constituted a "regular rather than unusual practice" against the African American citizens of Baltimore.[15]

---

14. Sheryl Gay Stolberg, "Findings of Police Bias Have Baltimore Asking What Took So Long," *New York Times*, August 11, 2016, A14.

15. DOJ, "Investigation of the Baltimore City Police Department" (August 10, 2016), www.justice.gov.

(3) *The serial sexual abuse and rape of African American women in Oklahoma City.* In December 2015, an Oklahoma police officer of white and Japanese descent was convicted of multiple accounts of sexually assaulting and raping eleven African American women during the period of March–June of 2014. Most of his victims had criminal histories, such as drug offenses and prostitution. Prosecutors and police investigators contend that Daniel Holtzclaw "used his position as an officer to run background checks to find information that could be used to coerce sex."[16] As one investigator noted, "They're the perfect victim. Nobody's going to believe them. If you believe them, who cares? 'A prostitute can't be raped.' . . . So that's why he was picking these kind of women, because they're the perfect victim."[17] While Holtzclaw declined to testify at his trial, his public comments since his conviction and sentencing to a 263-year prison term support this contention. Calling into question the reliability of one of his chief accusers, fifty-seven-year-old grandmother Jannie Ligons, Holtzclaw said, "She's not innocent the way people think she is. She had a [drug] bust in the '80s. . . . But we couldn't present that to the jury. This is not a woman that's, you know, a soccer mom or someone that's credible in society."[18]

The chilling horror, steady drumbeat, and numbing repetition of these events underscore how they are not isolated incidents. We are not dealing with a Milwaukee problem, a Baltimore issue, or an Oklahoma City outrage. These are, in the DOJ's terminology, "patterns and practices" illustrative of a pervasive national police culture. They constitute nothing less than the state-sponsored sexual violation of black bodies. To untangle the complex psychosexual dynamics at work in such behavior is far beyond the limits

---

16. Chris Gilmore, "Final Appeal Extension Expected to Be Filed for Holtzclaw Today," News 9 (February 1, 2017), www.news9.com.

17. Goldie Taylor, "White Cop Convicted of Serial Rape of Black Women," *The Daily Beast* (December 10, 2015), www.thedailybeast.com.

18. ABC News, "Ex-Oklahoma City Cop Spending 263 Years in Prison for Rape and His Accusers Share Their Stories" (April 21, 2016), abcnews. go.com.

of this essay. But the public exposure of the black body—a body both feared and prized[19]—as well as its sexualized debasement and humiliation—is a palpable display of the white ability to exercise dominance with impunity. In the words of one black Chicago youth, "It's society's way of saying, 'You ain't worth shit to us.'"[20]

Racist Interracial Pornography

This "pattern and practice" of the sexual abasement and humiliation of black bodies in the service of white dominance and erotic pleasure is unintelligible apart from a broader context of cultural sexual meanings and identities ascribed to these bodies. In order to excavate these cultural meanings and to demonstrate their contemporary relevance and salience, I now turn to an examination of the genre of racist interracial pornography.

The following observation provides the insight for why this examination is so pertinent to the task at hand: *"Pornography is the one media genre in which overt racism is still routine and acceptable.* Not subtle, coded racism, but old-fashioned racism—stereotypical representations of the sexually primitive black male stud, the animalistic black woman, the hot Latina, the Asian geisha."[21] Although

---

19. Ellis Cose, *The Envy of the World: On Being a Black Man in America* (New York: Washington Square Press, 2002). See also Meri Nana-Ama Danquah, *The Black Body* (New York: Seven Stories Press, 2009), 14.

20. Ta-Nehisi Coates quotes an African American young man in Chicago speaking of his understanding of the wider society's view of his peers: "'You ain't shit. You not no good. The only thing you are worth is working for us. You will never own anything. You not going to get an education. We are sending your ass to the penitentiary.' They're telling you no matter how hard you struggle, no matter what you put down, you ain't shit." See Coates, "The Case for Reparations," *The Atlantic* (June 2014). See also Van Thompson, "White Police Penetrating."

21. Robert Jensen, "Stories of a Rape Culture: Pornography as Propaganda," in *Big Porn Inc: Exposing the Harms of the Global Pornography Industry*, ed. Melinda Tankard Reist and Abigail Bray (North Geelong, Victoria, Australia: Spinifex Press, 2011), 31 (emphasis in the origi-

a provocative topic not commonly examined in Catholic theology, racist interracial pornography is important for several reasons. First, it is the fastest growing segment of Internet pornography.[22] Second, white males are by far the greatest producers and consumers of this kind of pornography; yet the dominant "performers" by far are black men and white women. This genre is "produced and marketed for a White male audience" and reflects "a White man's fantasy of Black sexuality."[23] This leads to perhaps the most important reason for turning to this medium for insight, for it provides an *unfiltered* access to the deep cultural meanings ascribed to the nonwhite body—especially, but not only the black male body—by a white patriarchal mentality, even when these associations are consciously denied or deemed inadmissible in contemporary public discourse. For these porn fantasies don't "work," and the industry would not be so profitable, in the absence of such deep and pervasive cultural (mal)formation.

In straight/heterosexual racist interracial pornography, one finds works with titles such as *Black Poles in White Holes*; *Huge Black Cock on White Pussy*; and *Monster Black Penises in Tight White Holes*.[24]

---

nal). I also want to clarify the limits and intent of this discussion. I am not interested in debating the morality of pornography *in se* in this project. Nor is it an indictment of all forms of interracial sexual representations in pornography. Rather, this project focuses upon *racist* interracial pornography, that is, that genre that trades upon racial stereotypes and degrading depictions that reflect and reinforce—that is, sexualize and eroticize—unequal societal racial relationships.

22. Gail Dines, "The White Man's Burden: Gonzo Pornography and the Construction of Black Masculinity," *Yale Journal of Law and Feminism* 18, no. 1 (2006): 285.

23. See Dines, "White Man's Burden," 285 and 289. Another study notes that such media are "produced and marketed for a White male audience. These films are a White man's fantasy of Black sexuality—the fact that Black men watch them is purely accidental" (Gloria Cowan and Robin R. Campbell, "Racism and Sexism in Interracial Pornography: A Content Analysis," *Psychology of Women Quarterly* 18, no. 3 [1994]: 325).

24. Dines, "White Man's Burden," 285 and 289.

In straight porn, racist interracial pornography performs two functions:

a. *It sexualizes inequality between white women and white men.* It is a curious phenomenon that much of this genre consists of white men watching sexual intercourse between black men and white women (who are often cast as being the wives of the white man who is watching the interracial coupling). One author provides this account for the popularity of these scenarios: "It is hard to conceive of a better way to degrade white women, in a culture with a long and ugly history of racism, than having them penetrated again and again by a body that has been constructed, coded, and demonized as a carrier for all that is sexually debased, namely the black male."[25] (One should note how such scenarios also *sexualize inequality between white men and black men*, as the scene is marketed to a white male audience for their erotic enjoyment. The black man "takes" the white woman, but only in a context that allows the white man to "get off" on seeing the white woman so "debased." The black man's sexual dominance is ultimately at the service of white male pleasure.)

b. *It sexualizes inequality between white men and women of color.* A staple feature of this genre of pornography is the sexual debasement and humiliation of women of color by white men. This function is perhaps the most pivotal one for this essay. I call attention to how certain films such as "Ghetto Gaggers" and "Degrading a Latina Slut" are marketed to a white male audience. Here is the description provided by the producers of "Ghetto Gaggers," informing potential viewers of the sexual fantasy and the erotic pleasure to be obtained [offensive language alert]: "Do you prefer seeing ghetto sluts being turned into submissive sistas? if so, Ghetto Gaggers is just what the doctor ordered. . . . You'll see black pornstars being destroyed by white cocks, and left in piles of puke and spit."[26]

There is much that is ethically problematic with such depictions. But it is important to emphasize this: an ethical reflection or evalu-

---

25. Ibid., 285.

26. Taken from www.degradingwomen.com. Note again the intended audience for this fantasy and to whom it is marketed.

ation of this genre that focuses only on the morality of pornography in general, or primarily upon the gendered violence present in these scenarios, misses the major and perhaps most salient feature of racist interracial pornography, namely, the nexus between racial identity and sexual behaviors—or, to say this more directly, the eroticization of white male dominance. As one author notes: "In pornography, all of the culture's racist myths become *just another turn-on*. Asian women are portrayed as pliant dolls; Latin women as sexually voracious but utterly submissive; and black women as dangerous and contemptible sexual animals."[27] This pornographic genre makes explicit the implicit cultural understandings of the bodies of persons of color that are at play in the sexual violation of black bodies by the police.

To further excavate the cultural meanings ascribed to the black male body, we also need to consider the phenomenon of gay racist interracial pornography. In such gay porn, representative titles include *Blackballed 8* (produced in 2011—self-described as "one of the most successful series in gay porn history has a new chapter"); *Poor Little White Guy 4* (released in 2008—"Oh poor little white guy, thrown down and gang-tagged by a group of fine black brothers. Don't cry too hard for him; he secretly loves it—and so will you!"); *Poor Little White Boy 5* (2005); and the *Thug Hunter* website (which features white men penetrating black men).[28] As with its straight counterparts, gay racist interracial pornography has two

---

27. Cited in Alice Mayhall and Alice D. H. Russell, "Racism in Pornography," *Feminism and Psychology* 3, no. 2 (June 1993): 277 (emphasis added). Another study notes, "Black women are portrayed as sexually uncivilized and promiscuous, essentially a whore. The black man is defined solely by the size, readiness, and unselectivity of his penis." Moreover, black men are portrayed as utterly devoid of capacities for intimacy, even given minimal porn standards for depicting genuine "intimacy." See Cowan and Campbell, "Racism and Sexism in Interracial Pornography," 325–26.

28. I quote from the descriptive liner notes that accompanied the various DVDs. These notes are found on the back covers of the original cases of the DVDs. At times, they are also found on various websites that advertise these DVDs or the scenes from them for purchase or downloading.

functions that are staple. Although they seem contradictory at first glance, upon deeper reflection the common purpose they serve is readily discerned.

a. When in the "top" or insertive/penetrating position, black men are depicted as powerful, dominant, and even dangerous. Yet, they are ultimately present to service the white "bottom," whose pleasure is the focus of the fantasy. The white "bottom" is the center of attention and the "star" of the film. This is conveyed through the white actor's central positioning on the films' cover and the fact that the white actor is often the only one who is named as starring in the film. Black men are often only credited in reference to the size and color of their phallus (e.g., as a "BBC"—"big black cock"). The fantasy turns on the culturally ascribed hypersexuality of the black man, who is presented as devoid of affection and as the "forbidden fruit" whose sexual energy is alluring and fascinating. His sexual prowess and virility are at the service of the white male, to whom this fantasy is being marketed.

b. When white men are in the top or insertive/penetrating position, they become racially abusive and denigrating, using blatantly racist expressions during the sexual encounter (see, e.g., *Thug Hunter 4*).[29] Here the white male takes pleasure in aggressively subordinating and conquering the supposedly more virile black man.[30]

---

29. From the video's description: "Big Daddy's *Thug Hunter 4* [2013] is four scenes, each one dedicated to finding a hard, horny, and thugged-out man to wreak sexual havoc on." One reviewer, relating his unease with "racially demeaning gay porn," notes that only black "thugs" are depicted in the film and writes, "[T]hey also seem to enjoy furthering nonsensical stereotypes. Here are a few samples from the opening scene's dialogue: 'They all think they're tough,' 'They're all down to make money, and they all act like they don't like it,' 'That's why we came to this neighborhood here, by the train tracks,' and my favorite, 'Half of them are homeless and junkies.'" See "Thug Hunter 4 [Big Daddy]," www.tlavideo.com.

30. The following is a recent expression of this sentiment, where a white gay man tells his scene partner, "I've always wanted to have sex with a black guy. Or, excuse me, to *top* a black guy." This is the opening dialogue between "Roman Daniels" and "Ty Royal" at collegedudes.com (emphasis in the

The white male's socially superior position becomes even more con-firmed through his so-called mastery over and "taking" of the black man in the one area where the white cultural coding of black sexual-ity would give him a purported advantage. (The relevance of this cultural script for the sexual violation of black men by white police officers is more than obvious.)

Thus, regardless of the sexual role that white gay men are cast in, they "maintain a position of privilege and superiority in their interactions with African American men. They expect to be served sexually, or when they are in the top position, they become racially abusive."[31] Thus in its various manifestations, racist gay interracial pornography—as its straight counterpart—serves *to sexualize or eroticize inequality between white men and men of color, especially black men.*

No doubt, the reader is by now aware of the disturbing nature of the genre of racist interracial pornography. However, one should not lose sight of the larger point that motivated this seeming excur-sus: racist interracial pornography does not make sense—it is unin-telligible—apart from a wider cultural frame, namely, that of racial-ized sexual discourse and representation that both manifests and reinforces a social hierarchy of white male anti-black supremacy. *Such pornography makes manifest and explicit the pervasive racial-ized sexuality and sexual racism that is often left tacit and implicit in accounts of police sexual violation of black bodies.* This is directly relevant to the discussion of anti-black sexual violation at the hands of police officers. The pervasiveness of anti-black sexual behavior in U.S. policing reflects the influence of pervasive sexual racialization. We see in the police behaviors previously described the denigration,

---

original). Note that the white actor makes it clear that his desire is not simply to be sexually intimate with a person of a different race but to dominate over him. This discourse, and the fantasy it expresses, does not make sense apart from the sexual racism that is pervasive in U.S. culture.

31. Niels Teunis, "Sexual Objectification and the Construction of White-ness in the Gay Male Community," *Culture, Health & Sexuality* 9, no. 3 (May–June 2007): 273.

abuse, and exploitative use of black bodies for the sake of white erotic pleasure and social dominance. U.S. policing practices and culture perform, enact, and enforce by means of sexual behaviors the anti-black dominance that is deeply embedded in U.S. society, and indeed Western culture.

Theological Reflection: Toward an Anti-Racist Eroticism

At the beginning of this essay, I noted that deconstructing systems of oppression, like anti-black racism, also must entail the deconstruction of "deep-level investments in sexualized and even eroticized assumptions [and practices] of dominance and submission."[32] The question that now arises concerns the resources present in faith traditions, specifically Roman Catholicism, that can be employed to that end.

Catholic theological reflection on sexualized anti-black racism and its inherent violence faces several daunting challenges. For one, there is the burden of unacknowledged Catholic complicity in U.S. sexual racism. The Catholic Church, through its teachings and practices in such matters as interracial marriage, the ordination of nonwhite men to the priesthood, and the admission of nonwhite women to the religious life, both participated in and reinforced the nexus between racial privilege and sexual denigration existing in wider society.[33]

Another challenge is that Catholic theological engagement with racial injustice is still quite limited, as I detailed in a recent issue of

---

32. Schneider, "What Race Is Your Sex?," *Queer Religion*, 138.

33. This is more fully explicated in the larger project. See, for example, the historical studies of Cyprian Davis, *The History of Black Catholics in the United States* (New York: Crossroad, 1992); Stephen J. Ochs, *Desegregating the Altar: The Josephites and the Struggle for Black Catholic Priests, 1871–1960* (Baton Rouge: Louisiana State University Press, 1993); and M. Shawn Copeland's examination of the life of a free woman of color, Henriette Delille, who founded the Sisters of the Holy Family in nineteenth-century New Orleans: *The Subversive Power of Love: The Vision of Henriette Delille* (Mahwah, NJ: Paulist Press, 2009).

Theological Studies.[34] Even more to the point, a third challenge or obstacle to effective engagement with sexual racism is that Catholic theological ethicists tend to treat racism and sexuality as "standalone" topics. Catholic studies on sexual ethics abound, but do not name or examine racialized sexuality, that is, how racialization impacts sexual identity and behaviors. The limited Catholic ethical literature on racism is largely silent on its deeply sexual character.[35]

Thus engaging racialized sexuality and sexual racism lies at the frontiers of Catholic theological and ethical reflection. This current project, then, cannot but be considered as a work in progress, one inspired by the following intuition: If a root factor in U.S. racism is the still existing unease with racial amalgamation and a (largely unstated) continuing fascination with interracial—and in particular, black—sexuality, then effective efforts to challenge racism cannot avoid engaging both the U.S. racialized sexual ethos and the religious dimensions of racialized sexuality.[36]

---

34. Bryan N. Massingale, "Has the Silence Been Broken? Catholic Theological Ethics and Racial Justice," *Theological Studies* 75, no. 1 (March 2014): 133–55.

35. The limited work on this issue has been done by M. Shawn Copeland, when she discusses the situation of enslaved women. However, she does not subject racialized sexuality and race-based sexual violence to in-depth theological or ethical analysis. See her works *The Subversive Power of Love* and *Enfleshing Freedom: Body, Race, and Being* (Minneapolis: Fortress Press, 2010).

36. For recent examples of the continuing fascination and unease with interracial sexuality consider (1) that almost 30 percent of Mississippi primary voters in 2012 believed that interracial marriages should be illegal; (2) that in 2011, a Louisiana justice of the peace refused to issue a marriage license to an interracial couple; and (3) in 2011, a Baptist church in Kentucky banned interracial couples from membership in the church. Nationally, although 75 percent of whites approve of interracial marriage in the abstract, less than half (43 percent) of white college students report a willingness to date interracially, with blacks being the least preferred dating prospects. See Erik Hayden, "46 Percent of Mississippi GOP Want to Ban Interracial Marriage," *The Atlantic* (April 7, 2011), https://www.theatlantic.com; and "Interracial Marriage: Many Deep South Republican Voters Believe Interracial Marriage Should Be

Given its nascent development, perhaps a useful contribution for an anti-racist sexual ethics would be to state questions that Catholic theological ethics must consider or address: If one of the core functions of sexual racism and racialized sexual discourse is to eroticize social and racial inequality, what resources exist within religious faith traditions—and, specifically, the Catholic faith tradition—and faith-based sexual discourses that would "encourage [racially differentiated] people to express their freedom and eroticize their equality?"[37] How can Catholic theological ethics contribute to the overcoming of black "somatic alienation," that is, a deep estrangement from their own embodied realities and sexual selves, brought about in reaction to white pejorative depictions of their sexuality?[38] How must Catholic sexual ethics be reconstructed so as to facilitate the racial "erotic conversion" so desperately needed in both church and society?[39]

Or, to express the challenge less prosaically and perhaps more adequately: How can Catholic sexual ethics contribute to the building of a world where interracial (and intra-racial) sexual partners

---

Illegal," *Huffington Post* (March 12, 2012); http://www.huffingtonpost.com. Even more recent reports relate a continuing unease over interracial coupling and sexuality: "People Say They Approve of Interracial Couples but Studies Uncover Bias," https://www.washingtonpost.com.

37. Anthony B. Pinn, *Embodiment and the Shape of Black Theological Thought* (New York: New York University Press, 2010), 97.

38. I borrow the term "somatic alienation" as a consequence of white supremacy from Charles W. Mills, *From Class to Race: Essays in White Marxism and Black Radicalism* (New York: Rowman & Littlefield, 2003). The estrangement of African Americans from their sexuality in reaction to white Christianity has been well described in the works of Kelly Brown Douglas, *Sexuality and the Black Church* (Maryknoll, NY: Orbis Books, 1999), and *What's Faith Got to Do with It? Black Bodies/Christian Souls* (Maryknoll, NY: Orbis Books, 2005).

39. On erotic conversion, see the work of Paul Gorell, "Erotic Conversion: Coming Out of Christian Erotophobia," in *Queer Religion*, 21–48. However, note that Gorell does not avert to racial dynamics in his understanding of erotic conversion.

"accept [their] nakedness as sacred, and hold sacred the nakedness of another,"[40] that is, a world that facilitates racialized persons' ability to love themselves and others through erotic love?[41]

My intuition is that a fruitful direction could lie in developing what might be called "the racially erotic Trinity." In my monograph *Racial Justice and the Catholic Church,* I noted how appeals to the Trinity are made in the struggle against racism. The nonhierarchical, nonsubordinate relationships constitutive of the Godhead are used to ground models of noncoercive, mutual, and nondomineering personal and social relationships:

> We believe the diversity of the human family reflects the interior life of the Triune God. Christians believe in a Trinitarian God, a community of persons who exist in a communion of life and love. In God, the Divine Persons relate to one another in neither domination nor subordination. In God, there is distinction without separation, unity without uniformity, difference without division. Since we are created in the image of this God, God's own life becomes the model for human social life. The variety of languages, cultures, and colors in the human family, then, is a mirror of the Trinitarian God whose essence is a loving embrace of difference.[42]

"A loving embrace of difference." This phrase inspires reflection on eros and the Trinity. The Jungian therapist and theologian Ann Belford Ulanov describes "eros" as "the psychic urge to relate, to join, to be in the midst of, to reach out to, to value, to get in touch with, to get involved with concrete feelings, things, and people, rather than to abstract or theorize."[43] Eros, then, connotes passion-

---

40. James Baldwin, *Just Above My Head* (New York: Dell Publishing, 1979), 309–10.

41. Pinn, *Embodiment,* 89.

42. Bryan N. Massingale, *Racial Justice and the Catholic Church* (Maryknoll, NY: Orbis Books, 2010), 127.

43. Ann Belford Ulanov, *The Feminine in Jungian Psychology and in Christian Theology* (Evanston, IL: Northwestern University Press, 1971), 155,

ate, loving connection. Eros is a passion, that is, it is invested and committed, sensual and sensuous. Another author, John Neary, describes eros as "a passionate attraction to the valuable and a desire to be united with it."[44] "Trinity," then, might be understood as Christian shorthand for speaking of a relational God, an "erotic" God, a God who is constitutively both a relationship and a passion for nondominative and noncoercive relating. Only because God draws near to us erotically, that is, passionately and with desire, are humans enabled or even enticed to engage in "logos" thinking or theologizing about the Divine.

Yet, the Incarnation makes this erotic Godhead *in-bodied,* that is, enfleshed with suffering and partaking in physical delight. Elizabeth Johnson vividly describes how an incarnational commitment makes the Divine bodily and physically expressive: "Bodiliness opens up the mystery of God to the conditions of history, including suffering and delight. She becomes flesh . . . irrevocably, physically connected to the human adventure."[45] This embodied/"in-bodied" God gives further insight, impetus, and audacity to speak of an erotic God— and the courage to redeem eros from the realm of the titillating, dirty, and forbidden.

If we are created in the image of the Divine Mystery, whose essence is a loving—dare I say, erotic—embrace of difference, how might this inform human interracial sexual relating? I am not prepared or able to give a fully coherent response to that question; it demands a fuller and more developed study of eros and Trinitarian belief that is beyond the space constraints of this essay. Yet, I believe that such an understanding of the Divine Mystery provides a faith basis for a nondominative eroticism that challenges and subverts the malformed ways that we are socialized into racist sexual identi-

---

as cited by John Neary, "The Erotic Imagination and the Catholic Academy," in *Professing in the Postmodern Academy,* ed. Stephen R. Haynes (Waco, TX: Baylor University Press, 2002), 150.

44. Neary, "The Erotic Imagination," 160.

45. Elizabeth Johnson, *She Who Is: The Mystery of God in Feminist Theological Discourse* (New York: Crossroad, 1987), 168.

ties and behaviors. It would ground what might be considered an essential ethical question concerning any intimate and sexual relation: "Does it embody and promote affection, mutual respect, and equality between the partners—and contribute to the realization of equality between men and women [of all colors]—or does it constitute and further contribute to the degradation of people," especially by eroticizing racial and social inequality?[46]

This essay ends on an unfinished note, raising more questions than answers about where Catholic theological ethics needs to go in developing an anti-racist sexual ethics. Yet my intuition suggests that in these first and provisional reflections lies a key needed to rectify the compounded lacunae and omissions that render Catholic theological ethics inadequate, complicit, and impotent (pun intended) in the face of the challenge of anti-black sexual racism and the violence it breeds in our world.

46. Bob Avakian, *Break All the Chains: Bob Avakian on the Emancipation of Women and the Communist Revolution* (Chicago: RCP Publications, 2014), 54–55.

Selected Bibliography

Barad, Karen. *Meeting the Universe Halfway: Quantum Physics and the Entanglement of Matter and Meaning.* Durham, NC: Duke University Press, 2007.

Brand, Dionne. *A Map to the Door of No Return: Notes to Belonging.* Toronto: Vintage Canada, 2001.

Brown Douglas, Kelly. *Stand Your Ground: Black Bodies and the Justice of God.* Maryknoll, NY: Orbis Books, 2015.

Carter, J. Kameron. "Paratheological Blackness." *South Atlantic Quarterly* 112, no. 4 (2013): 589–611.

Cassidy, Laurie M., and Alexander Mikulich, eds. *Interrupting White Privilege: Catholic Theologians Break the Silence.* Maryknoll, NY: Orbis Books, 2007.

Copeland, M. Shawn. *Enfleshing Freedom: Body, Race, and Being.* Minneapolis: Fortress Press, 2009.

Cone, James. *The Cross and the Lynching Tree.* Maryknoll, NY: Orbis Books, 2011.

Cox, Aimee Meredith. *Shapeshifters: Black Girls and the Choreography of Citizenship.* Durham, NC: Duke University Press, 2015.

Crawley, Ashon. "Let's Get It On! Performance Theory and Black Pentecostalism." *Black Theology: An International Journal* 6, no. 3 (2008): 308–29.

Danquah, Meri Nana-Ama, ed. *The Black Body.* New York: Seven Stories Press, 2009.

DeFrantz, Thomas F., and Anita Gonzales. *Black Performance Theory.* Durham, NC: Duke University Press, 2014.

Edwards, Erica R. *Charisma and the Fictions of Black Leadership.* Minneapolis: University of Minnesota Press, 2012.

Eisentein, Zillah R. *Hatreds: Racialized and Sexualized Conflicts in the 21st Century.* New York: Routledge, 1996.

Ferreira da Silva, Denise. *Toward a Global Idea of Race.* Minneapolis: University of Minnesota Press, 2007.

Gilroy, Paul. *Against Race: Imagining Political Culture Beyond the Color Line.* Cambridge, MA: Harvard/Belknap, 2002.

Glissant, Édouard. *Poetics of Relation.* Translated by Betsy Wing. Ann Arbor, MI: University of Michigan Press, 1997.

Gordon, Lewis R. *Existentia Africana: Understanding Africana Existential Thought.* New York: Routledge, 2000.

Grimes, Katie M. "Racialized Humility: The White Supremacist Sainthood of Peter Claver, SJ." *Horizons* 42, no. 2 (Dec. 2015): 295–316.

Hartman, Saidiya. *Lose Your Mother: A Journey along the Atlantic Slave Route.* New York: Palgrave Macmillan, 2008.

Lemert, Charles C. *Durkheim's Ghosts: Cultural Logics and Social Things.* New York: Cambridge University Press, 2006.

Lloyd, Vincent. *Black Natural Law.* New York: Oxford University Press, 2016.

Kelley, Robin D. G. *Freedom Dreams: The Black Radical Imagination.* Boston: Beacon Press, 2002.

Maldonado-Torres, Nelson. *Against War: Views from the Underside of Modernity.* Durham, NC: Duke University Press, 2008.

Massingale, Bryan N. *Racial Justice and the Catholic Church.* Maryknoll, NY: Orbis Books, 2010.

McKittrick, Katherine. *Demonic Grounds: Black Women and the Cartographies of Struggle.* Minneapolis: University of Minnesota Press, 2006.

———, ed. *Sylvia Wynter: On Being Human as Praxis.* Durham, NC: Duke University Press, 2015.

Melamed, Jodi. *Represent and Destroy: Rationalizing Violence in the New Racial Capitalism.* Minneapolis: University of Minnesota Press, 2011.

Mignolo, Walter. *Local Histories/Global Designs: Coloniality, Sub-altern Knowledges, and Border Thinking*. Princeton, NJ: Princeton University Press, 2000.

Nagel, Joane. *Race, Ethnicity and Sexuality: Intimate Intersections, Forbidden Frontiers*. New York: Oxford University Press, 2003.

Ortega-Aponte, Elias. "Democratic Futures in the Shadow of Mass Incarceration: Toward a Political Theology of Prison Abolition." In *Common Goods: Economy, Ecology, and Political Theology*. Edited by Melanie Johnson-DeBaufre, Catherine Keller, and Elias Ortega-Aponte. New York: Fordham University Press, 2015.

Patterson, Orlando. *Slavery and Social Death: A Comparative Study*. First edition. Cambridge, MA: Harvard University Press, 1985.

Prevot, Andrew. *Thinking Prayer: Theology and Spirituality amid the Crises of Modernity*. Notre Dame, IN: University of Notre Dame Press, 2015.

Sexton, Jared. *Amalgamation Schemes: Antiblackness and the Critique of Multiracialism*. Minneapolis: University of Minnesota Press, 2008.

———. "People-of-Color-Blindness: Notes on the Afterlife of Slavery." *Social Text* 28, no. 2 (2010): 31–56.

Slabodsky, Santiago. *Decolonial Judaism: Triumphal Failures of Barbaric Thinking*. New York: Palgrave Macmillan, 2014.

Taylor, Charles. *The Ethics of Authenticity*. Cambridge, MA: Harvard University Press, 1991.

Thompson, Carlyle Van. "White Police Penetrating, Probing, and Playing in the Black Man's Ass: The Sadistic Sodomizing of Abner Louima." In *Eating the Black Body: Miscegenation as Sexual Consumption in African American Literature and Culture*. New York: Peter Lang, 2006.

Townes, Emilie M. *Womanist Ethics and the Cultural Production of Evil*. New York: Palgrave Macmillan, 2006.

Turman, Eboni Marshall. *Toward a Womanist Ethic of Incarnation: Black Bodies, the Black Church, and the Council of Chalcedon*. New York: Palgrave Macmillan, 2013.

Weheliye, Alexander. *Habeas Viscus: Racializing Assemblages, Bio-politics, and Black Feminist Theories of the Human.* Durham, NC: Duke University Press, 2014.

Wilderson, Frank B. *Red, White, and Black: Cinema and the Structure of U.S. Antagonisms.* Durham, NC: Duke University Press, 2010.

Yancey, George A. *Who Is White? Latinos, Asians, and the New Black/Nonblack Divide.* Boulder, CO: Lynne Rienner Publishers, 2003.

Index